The Cambridge Introduction to
Jacques Lacan

The difficulty of Jacques Lacan's thought is notorious. *The Cambridge Introduction to Jacques Lacan* cuts through this difficulty to provide a clear, jargon-free approach to understanding it. The book describes Lacan's life, the context from which he emerged, and the reception of his theory. Readers will come away with an understanding of concepts such as jouissance, the *objet a*, and the big Other. The book frames Lacan's thought in the history of philosophy and explains it through jokes, films, and popular culture. In this light, Lacan becomes a thinker of philosophical importance in his own right, on a par with Jean-Paul Sartre and Simone de Beauvoir. Lacan's great contribution is the introduction of the unconscious into subjectivity, which results in a challenge to both the psychoanalytic establishment and to philosophers. *The Cambridge Introduction to Jacques Lacan* provides readers with a way of understanding the nature of Lacan's contribution.

Todd McGowan teaches theory and film at the University of Vermont. He is the author of *Embracing Alienation*, *The Racist Fantasy*, *Emancipation After Hegel*, *Capitalism and Desire*, *Only a Joke Can Save Us*, and other works. He is also the cohost of the *Why Theory* podcast with Ryan Engley.

The Cambridge Introduction to
Jacques Lacan

TODD MCGOWAN
University of Vermont

Shaftesbury Road, Cambridge CB2 8EA, United Kingdom

One Liberty Plaza, 20th Floor, New York, NY 10006, USA

477 Williamstown Road, Port Melbourne, VIC 3207, Australia

314–321, 3rd Floor, Plot 3, Splendor Forum, Jasola District Centre, New Delhi – 110025, India

103 Penang Road, #05-06/07, Visioncrest Commercial, Singapore 238467

Cambridge University Press is part of Cambridge University Press & Assessment, a department of the University of Cambridge.

We share the University's mission to contribute to society through the pursuit of education, learning and research at the highest international levels of excellence.

www.cambridge.org
Information on this title: www.cambridge.org/9781009300728

DOI: 10.1017/9781009300742

When citing this work, please include a reference to the DOI 10.1017/9781009300742

First published 2025

A catalogue record for this publication is available from the British Library

A Cataloging-in-Publication data record for this book is available from the Library of Congress

ISBN 978-1-009-30072-8 Hardback
ISBN 978-1-009-30075-9 Paperback

In memory of Mari Ruti,
a singular being

Contents

Preface

Jacques Lacan is the most misunderstood theorist of the twentieth century. The problem of understanding him begins with the fact that he never published one central book laying out his doctrine, such as Jean-Paul Sartre's *Being and Nothingness* or Simone de Beauvoir's *The Second Sex*. Access to his thought was possible only through the occasional essays that he wrote and the limited diffusion of the seminars that he gave starting in 1953 and continuing to the end of his life in 1981. He didn't write a major book articulating his theory because he considered publication primarily a vehicle for misunderstanding, not understanding.

Lacan was fond of calling publication "*poubellication*," a neologism that works in French to bring together publication with garbage. A *poubelle* is a trash can. The use of the portmanteau *poubellication* indicates Lacan's derision for publication due to the way that readers typically approach books as commodities to be consumed (and then discarded in the trash) rather than as challenges to be wrestled with. Despite this disdain, Lacan did not completely forswear producing a written form of his work for the public.

Beginning in the 1930s, Lacan wrote a series of essays that he published in a variety of venues. The most important of these came to constitute his collected writings known as the *Écrits*, which just means "writings" in French. The collection appeared in print in 1966.[1] This one book publication makes no attempt to bring coherence to the essays that Lacan wrote in different times and contexts. They do not hold together to articulate a systematic doctrine but reflect the occasional manner in which Lacan wrote them. What's more, when Lacan wrote essays, he employed an idiosyncratic style.

The misunderstanding surrounding Lacan stems not just from the absence of a major written work or the nonsystematic form of the *Écrits*. It is also the product of his own obfuscatory style. The difficulty of Lacan's style is not an accident or the product of a lack of skill. Lacan's sensitivity to the reception of Freud's thought informed both his opposition to publication and the stylistic choice in his writing. As Lacan saw it, the directness of Freud's prose allowed readers to understand his point too quickly and thus not fully engage with its disruptiveness. Thanks to Freud's accessible style, followers easily assimilated his theoretical innovations to already existing positions. Lacan vowed not to make the same mistake himself. He believed that writing forbidding prose would hinder attempts to reduce his ideas to preexisting formulas and demand instead careful engagement.[2] His aim was to prevent readers from understanding too quickly so as to avoid thinking fully and questioning their own preconceptions.[3]

With the perspective of several decades, we can safely judge this project to be a failure. Rather than preventing facile misunderstandings with tortuous prose that demanded attentive reading, Lacan ended up making himself even more misunderstood than Freud had been. As a result of the stylistic choice that Lacan made in his written work, understanding Lacan's philosophy requires turning from his written work to the seminars that he gave. Focusing solely only on what Lacan wrote and not on his oral seminars makes it impossible to grasp his philosophical project.

Without question, Lacan disseminated his most important – and most lucid – ideas orally in his seminars, not in written form. This was the result of a conscious decision on his part, a decision that had extreme ramifications for how both contemporaries and subsequent generations would receive his thought. While the seminars were much more accessible than the written essays, they were for a long time also unavailable to the public. Only a privileged inner circle who attended the seminars or who obtained typescripts of them were able to interact with this primary dimension of Lacan's thought.[4] Although his son-in-law and literary executor Jacques-Alain Miller began to publish the seminars toward the end of Lacan's life, important seminars remained unpublished even forty years after his death. During Lacan's lifetime and immediately after, the arcane formulations of the written doctrine dominated the perception of his philosophy.[5] The result was a widespread misperception.

In addition to the difficulties in understanding that Lacan's prose causes, his emphasis on language creates further problems. He uses the term *symbolic order* rather than just discussing *language* and refers to *signifiers* rather than *words* in order to focus on the breadth of the impact that this order has on us. The symbolic order is the order of language but also includes the different values assigned to identities. The symbolic identity that organizes our social existence is more than just our name but includes profession, education, class, ethnicity, gender, religion, and everything else that goes into how we identify ourselves. The signifiers that make up the symbolic order underwrite all social existence. Words are signifiers, but so are the clothes we wear, the hairstyle we have, and the type of food we eat. The symbolic order with its mass of signifiers defines the social terrain, even going so far as to indicate to us how we should navigate it.

The symbolic order – the order of language – plays an outsized role in Lacan's system. It provides the basis both for his critique of other psychoanalysts and for the philosophical impact of his thinking. Lacan theorizes the subject as the product of the imposition of the symbolic order on the human animal. He tends to use the term *subject* for what we might call a *person* or *human* to indicate that we are first and foremost speaking beings caught up in the process of signification, a universe of meaning that informs everything in our lives. The subject is neither a biological entity nor a social one. It is the result of the collision between the human animal and the social order. This collision produces unconscious desires that are distinct from animal instincts and from social determinations. The subject doesn't exist prior to its encounter with the signifier but is a subject of the signifier. A signifier is a word or any element within the symbolic order that conveys meaning.

This emphasis on signification leads to misunderstanding because it prompts people to assume that Lacan is a social constructionist, someone who believes that we are just what our society makes of us. Social constructionism draws a straight line from the social structure that we live within to our actions, our words, and even our thoughts. It credits society, rather than biology or our own choices, with making us what we are. This is not Lacan's position. Although the encounter with the symbolic order produces subjectivity, the symbolic order does not determine the subject. This is a key distinction. Subjectivity, according to Lacan, is not just an effect of language – it is not socially constructed – but what emerges at the point where signification fails, where the symbolic order isn't determinative. But for many years, it became commonplace to view Lacan as a thinker who undermined the notion of the subject through drawing attention to the power of the signifier. This was an error with unfortunate consequences for making sense of Lacan's project.

According to this doxa, subjectivity is nothing but a construction of the symbolic order in Lacan's philosophy. The symbolic order imposes certain desires on us. We believe that we are free agents acting out our conscious will, but what we desire is just the effect of the signifiers that structure this desire on our behalf. As Kaja Silverman puts it in *The Subject of Semiotics*, "Lacan indicates that the subject's desires are manufactured for it. The factory – the site of production – is the symbolic."[6] Silverman views Lacan's theory as a referendum on the ultimate power of the signifying structure over those caught within its grasp. For instance, according to this way of thinking about

Lacan, I believe that I seek out a new television because of my own private desire, but I am just playing out the desire that the capitalist symbolic order has given to me. Whatever symbolic order we live within determines what we desire. Lacan allows us to recognize these determinations. The problem with this position on Lacan lies in the relationship between the symbolic order and the subject that it assumes.

Given the way that reference to the symbolic order dominates Lacan's thinking, this misunderstanding is itself readily comprehensible, especially for those considering him solely or primarily through his written work. But according to Lacan, subjectivity is not reducible to an effect of the symbolic order. Although this order produces the subject, it doesn't do so in a direct fashion. The symbolic order issues a demand. The subject is a subject and not a pure product of the symbolic order because it never responds to this demand properly. Every demand goes awry when the subject interprets it, and this interpretation is the subject's desire. The symbolic order may demand that I purchase a television, but my desire might respond by turning to books rather than the television – even books that challenge the society of consumption. In contrast to what Silverman claims, unconscious desire stems from the failure of the symbolic order's imposition of a demand on the subject. To desire is always to desire askew from the demand articulated in the signifier.

Despite a desire that doesn't coincide with social demands, the subject still makes strenuous efforts to conform. The disjunction between the symbolic order and the subject opens the space for a radical unconscious desire, but it also leads the subject to yearn to find a place for itself within the symbolic order. Every subject experiences its disjunction from the symbolic order as a wound that it tries to heal by aligning itself with a symbolic identity. One tries to really become a police officer or a judge or even a criminal in order to have a place, but subjectivity cannot ever fully overcome its displacement, its inability to belong to the symbolic order. To be a subject is to be riven between one's unconscious desire and the symbolic identity that promises respite from this desire. For Lacan, there is no solution to this split other than living with it.

Subjectivity is our inescapable problem. Lacan stands out from all forms of constructivism through the privileged position that subjectivity has in his philosophy. He contrasts subjectivity and symbolic identity in a way that social constructivism doesn't. Lacan is first and foremost a theorist of the subject. Rather than trying to dismantle the philosophical tradition that focuses on subjectivity, Lacan integrates the psychoanalytic discovery of the unconscious into this philosophizing.

Lacan's emphasis on subjectivity separates him from the thinkers often mistakenly grouped with him, typically under the moniker *poststructuralism*. People tend to use this term to refer to a group of French thinkers including Jean Baudrillard, Gilles Deleuze, Jacques Derrida, Michel Foucault, Luce Irigaray, Julia Kristeva, and Jacques Lacan. This term, one invented in the United States and not used by any of the theorists themselves, papers over dramatic conflicts between them that makes any grouping of them impossible. It is a term that should not be used because it creates needless confusion. But if there is one idea that these supposed poststructuralists hold in common – an idea that would bridge the sometimes bitter opposition between Derrida and Foucault, for instance – it would be the critique of subjectivity. With the stark exception of Lacan, these thinkers tend to see the subject as a theoretical dead end that has entrapped Western philosophy. From this perspective, to invest oneself in the idea of subjectivity is to succumb to a myth perpetuated by the Enlightenment and its adherents.

Although Deleuze, Derrida, and Foucault disagree with each other, sometimes even vehemently, what links them together is their shared critique of the subject. They launch this criticism in different ways, but each of them insists on it.[7] Lacan believes that giving up on the subject would be akin to theorizing away the unconscious. It is the unconscious that alienates us from what the symbolic order would make of us. Subjectivity indicates the ability to be other than what one was made to be, an ability that we have thanks to the unconscious, which is the point at which we do not know ourselves. Psychoanalysis intervenes at this point not to know our unconscious but to help us find a way of relating to it, of recognizing its impact.

The task of introducing Lacan involves traversing a labyrinth of misunderstandings, many of which Lacan himself introduced intentionally to make things even more tortuous. Although it's tempting with a difficult thinker who strives to render his prose as arduous as possible to dismiss him as unintelligible and move on to those who express themselves clearly, Lacan is worth the time that it takes to work one's way through all the misunderstandings. One can reject his stylistic choices – I believe that we must – while still granting the perspicuity of his central insights. Fewer people today should try to write like Lacan, but more people today should pay attention to his thought. His unsurpassed originality lies in offering a reconception of subjectivity that integrates the unconscious into it without eliminating the subject's freedom. Lacan is a philosopher of the subject who avoids the Scylla of biologism and the Charybdis of culturalism. This is what makes him worth the trouble.

Notes

1 A selection of the *Écrits* first appeared in English in 1977. In France, a subsequent compilation of his writings came out posthumously in 2001 with the title *Autres écrits.* In 2023, another posthumous volume appeared that collected his earliest writing. It is entitled, appropriately enough, *Premiers écrits.* The writing in the work predates Lacan's turn to psychoanalysis and reflects his position as a psychiatrist.

2 The intervening years have made Lacan's written works more accessible, not because his prose miraculously became more intelligible on its own but because a group of Lacanian thinkers collected a series of commentaries that provided a meticulous reading of each essay published in the *Écrits.* Anyone invested in Lacan's thought owes an immense debt to Stijn Vanheule, Derek Hook, and Calum Neill. See Stijn Vanheule, Derek Hook, and Calum Neill, *Reading Lacan's Écrits from "The Signification of the Phallus" to "Metaphor of the Subject"* (London: Routledge, 2018); Stijn Vanheule, Derek Hook, and Calum Neill, *Reading Lacan's Écrits from "The Freudian Thing" to "Remarks on Daniel Lagache"* (London: Routledge, 2019); and Stijn Vanheule, Derek Hook, and Calum Neill, *Reading Lacan's Écrits from "Logical Time" to "Response to Jean Hyppolite"* (London: Routledge, 2022). To give an idea of how difficult Lacan's written work is, two of the contributors to these volumes, tasked with writing an essay explaining one of Lacan's articles, ended up writing a book-length treatment that had to be published in a different form because its length so exceeded the limits of a standard essay. This shows that sometimes it takes a whole book to explain a twenty-five-page article, at least when Jacques Lacan has written it. That said, both books are invaluable contributions to understanding not just the particular essay they discuss but also Lacan's theory in general. See Adrian Johnston, *Irrepressible Truth: On Lacan's "The Freudian Thing"* (London: Palgrave, 2017), and Dany Nobus, *The Law of Desire: On Lacan's "Kant with Sade"* (London: Palgrave, 2017).

3 Lacan makes this point to those attending his seminar on several occasions. For instance, while going over the ethics of psychoanalysis, he tells his auditors, "I have always told you that it is important not to understand for the sake of understanding." Jacques Lacan, *The Seminar of Jacques Lacan, Book VII: The Ethics of Psychoanalysis, 1959–1960*, ed. Jacques-Alain Miller, trans. Dennis Porter (New York: Norton, 1992 [1986]), 278. Although Lacan says this in an oral seminar, it is primarily in his writing that he attempts to forestall understanding through an unapproachable style.

4 The members of the audience at Lacan's seminars were primarily psychoanalysts. He thought of himself as first and foremost someone introducing others into the practice of psychoanalysis. This will not be my focus here. There are, however, several excellent introductions to the practice of Lacanian psychoanalysis. See especially Bruce Fink, *A Clinical Introduction to Lacanian Psychoanalysis: Theory and Technique* (Cambridge, MA: Harvard University Press, 1997) and Dany Nobus, *Jacques Lacan and the Freudian Practice of Psychoanalysis* (London: Routledge, 2000).

5 Typically, a thinker's esoteric work given to the inner circle is more difficult than the exoteric work available to the general public. Lacan reverses this structure, which leads to lasting difficulties in the widespread dissemination of his thought. In Lacan's case, the esoteric texts are the accessible ones.

6 Kaja Silverman, *The Subject of Semiotics* (Oxford: Oxford University Press, 1983), 178.

7 Late in his life, Foucault takes up a more sanguine attitude toward the subject, as he turns his thought toward ancient Greece. Even here, however, Foucault's conception of the subject remains at a distance from Lacan's. He tries to consider subjectivity outside of the subjection to the symbolic law that Lacan views as necessary.

Acknowledgments

Mari Ruti asked me to write this book with her and then wouldn't take no for an answer. It would been a better book had she written it, but she died tragically before she was able to get started on it. I heard her in my head every day that I worked on the book, usually voicing a slight critique of how I was putting things.

Ray Ryan at Cambridge University Press has been uniquely supportive. He gave me all the space that I needed after Mari's death, while at the same time encouraging me to finish the book myself. I'm indebted to him for this. Thanks to Luke Thurston for an incredible reading.

Thanks to my brother, Wyk McGowan, who helped me navigate the centrality of symbolic castration in our upbringing. My in-laws, Jane Neroni and Del Neroni, managed to produce a profound psychoanalytic theorist, for whom I am grateful every day. My twin sons, Dashiell and Theo Neroni, function as ersatz Lacanian analysts for me. In their responses to my lack of authority, I see the analyst as *objet a*.

At the University of Vermont, Andrew Barnaby, Emily Bernard, Bill Falls, Daae Jung, John Waldron, and Hyon Joo Yoo help to punctuate the session.

Thanks to those who don't belong to LACK, including Bea Bookchin, Clint Burnham, Daniel Cho, Joan Copjec, Ryan Engley, Matthew Flisfeder, Sheldon George, Scott Krzych, Anna Kornbluh, Don Kunze, Juan Pablo Lucchelli, Hugh Manon, Quentin Martin, Jonathan Mulrooney, Carol Owens, Kenneth Reinhard, Frances Restuccia, Molly Rothenberg, Russell Sbriglia, Stephanie Swales, Louis-Paul Willis, Jean Wyatt, Cindy Zeiher, and Alenka Zupančič.

Thanks to Slavoj Žižek for interrupting my dismissal of Lacan. When I first read the *Sublime Object of Ideology*, it occasioned a revaluation of all values.

Sheila Kunkle has been with me from the beginning of my exploration of Lacan. Meeting her in the way that I did must have been a felicitous encounter with the real, if such a thing were possible.

Walter Davis knew just where the book was lacking and showed me how to lean into the lack rather than filling it in. I'll always be thankful for the critical eye toward Lacan that he brings.

I'm grateful to Jennifer Friedlander and Henry Krips for constantly challenging my assumptions about Lacan by actually paying attention to the text in a way that I prefer not to.

Thanks to Richard Boothby for his devotion to *das Ding*. Talking to him puts a hole in my signifying universe.

I appreciate the careful readings of this book from Michael Blouin, Nick Kaldis, Anna Karnedy, Dashiell Neroni, Maris Poepsel, and David Shields. Each of these readings allowed me to reshape things to make the book more accessible.

Hilary Neroni has corrected what could be corrected. Her generous attention to the manuscript at various stages stopped it from going off the rails. Unfortunately, every book that I write takes time away from every book she would write, and mine are worse.

Thanks to Walter Davis, Paul Eisenstein, and Hilary Neroni. Lacan must have had them in mind when he decided to foreground jouissance.

Chapter 1

Context

Sigmund Freud had the most influence on Lacan's thinking. Lacan's debt to Freud is evident throughout everything that he says and writes. Freud's theorization of the unconscious in *The Interpretation of Dreams* in 1900 strikes Lacan as a great philosophical event, one that he would try to develop and keep alive. The discovery of the unconscious gives psychoanalysis its philosophical importance.

For both Freud and Lacan, the unconscious is an agency in the psyche that evades our attempts at conscious control. The unconscious is not just what we aren't conscious of at any moment but what is irreducible to consciousness. It follows a logic distinct from consciousness that we cannot integrate into conscious thought processes. We can become aware of the unconscious – this is what psychoanalysis strives for – but we cannot intentionally think unconsciously. It takes us by surprise because it pushes us in directions that we wouldn't consciously want and that we might even find repulsive. A slip of the tongue might, for instance, reveal that I unconsciously favor one of my children over the other. I don't consciously intend to say *Hannah* instead of *Rene*, but the unconscious makes itself manifest despite my intentions. While it is disruptive to consciousness, the concept of the unconscious provides a compelling way of understanding both our subjectivity and the social order, when we pay attention to it. The importance of the unconscious draws Lacan to psychoanalysis.

Lacan illustrates how Freud's conception of the unconscious, unbeknownst to Freud himself, actually reveals itself as an effect of language. This leads Lacan to one of his most well-known pronouncements, which he repeats in slightly different ways. It receives its canonical form in *Seminar XI: The Four Fundamental Concepts of Psychoanalysis, 1963–1964*, where he states, "*the unconscious is structured like a language.*"[1] The point is not that the unconscious is language but that it bears the imprint of language. It emerges through the points where language malfunctions, through what cannot be said. Psychoanalysis pays attention to gaps and failures.

But when Lacan became interested in psychoanalysis in the 1930s, something was amiss in the field that he felt the need to correct. In *The Interpretation of Dreams*, Freud divided the psyche into the consciousness (what we aware of at this moment), the preconscious (what we could recall without difficulty), and the unconscious (what we cannot make conscious). This became known as the topographical model of the psyche, but in the early 1920s, things in the psychoanalytic world underwent a dramatic change. Freud developed a structural model of the psyche to supplement the topographical model. This new model split the psyche into the id, the ego, and the superego. Freud added the structural model because he sensed the inability of the topographical model to explain all the psychic phenomena that he encountered. He meant it as a supplement to his earlier view. But the structural theory quickly gained adherents and thoroughly displaced the topographical theory among most psychoanalytic thinkers and among the public. It allowed psychoanalysts and lay people to discuss the psyche while avoiding the disruptiveness of the unconscious, which subtracted the most important idea from the theory. This is where Lacan intervened.

One might profitably interpret Lacan's emergence as a response to the deleterious effects associated with this turn to the structural theory, effects that were directly not the fault of Freud himself but of followers too eager to escape the radicality of the initial psychoanalytic discovery. These psychoanalysts practicing in Freud's wake took the image of a healthy ego as the ideal that could animate psychoanalytic treatment. Psychoanalysis became a treatment aimed at normalizing patients and adjusting them to the social reality. Building up the patient's ego, so the thinking went, would lead to a more profitable existence in society.

The psychoanalytic investment in the ego betrayed the discovery inherent in the topographical theory that defined psychoanalysis as a project – that of the unconscious. The unconscious follows a different logic than consciousness, a logic that embraces contradictions rather than dissolving them, that leads to destruction rather than construction, and that aims at failure rather than success. When the unconscious manifests itself, our conscious plans go awry. The unconscious plays out a drama that cannot be integrated into consciousness. All we can do is try to take stock of it. Although Freud himself continued to focus on the unconscious after the introduction of the structural theory, many of his adherents marginalized it in favor of the ego. By doing so, they turned psychoanalysis into just another form of therapy designed to integrate patients back into the confines of capitalist society's norms. Lacan's return to Freud began as an attempt to place the unconscious back at the center of the psychoanalytic project.[2]

Lacan's early essays often come back to a single note: The ego cannot be the bedrock of psychoanalytic treatment because it is an imaginary entity. There is no such thing as a healthy ego that the analyst can shore up. The psychoanalysts that attempt to support the patient's ego end up pushing the patient toward an imaginary illusion rather than facilitating any type of cure. This version of psychoanalysis – commonly known as ego psychology – not only fails, but it points the subject in a conformist direction alien to the fundamental insights of psychoanalysis.

Lacan reacts against the conformism that predominates in psychoanalytic practice in the late 1940s and early 1950s. He even identifies an ethical dimension of psychoanalysis that pushes against the conformity that he sees operative in so many other analysts. He makes this clear in *Seminar VII: The Ethics of Psychoanalysis, 1959–1960*, where he states, "There's absolutely no reason why we should make ourselves the guarantors of the bourgeois dream. A little more rigor and firmness are required in our confrontation with the human condition."[3] Lacan's early aim is to turn psychoanalysis back into a practice that discovers the subject's singularity rather than encouraging adaptation to oppressive norms.

The critique of the ego that dominates Lacan's early psychoanalytic theorizing takes the structure of signification as its starting point. As Lacan sees it, the mediation of the symbolic order displaces the ego from the center of the subject's experience. Focus on the ego leads psychoanalysts and their patients to miss the role that the symbolic order plays in structuring the subject. To imagine oneself identical with one's ego is to miss how the unconscious, which emerges from signification, constantly undermines the ego's authority. Through his emphasis on the structuring priority of the symbolic order, Lacan builds on Freud's claim that "*the ego is not master in its own house.*"[4] When psychoanalysis focuses on the ego, it misses the society that lays down the strictures in which the ego remains confined.

When it comes to thinking about society in psychoanalytic terms, no one looms as a more important figure than Lacan. This includes Freud himself, the founder of psychoanalysis. As the founder, Freud obviously has an outsized significance for every direction that psychoanalytic theory takes. Without Freud's groundbreaking innovations, Lacan's contributions would not be possible. Specifically, Freud introduces the unconscious, which enables theorists to recognize how people might act contrary to their conscious will and their self-interest. This provides a new direction for thinking about social relations, one that eschews recourse to the struggle for power on the one hand or the pursuit of the good on the other. For Freud, the priority of the unconscious drives societies to undermine their own power and to threaten their own good. There is a theory of how the social order functions lurking within Freud's thought, but developing this theory is not Freud's primary concern.[5]

When he originates psychoanalysis, Freud focuses on the individual in relation to others whom it desires. The individual psyche is Freud's starting point. Although Freud speculates about the social background of the psyche, the specific role that the social structure plays in constituting it does not play a central part in his theory. He takes the individual psyche as the point of departure for developing his original conception of psychoanalysis. But Lacan makes the radical gesture of socializing Freud's thought, framing the psychoanalytic understanding of subjectivity in terms of how the social structure imprints itself on the subject through language.[6] He doesn't do this as a critique of Freud but as a development of Freud's thought.[7] Lacan takes up subjectivity as the fundamental problem, subjectivity that emerges through the signifying effect of language.

The signifying structure of language is distinct from culture. Culture uses signifiers but arranges them so that they appear to have a substantial meaning. Culture gives the illusion of a grounded identity that the signifier doesn't. Lacan is not a culturalist who believes that our specific culture makes us what we are. He is not concerned with how cultural influences imprint themselves on subjectivity, with how they produce particular tastes or proclivities that are specific to a social situation. He doesn't reduce subjectivity to the effects of the culture in which it emerges or the historical period that contains it. As Lacan sees it, thinking this way amounts to a psychoanalytic heresy. His focus on socializing psychoanalysis occurs entirely through the structure of signification, a structure he theorizes as separate from the influence of culture. Culture promises us that we can be part of it and fit in, while signifiers constantly confront us with our inability to fully identify ourselves with them. Unlike culture, signification occasions a rupture that leaves the subject divided from itself and unable to achieve any self-identity. Culture promises to give us an undivided identity, but the very signification of that identity results in a subject divided from itself.

Lacan emphasizes the linguistic background of subjectivity to such an extent that he theorizes subjectivity primarily in terms of its relationship to the signifier. The subject for Lacan is the subject of the signifier. Subjectivity does not exist prior to the relationship that it has to the signifying order. This order enables the subject to relate to itself – it makes self-consciousness possible – but it also introduces an obstacle into the subject's self-relation. This obstacle is the unconscious. Lacan sees the conception of the unconscious as Freud's lasting theoretical contribution. The unconscious is the sine qua non of psychoanalysis. In a way that remains only implicit in Freud's thinking, Lacan locates the unconscious at the juncture of animality and the signifying structure.

In Lacan's way of conceiving it, psychoanalysis wrestles with the results of the collision that takes place between the instincts of the human animal and the structure of signification. This collision is more violent than a highspeed crash on the highway. In its aftermath, the instincts of the human animal become unrecognizable. They become the unconscious drives of the subject, an entity forever divorced from its animal origin. Psychoanalysis doesn't discover the animal within the human but how the structure of signification deforms this animal into an inhuman subject. Lacan contends that the unconscious is not our hidden animal instincts but an effect of the separation from animality.

This deformed animal or inhuman subject has a skewed relationship to the social order within which it exists. The collision between the biological entity and the structure of signification produces a subject that doesn't belong to the social order but sticks out from it. The deformed status of subjectivity separates it from the coercive power of society. The subject is not just the whim of social forces that constitute it. Lacan focuses on subjection to the signifier in order to distinguish the subject from the socially constituted symbolic identity. The split between the lacking subject of the signifier and the symbolic identity that fills in this lack with some social content is fundamental. Everyone must wrestle with this conflict. No one is a pure subject, and no one can attain a pure symbolic identity.

Subjectivity is a form without any content. Symbolic identity provides a content. It fills the gap within desiring subjectivity by supplying what subjectivity lacks. A series of signifiers comes together to constitute symbolic identity. In contrast to the lack of any foundation that characterizes subjectivity, symbolic identity offers points of anchorage. Signifiers of symbolic identity include nationality, economic status, ethnicity, gender, sexual orientation, career, and even attractiveness. The subject can tell itself that it is a German, that it is wealthy, that it is a dentist, that it is a heterosexual, and so on. These signifiers offer symbolic answers to the question of subjectivity, but these answers are only symbolic.

No matter how ardently I identify with some aspect of my symbolic identity, my subjectivity always exceeds it. Another way of understanding the unconscious is as the name that psychoanalytic theory gives to this mismatch between subjectivity and symbolic identity. The unconscious manifests itself through our inability to reduce subjectivity to the markers of identity. The harder I try to see myself as German, for example, the more this effort itself betrays the absence of identity with the signifier. The moment I assert a symbolic identity for myself, just as quickly I avow my failure to be it fully. If I have to say it, my statement reveals that I am not identical with what I claim for myself. True self-identity would have to go unsaid. It could not even be thought. Because identity is always articulated through the signifier, the subject always remains alien to it.

This is evident in a joke about a terrible golfer. After finishing an especially poor round, the disappointed golfer takes out his frustration on his caddie. He says, "You must be the worst caddie in the world." The caddie responds, "No, I don't think so. That would be too much of a coincidence." Here, the golfer identifies the caddie as the source for his own inadequacy as a golfer. He does so to shore up his own symbolic identity as a golfer and avoid confronting his lacking subjectivity. But the caddie corrects him, pointing out the golfer hasn't rightly recognized who is the failure and who is the innocent bystander.

The key to the joke lies in what is not said: The caddie doesn't just state directly that the golfer is terrible. Instead, he makes this point indirectly through a comment on his own ability as a caddie. This unspoken evaluation indicates the unconscious status of the golfer's subjectivity and its distance from the symbolic identity he claims for himself. Thanks to the unconscious, every subject is in the position of this golfer – asserting a symbolic identity out of step with the subject itself. We all consciously think we're good golfers derailed by bad caddies, but the unconscious knows better. The caddie in this joke gives voice to the unconscious, which is why he must speak elliptically rather than directly. The assertion of symbolic identity always misses subjectivity because it cannot account for the distortion that the unconscious introduces.

The distinction between the subject and its identity allows us to recognize what separates Lacan from the theory of social construction. For the constructionist, subjectivity and identity are the same. One is nothing outside of one's symbolic identity, which the historical situation determines. According to this position, if I live in a historical epoch structured around hierarchies, I will think in terms of hierarchy.[8] If I live in a capitalist society, I will think like a capitalist. There is no possibility for a break within the epoch, only a break between one epoch and the following one. There is no subject that exists in a disjunctive relationship to the social order that constitutes it. This constructivist view reduces every subject to its social place. But according to Lacan, subjectivity can never find a place within society. An emphasis on the failure of the subject to fit in its society establishes the groundwork for Lacan's philosophical system.[9]

The emphasis that Lacan places on the social order enables him to grasp the philosophical bearing of psychoanalysis in a way that Freud cannot. Lacan often characterizes himself as a faithful interpreter of Freud who advocates a return to Freud. But Lacan's return adds a philosophical dimension to psychoanalytic theory that Freud himself never fully worked out. Throughout his seminars, Lacan elaborates a theory of the subject in relation to the social order that goes beyond anything Freud could articulate. Although as a youth Freud aspired to become a philosopher, he takes pains to separate psychoanalysis as a science from philosophical speculation. For Freud, philosophy struggles with a fundamental uncertainty about its claims that psychoanalytic thinking can overcome due to its scientific bent. As a result of his investment in the experimental work of psychoanalysis as a proving ground for his ideas, Freud believes that psychoanalysis can approach nearer and nearer to the status of a science. Ultimately, he hopes that it will attain a position next to sciences such as physics and biology. Lacan gives up this dream of establishing psychoanalysis as a scientific mode of inquiry in favor of asserting its philosophical significance. Freud's inability to recognize the parallels between psychoanalytic inquiry and philosophical thought stems from his lack of knowledge of philosophy. Lacan makes up for this lacuna.

Lacan is a psychoanalytic philosopher. In contrast to Freud, Lacan engages himself seriously with the history of Western philosophy. His seminars discuss various philosophical figures as much as they do Freud himself and much more than they do other psychoanalysts. Lacan's interlocutors are René Descartes, Blaise Pascal, and Baruch Spinoza, not so much psychoanalysts like Carl Jung, Alfred Adler, and Melanie Klein.

The majority of the attendees at Lacan's seminars were psychoanalysts or fledgling psychoanalysts. When he gave the seminars, he wasn't just trying to construct a theory of subjectivity but to train analysts in a specific practice of psychoanalysis. In fact, despite his philosophical orientation, Lacan explicitly resists taking up the mantle of the philosopher of psychoanalysis.[10] He sees himself as a psychoanalyst who teaches others about the practice. But his concerns are also philosophical ones. He engages in philosophical speculation every bit as much as his contemporaries Jean-Paul Sartre and Simone de Beauvoir.

Lacan announces his respect for the philosophical tradition in *Seminar II: The Ego in Freud's Theory and in the Technique of Psychoanalysis, 1954–1955*, a respect that he conceives in opposition to the intellectual trends of the midcentury. It had become fashionable to declare philosophical authors passé, their positions no longer relevant in the contemporary world. Lacan has none of this. He tells those attending his seminar, "I don't much like hearing that we have *gone beyond* Hegel, the way one hears we have *gone beyond* Descartes. We go beyond everything and always end up in the same place."[11] Instead of going beyond figures such as Descartes and Hegel, Lacan attempts to further their conception of subjectivity through recourse to the discoveries of psychoanalysis. Lacan's implicit wager is that psychoanalysis gives him a path to extend the philosophy of subjectivity. Insofar as he is a philosopher, he is a philosopher of the subject.

Subjectivity is a nodal point for modern Western philosophy beginning with René Descartes. Appropriately, Lacan's theorization of subjectivity takes Descartes as its point of departure. Although Descartes doesn't use the term *subject*, he is the first to theorize subjectivity as the beginning of philosophical inquiry, which leads him to claim, "I think, therefore I am."[12] He starts his philosophy with radical doubt, the questioning of all his assumptions about himself and the world, even his own sense perceptions. Both our senses and our minds deceive us all the time, which leads Descartes to install doubt as his philosophical starting point. Descartes doesn't doubt for the sake of doubting – he is not a skeptic – but in order to attain certitude. He wonders what he can be certain about if he casts doubt on everything that our senses and our minds lead us to believe.

Doubt leads to certitude because one has certainty that one doubts. Even at the moment that one doubts everything, one remains aware of oneself as a thinking subject doing the doubting. For Descartes, there is no act of doubting possible without a thinking subject who doubts. This is why we can be certain of our existence on the basis of knowing that we are thinking. The act of doubting and the certainty it provides generate subjectivity in Descartes's philosophy. The Cartesian subject is a subject of doubt. The discovery of this subject is Descartes's great breakthrough.

Taking up radical doubt as the basis for the discovery of certainty links Descartes with psychoanalytic thinking. Freud also proceeds through doubt to discover where subjectivity emerges. For Descartes, doubt enables us to attain certitude about the thinking subject. For Freud, doubt reveals the influence of unconscious desire. When doubt intervenes in the recollection of a dream, this is how consciousness resists – and reveals – unconscious desire. In *The Interpretation of Dreams*, Freud writes, "Doubt whether a dream or certain of its details have been correctly reported is once more a derivative of the dream-censorship, of resistance to the penetration of the dream-thoughts into consciousness."[13] Doubting details of the dream underlines the presence of unconscious desire in these details. Doubt about what happens in the dream expresses to Freud the certainty of the subject's unconscious desire in what the subject doubts. The psychoanalytic method prioritizes the subject's doubts because they evince ripples in consciousness where the unconscious manifests itself. Although Freud does not recognize the parallel with Descartes, Lacan does. According to Lacan, Freud's sense of the importance of doubt in recounting the dream reveals that the subject at work in psychoanalysis is the same subject that Descartes discovers in his philosophy.[14]

Descartes doesn't discover the subject by assuming it as his philosophical starting point but by questioning everything that seems certain. Descartes directs his philosophical inquiry through radical doubt, which enables him to grasp that the subject finds itself only at the point where it loses itself. This anticipates the psychoanalytic discovery of the subject's unconscious. The unconscious marks the point at which the subject is at home in what appears most foreign to it. To theorize the subject through the unconscious, Lacan must see the connection from Descartes, but he also must pass through Immanuel Kant and G. W. F. Hegel, his two primary philosophical touchstones.

As figures within the movement known as German Idealism (which began in 1781 when Kant wrote the *Critique of Pure Reason* and ended in 1831 when Hegel died), Kant and Hegel theorize the connection between subject and object by bridging the gap between them. They don't do this in either of the ways that we might suspect. The idealist tack would reduce the object to the subject by rejecting the existence of any external objects outside the subject. All would exist within our act of perceiving.[15] In contrast, the materialist gesture would reduce the subject to the object and view the subject as nothing but another object. According to this theory, the problem of how we access objects never arises because there is no subject to struggle with this question.[16] Despite the name, German Idealism avoids the facile solutions of both idealism and materialism.

Prior to the revolution of German Idealism, philosophers conceive of the subject on one side and the object on the other of a fundamental divide. There are subjects in the world with objects external to them. Through this oppositional understanding, subjects come to know objects by reaching out and grasping them through the act of knowing. Despite this outreach on the part of the subject, at no point does the opposition between subject and object break down. It is only with Kant's theorization of the subject in the *Critique of Pure Reason* that this changes.

Even though he mentions Kant less than Descartes or Hegel, Lacan is first and foremost a psychoanalytic Kantian, which is why grasping Lacan's thought requires looking briefly at the contours of Kant's theoretical philosophy. There is a clear parallel between Kant's conception of subjectivity and

Lacan's. Both view subjectivity as the vehicle for understanding the world while at the same time the limit that restricts our understanding.

Objects become accessible for the subject, Kant believes, because the structure of subjectivity makes them accessible. There is no simple or immediate apprehension of objects that doesn't occur through the structure of accessibility in the subject. Instead, in Kant's theory, subjectivity has a form of apprehension that makes all objects available to it. This structure will provide the basic model for Lacan to construct his own theory of the subject.[17] Kant divides subjectivity into three faculties that regulate the subject's access to objects: the sensibility, the understanding, and reason. Perceptions occur through the sensibility, while the understanding organizes these perceptions into a meaningful structure. Reason stops the understanding from indulging in misleading speculative excesses. Lacan's version of these faculties is the three registers of imaginary, symbolic, and real.

In Kant's philosophy, the sensibility allows the subject to perceive sense impressions by structuring them through space and time. The framing structure of space and time opens up access to sense impressions by limiting them to a specific spatiotemporal form. If we lacked the strictures of spatiality and temporality, our sense impressions would lose their coherence and no longer be conducive to meaning. There would be no possibility of ordering our sense impressions in any meaningful fashion. We would be unable to distinguish between what happened earlier and what happened later, between what was near and what was far. Our sense impressions would remain a complete jumble without the form of space and time that the sensibility provides. We can make sense of what we sense because there are clear limits – those of space and time – that govern how our perception works. This is Kant's theory of the sensibility, our first faculty of knowing.

The same thing occurs with the understanding, which is the second faculty. The understanding orders sense impressions that the sensibility produces in a conceptual apparatus. Kant contends that the understanding has categories that organize all the spatial and temporal sense data that we take in. These categories dramatically confine our experience to preestablished laws such as that of causality. Nothing in our understanding can violate the law of causality: The understanding assures us that there is no event that occurs without a cause driving it. The law of causality governs all our experiences. Just as in the case of the sensibility, this limit on the understanding is generative. The limit that the categories provide allows us to access the mass of sense data in an orderly fashion.

The last faculty, for Kant, is reason. Unlike the sensibility and the understanding, each of which play a productive role in our knowing, reason is purely limiting. It limits the subject's ability to speculate beyond what it can experience. This ultimate limit on knowledge provides the subject with access to objects by confining it to appearances and restricting it from trying to access things in themselves. Reason's attempts to think beyond the field of what we can experience lead to irresolvable contradictions. But reason also has the ability to recognize the contradictions that emerge when it goes too far. For instance, we can grasp that it is impossible to know if the world has a temporal beginning to it. Any attempt to isolate the beginning point would lead to the question of what came before that beginning. Kant sees that this line of questioning could never reach a satisfying end. Reason tells us that we cannot speculate about the world as a totality. We must think only about the field of possible experience (which is the product of the faculties of the sensibility and the understanding). This recognition establishes the limit that makes all knowledge possible.

Philosophy encounters a necessary limit – what we cannot know, such as the origin of the world. According to Kant, this limit always remains external to our reason. No matter how much self-reflection we engage in, we cannot integrate the limit into our thinking. We come up against it as if we were butting our heads against a wall. What is impossible for us provides only a negative form of knowledge: We know only that we must stop our thinking at the limit.

Hegel is much more sanguine about the prospects for thinking than Kant. When thinking runs into a limit that it cannot traverse, this limit isn't simply negative. It is also revelatory. It marks a form of knowing through the revelation of what is impossible. An impossibility for thinking is not just a failure to know but also a way of knowing. We know the truth through the failure of knowledge. According to Hegel, this is what Kant fails to see.

Kant doesn't recognize that theorizing a limit includes that limit within one's thinking. No limit can have a purely external status, which is how Kant conceives the limit on reason. Hegel writes, "Something can be known, even felt to be a *barrier* ... only insofar as one has at the same time *gone beyond* it."[18] Hegel's step beyond Kant involves grasping the immanence of the limit that we encounter. By showing the existence of points of impossibility within our thinking, we expose the internal gaps within our thought, not external limits that we must accept as unbreachable. The contradictions that upend reason's attempt to know the world as a totality are not just dead ends. They pinpoint the impossible within the field of the possible.

Hegel's conception of subjectivity embraces contradiction in a way that Kant's does not. When thought tries to know the totality and encounters a contradiction, Hegel views this as the utmost expression of the subject's own truth. In his conception, truth arises where knowledge fails. Where Kant sees nothing but a limit on knowledge, Hegel sees how truth corresponds to enacting of this limit. But Hegel's thought about the truth of subjectivity can only emerge against the background of Kantian philosophy. Kant establishes the foundations on which Hegel is able to build his system and which informs Lacan's as well.

Kant's tripartite conception of subjectivity represents such a philosophical revolution because in each faculty he grasps the necessity and fecundity of the limit. As Kant sees it, the subject encounters objects not when it reaches out beyond itself but through its forms of self-limitation. The inability of the subject to know everything permits it to know something. What the subject cannot access in the object is what makes the object available to it. The link between Kant and psychoanalysis runs through the fecundity of the limit.

Kant explores how our subjectivity provides the form for the world that we experience, a project that Lacan repeats with a psychoanalytic twist. Where Kant divides the subject between the sensibility, the understanding, and reason, Lacan theorizes subjectivity through the imaginary, the symbolic, and the real. There is an almost exact overlap between Kant's three faculties and Lacan's three registers.

Lacan completes Kant's transcendental account of subjectivity by showing the role that the unconscious must play in each of the Kantian agencies. Once we take the unconscious into account, the way that the subjectivity forms its reality becomes less easily recognizable for the subject itself. Unlike Kant, Lacan believes that the structure of our perception deceives us about the act of perception itself. It's not that our experience is confined to appearances and can say nothing about things in themselves but rather that the unconscious blinds us to what we actually experience. Kant thinks that the subject can be self-conscious about its consciousness, but Lacan shows how the unconscious gets in the way of this self-knowledge.

The imaginary is Lacan's term for the agency that structures the subject's sense impressions. In this sense, it parallels Kant's sensibility. But unlike Kant's theory of the sensibility, Lacan's imaginary doesn't privilege space and time. The basic property of the imaginary register is that it constructs what we perceive as whole. This is how the imaginary misleads us. When we think in terms of the imaginary, we see ourselves as a whole, as an ego that exists independent from the world outside of it. The belief in the independence of the ego is, for Lacan, an imaginary illusion, the result of an inability to perceive the structural interdependence that shapes our subjectivity. The imaginary sees whole beings and harmonious relations rather than ruptures and contradictions. In this sense, when we cleave to the imaginary, we fall for an essential deception.

Lacan is critical of the imaginary in a way that Kant is not critical of the sensibility. Kant invests himself in the sensibility as the bedrock for knowledge that the understanding further develops. For Kant, the sensibility doesn't deceive. But in the case of both the sensibility and the imaginary, the faculty itself acts as the source for sensory information that otherwise would not be available to the subject. In Lacan's theory, one must go through the imaginary deception in order to have access to the world at all. It's just that Lacan, in contrast to Kant, sees the need for a corrective to the imaginary. To fall completely victim to the imaginary illusion of wholeness and isolation is, for Lacan, to be incapable of living in society. The imaginary order on its own lacks the power of mediation.

As a result, imaginary thinking always operates according to the model of either/or. Either the ego has the object, or the other does. On the imaginary level, there is no possible mediation between this opposition. It's akin to an opposition between teams in a sporting event: One team's victory is the other team's loss. They can't compromise and decide to get along without betraying the nature of the game. To remain under the dominance of the imaginary is to succumb to unrelenting aggressiveness because one lacks the symbolic mediation to bring a third party into the imaginary dualism.[19] This is what the example of sports captures. Especially early on in his trajectory, Lacan sees the act of making evident the symbolic structure beneath the imaginary relations as the point of the psychoanalytic intervention.

Treating others as imaginary entities grants them a wholeness or a substantiality that they don't actually have. Lacan criticizes imaginary thinking because it fails to grasp that every entity suffers from a self-division, a division that depends on the symbolic function. The symbolic function is a third party that mediates all imaginary encounters and dissipates the aggressiveness that would otherwise animate them. It is the sports league that regulates when the teams play the game and the rules under which they play it. The imaginary conflict occurs within the frame that the symbolic order provides. The realm of the signifier – the symbolic order – allows subjects to speak to each other rather than punching each other in the face.

The symbolic order mediates every interaction. No subject can exist entirely in the imaginary realm because the symbolic order provides the foundation for all imaginary relations. Before it misrecognizes itself as an autonomous ego, a subject emerges through the encounter between the human animal and the signifying structure. This structure provides the subject with the signifiers that allow it to make sense of the world. In this sense, the symbolic order operates in the manner of Kant's faculty of the understanding.

But the symbolic order is not a neutral mechanism. It does order our sense impressions in the way that Kant's understanding does, but it does so by making demands on us and telling us what has value and what doesn't. Whereas the Kantian understanding provides us with an objective conception of the field of possible experience, the symbolic order in Lacan's thought indicates the impossibility of any neutral view of the world. Every symbolic order is slanted.

And yet, Lacan believes that the tilt of the symbolic order offers an important corrective of our imaginary deception. Recognizing the mediating role of the symbolic order allows the subject to escape the inherent aggressiveness of the imaginary realm. For a number of years, Lacan simply takes the side of the symbolic against the imaginary and affirms this as the role of the psychoanalyst. The early period (until *Seminar VII: The Ethics of Psychoanalysis, 1959–1960*) in Lacan's intellectual trajectory represents him at his most Kantian, the time when the real remains just that which is out of reach. It is what the symbolic order butts up against without including. We know that it's there, but we don't know anything about it.

Both Kant's reason and Lacan's notion of the real center on contradiction. In contrast to the understanding, reason falters, as Kant sees it, by leading our thinking into contradictions. This is why we must understand how to limit it. While Kantian reason falls into contradiction by trying to think beyond what we can process in our sense experience, Lacan contends that contradictions prove the existence of the real. The contradictions of the symbolic order indicate that there is a real irreducible to this order. The real is the site of the subject's unconscious desire.

Like reason, the real is a limit concept or the limit of all conceptualization. It marks a point at which the mediating structure of the symbolic order runs into an impasse that it cannot explain on its own terms. We can recognize the effects of the real but cannot explain it in terms of the symbolic order. The real is where the signifying order is at odds with itself. It is here that the subject finds its unconscious desire aroused.

Psychoanalysis permits Lacan to introduce the unconscious into subjectivity, something that no prior thinker had the conceptual tools to do. Thanks to the unconscious, the subject is always outside itself, desiring in a way at odds with what it consciously wants. Philosophers such as Kant and Hegel lacked any conception of the unconscious, while Freud didn't have the background in philosophy to take the step that Lacan does. By bringing the unconscious to the philosophy of the subject, Lacan accomplishes an advance in the understanding of subjectivity. This is his major theoretical contribution. With this step, the subject's relationship to objects can be understood in a way that hadn't hitherto been possible.

Understood psychoanalytically, subjectivity implies that our desire shapes the world that we perceive. This seems straightforward and relatively uncontroversial. Everyone knows that our desires influence how we grasp things. But psychoanalytic theory complicates the picture by positing that our desire structures the world through what escapes our conscious knowledge. The world emerges through the gaps within our conscious apprehension of it, not through the structure of our knowledge. These gaps are real.

Lacan keeps the Kantian project alive in the twentieth century not by faithfully echoing Kant's original insights but by remaking his theory through introducing the unconscious into it. Once we think in terms of the unconscious rather than just consciousness, the sensibility becomes the imaginary, the understanding becomes the symbolic, and reason becomes the real. This rethinking of the Kantian enterprise enlivens not just Kantian philosophy itself but also the domain of psychoanalysis. Thanks to his background in philosophy, Lacan gives psychoanalytic thought a unique philosophical turn.[20]

Throughout his intellectual trajectory, subjectivity remains at the fore of Lacan's thinking. He is a theorist of the subject, one who takes into account the formative role of the unconscious for this subject. This is the one constant. Everything else about Lacan's thinking changes several times in his life in ways that aren't immediately self-evident. These dramatic changes create a philosophy that differs according to the historical point at which we examine it. The result is that it is impossible to adhere to Lacan's theory from beginning to end. If one wants, one can be an early Lacanian, a middle Lacanian, or a late Lacanian. One cannot simply be a Lacanian.

Lacan is a thinker who constantly revolutionized his own thought without ever saying directly that he was doing so. This makes it difficult to piece together what aspects of his theory cohere and what parts are at odds with each other. Sometimes, he will introduce changes so dramatic from one year to the next in his seminar that they reorient his entire theoretical system. And yet, he often continues to employ the same terminology through the period of radical change, so that this terminology comes to acquire a new significance. Never at any point does he acknowledge that he has changed his mind about his ideas, which makes it even more difficult to keep track of the changes.[21] It falls on those reading his works to clarify when things shift without warning.

The same term might appear from one year to another in the seminars and have acquired an entirely new significance during this transition. This variability separates Lacan from every other major theorist. Even those who underwent well-known transformations – Karl Marx in the mid-1840s, Martin Heidegger in the early 1930s – usually have no more than two distinct periods in their intellectual trajectory. More often than not, a thinker's mature work remains more or less constant. Not so with Lacan. Whereas someone like Hegel remained conceptually consistent throughout his mature life, Lacan upended his own theory on several occasions. As a result, one can be Hegelian without pinpointing the period of Hegel's work to which one adheres, but the same claim cannot be made for Lacan. The differences between Lacan's theory at the time of his first seminar in 1953 and that of his twenty-third seminar in 1975 are so substantial that it is impossible to merge them together without disfiguring both. In between, Lacan changed his mind about the structure of desire, the form that enjoyment takes, the possibility for a social bond, and how we should conceive sexual difference.

There are three fundamental movements in Lacan's thought: the early more structuralist phase, the middle *objet a* phase, and the later sexuation phase.[22] Although there are clear continuities between these different periods – Lacan retains the ideas of symbolic, imaginary, and real throughout each – the ruptures between them are almost impossible to miss.[23] Early on, the determinative role of the symbolic order comes to the fore. Lacan calls attention to the functioning of the symbolic order shaping the illusions of the imaginary. In the middle period, the emphasis turns to the relationship between the symbolic order and the real. Lacan focuses on the real as it disrupts the functioning of the symbolic. In the third one, the real ends up taking priority over the symbolic. The relationship between the symbolic order and the real ceases to be universally valid.

The claim of this book will be that Lacan's most philosophically important period occurs when he develops the concept of the *objet a*, a period from *Seminar IX: Identification, 1961–1962* to *Seminar XVI: From an Other to the other, 1968–1969*. This is the one period where Lacan is the least Kantian in his thinking, the least concerned with emphasizing what structures our experience. For this span of a few years, one can align Lacan's theoretical project more with that of Hegel than with that of Kant. During this period, Lacan conceives the real as a point of impossibility within the symbolic order, but it is an impossibility that nonetheless occurs. This is an idea that recalls Hegel's insistence that contradiction actually takes place. The Lacan of the middle period is a dialectical thinker in the spirit of Hegel.

During this middle period, Lacan stresses that the connection between the subject and the society occurs through the failures of each. As a result, subjectivity is by its very existence a challenge to the smooth running of the ruling order. The subject's unconscious desire bespeaks the inability of the subject to master itself and the society's inability to stamp out all challenges. Here, Lacan locates subjectivity at the point of contradiction within the symbolic totality. Although Lacan himself didn't theorize it, there is a political dimension to his theory in the middle period that inspired many others in his wake.

But Lacan sustains this view for only a few years. When he develops the theory of the four discourses in *Seminar XVII: The Other Side of Psychoanalysis, 1969–1970*, he implicitly reasserts his allegiance to Kantian philosophy by returning to an emphasis on the structuring limits that arise through different relationships to the symbolic order. In this late period, the real isolates each subject in its own way of structuring itself. The structure ceases to be the shared reality of the symbolic order. It becomes individualized and unique to each subject. Contradiction gives way to difference as Lacan moves away from his most far-reaching insights.

What stands out about the period from *Seminar IX* to *Seminar XVI* is that during this time Lacan locates the universality of subjectivity in the subject's break from the symbolic order.[24] At this point, subjectivity has a singular form. Although there are an infinite number of subjects, we can recognize the universal form that each takes on through its failure to fit in the symbolic order. Before this period, in the early structuralist years, Lacan doesn't associate the subject's desire with the real. As a result, he fails to see how decisive the break between the subject and the symbolic order must be. In the years afterward, he will become caught up in analyzing the different forms that subjectivity assumes in its masculine and feminine versions. One's form of enjoyment will come to depend on how one is sexed. He will define the different forms of sexuation by their nonrelation with each other. Subjects exist in isolation rather than through the contradictions of a shared symbolic space in Lacan's late theory. This isolation of the subject in the form of nonrelation represents a turn from Hegel back to Kant. Hegel's consideration of the totality gives way to Kant's prioritizing of the individual subject. This cuts into the political resonance of the late period.

Although Lacan socializes the psychoanalytic project, he does so in order to establish the basis for a theory of subjectivity, which is what doesn't belong to the social order of which it is a part. After Kant and Hegel, Lacan is one of the foremost thinkers of the subject. The implications of the unconscious lay the groundwork for his transformation of Kant and Hegel's philosophy. Lacan shows that the subject appears where the social order cannot make sense of it.

Notes

1 Jacques Lacan, *The Seminar of Jacques Lacan, Book XI, The Four Fundamental Concepts of Psychoanalysis, 1963–1964*, ed. Jacques-Alain Miller, trans. Alan Sheridan (New York: Norton, 1978 [1973]), 20.

2 Although Lacan criticizes the emphasis on developing a healthy ego and disparages the turn to the structural theory, he does not reject it entirely. The role that the superego plays in the psyche and in society takes on an important role in Lacan's theoretical framework.

3 Jacques Lacan, *The Seminar of Jacques Lacan, Book VII: The Ethics of Psychoanalysis, 1959–1960*, ed. Jacques-Alain Miller, trans. Dennis Porter (New York: Norton, 1992 [1986]), 303.

4 Sigmund Freud, "A Difficulty in the Path of Psycho-Analysis," trans. Joan Riviere, in *The Complete Psychological Works of Sigmund Freud*, vol. 17, ed. James Strachey (London: Hogarth Press, 1955 [1917]), 143.

5 Years after he initially develops psychoanalytic thinking, Freud does turn to speculation about the origins of society in *Totem and Taboo* (1913) and the relationship between society and the individual psyche in *Civilization and Its Discontents* (1930). In both works, he addresses society from the perspective of the individual. He never takes the social order itself as the starting point for theoretical speculation.

6 Lacan stresses that the ambit of psychoanalysis extends beyond the Oedipal triangulation of the child, the mother, and the father. While Lacan doesn't openly abandon the Oedipus complex and even invokes it on several occasions, his theory definitely doesn't center on it in the way that Freud's does, at least early on before Freud writes *Beyond the Pleasure Principle* in 1920. This is why Lacan comes off remarkably well in *Anti-Oedipus*, Gilles Deleuze and Félix Guattari's otherwise scathing indictment of psychoanalysis. Deleuze and Guattari view Lacan as one psychoanalyst who has already internalized their critique of the concept of the Oedipus complex.

7 Even when Lacan breaks from Freud, he usually insists that he is simply expanding on Freud's insights. Except on very rare occasions, he doesn't announce where he stops following Freud's lead. But Lacan does avow his departure from Freud's argument when it comes to religion. Freud dismisses religion as a mass delusion worthy of children and comes down harshly on Christian love for one's neighbor. He finds the Christian commandment nonsensical and even dangerous for the subject. Lacan, to the contrary, argues that this marks an existential retreat on Freud's part, a refusal of the openness to the other's enjoyment that the Christian commandment to love one's neighbor enjoins.

8 Michel Foucault is the representative figure of constructivism and the antipode of Lacan, despite the fact that people have a tendency to group them together theoretically. Foucault analyzes the determinative role that a prevailing mode of thought has in a series of historical epochs. If one exists within, say, the modern humanist epoch, one's thinking will bear the imprint of this humanism, no matter how radical the philosophy that one advances. According to Foucault, even Marxism fits perfectly within its epoch. We think of Marxism as a radical movement, but Foucault claims its radicality nonetheless remains within ruling ideas of its epoch. Foucault's insistence that everything fits in its historical time runs counter to Lacan's understanding of subjectivity as that which never fits, no matter how much it strives to do so.

9 Lacan does not organize his thought systematically but articulates it in a piecemeal fashion constantly under revision. This mode of presentation, however, doesn't detract from the systematic form that appears when one puts Lacan's theorizing together. In an early work written on Lacan's thought, Jean-Luc Nancy and Philippe Lacoue-Labarthe view the discovery of a Lacanian system as a scandal, as proof that Lacan's disruption of mastery works in service of a mastery over disruption. The fact that two of Lacan's more significant critics would consider systematic thinking as scandalous rather than as necessary reveals the topsy-turvy era in which he lived. If necessary, see Jean-Luc Nancy and Philippe Lacoue-Labarthe, *The Title of the Letter: A Reading of Lacan*, trans. Francois Raffoul and David Pettigrew (Albany: SUNY Press, 1992 [1973]).

10 In *Seminar III: Psychoses, 1955–1956*, Lacan distances his own work in the seminars from the practice of philosophy, although he does acknowledge the value of laying out the philosophical implications of Freud's breakthrough. He states, "there is no question … of my doing the metaphysics of the Freudian discovery and drawing out its consequences for what may be called being, in the widest sense of the term. This is not my intention. This would not be useless, but

I think that it can be left to others and that what we are doing here will indicate how it might be approached." Jacques Lacan, *The Seminar of Jacques Lacan, Book III: The Psychoses, 1955–1956*, ed. Jacques-Alain Miller, trans. Russell Grigg (New York: Norton, 1993 [1981]), 73. Lacan's commitment to training psychoanalysts holds him back from fully investing himself in the exploration of the philosophy of psychoanalysis, but when one reads his seminars, it quickly becomes evident that his concern for philosophy weighs as heavy as his concern for the practice of psychoanalysis.

11 Jacques Lacan, *The Seminar of Jacques Lacan, Book II: The Ego in Freud's Theory and in the Technique of Psychoanalysis, 1954–1955*, ed. Jacques-Alain Miller, trans. Sylvana Tomaselli (New York: Norton, 1991 [1978]), 71.

12 René Descartes, *Discourse on the Method of Rightly Conducting One's Reason and Seeking the Truth in the Sciences*, trans. Robert Stoothoff, in *The Philosophical Writings of Descartes*, vol. 1 (Cambridge: Cambridge University Press, 1985 [1637]), 127, translation modified.

13 Sigmund Freud, *The Interpretation of Dreams*, trans. James Strachey, in *The Complete Psychological Works of Sigmund Freud*, vol. 5, ed. James Strachey (London: Hogarth Press, 1953 [1900]), 515–516.

14 In *Seminar XI: The Four Fundamental Concepts of Psychoanalysis, 1963–1964*, Lacan gives Descartes credit for the discovery of subject and then points out that Freud allows us to pinpoint where the subject is at home in the world. He states, "I am not saying that Freud introduces the subject into the world . . . since it was Descartes who did this. But I am saying that Freud addresses the subject in order to say to him the following, which is new – *Here, in the field of the dream, you are at home.*" Lacan, *Seminar XI*, 44. When one is at the mercy of the unconscious in the dream, one encounters the truth of one's subjectivity. For Descartes, in contrast, the dream represents one possible deception that one must get beyond to discover the truth of one's subjectivity.

15 This is the philosophy of George Berkeley. See George Berkeley, *A Treatise on the Principles of Human Knowledge* (Oxford: Oxford University Press, 1998 [1710]).

16 Graham Harman is George Berkeley's opposite number. See Graham Harman, *Object-Oriented Ontology: A New Theory of Everything* (New York: Penguin, 2018).

17 Ruth Ronen maps Lacan's debt to the Western philosophical tradition and gives Kant a central place in this analysis. She recognizes that Lacan develops Kant's project rather than overturning it. Ronen insists, "Lacan's claim about what is real in the formal rules of the understanding does not deviate from the Kantian insight, but rather reveals its power." Ruth Ronen, *Lacan with the Philosophers*, trans. Michal Sapir (Toronto: University of Toronto Press, 2018), 147. Kant doesn't see the effect of the unconscious on subjectivity, but his system inadvertently reveals the necessity of including it.

18 G. W. F. Hegel, *Encyclopedia of the Philosophical Sciences in Basic Outline, Part I: Science of Logic*, trans. Klaus Brinkman and Daniel O. Dahlstrom (Cambridge: Cambridge University Press, 2010 [1817]), 107.

19 Lacan links the predominance of the imaginary with an unrelenting aggressiveness that only recognition of the symbolic link can dissipate. In his *Seminar III*, he states, "The aggressive tension of this *either me or the other* is entirely integrated into every kind of imaginary functioning in man." Lacan, *Seminar III*, 95. Once we grasp the role of symbolic mediation in our relations, it becomes possible to think of multiple people having access to an object.

20 According to Mikkel Borch-Jacobsen, Lacan is a bricoleur who doesn't generate new ideas of his own. He begins his takedown of Lacan by stating, "Lacan was an inspired autodidact – that is, a prodigious *assimilator*, open to every influence, quick to grasp resemblances and analogies among the most diverse fields. He was also incredibly agile at appropriating others' ideas." Mikkel Borch-Jacobsen, *Lacan: The Absolute Master*, trans. Douglas Brick (Stanford: Stanford University Press, 1991), 1–2. While what Borch-Jacobsen says here is undoubtedly true, this claim has the effect – like the entirety of his book – of eliminating the genuine originality of Lacan's conception of subjectivity. He brings the unconscious into the subject of German Idealism and thereby radically transforms it.

21 Near the end of his life, Lacan does confess to a theoretical failure, but this does not lead to the development of a major theoretical overhaul. In *Seminar XXVI: Topology and Time, 1978–1979*, he admits that the Borromean knot doesn't express the form of the sexual nonrelation as he hoped that it would. This leads him to say, "It is clearly evident that I was wrong, that I let myself slip. It's irritating, even more than annoying. It's even more annoying because it's unjustified." Jacques Lacan, *Le Séminaire, livre XXVI: La topologie et le temps, 1978–1979*, unpublished manuscript, session of January 9, 1979.

22 Colette Soler insists that Lacan was never a structuralist because he insisted on the importance of the subject. This separates him definitively from structuralists like Ferdinand de Saussure and Claude Lévi-Strauss, who theorize structure without subjectivity.

23 Lacan's most well-known seminar, *Seminar VII: The Ethics of Psychoanalysis, 1959–1960*, stands out because it occurs between the first and second periods but doesn't belong to either.

24 When we consider Lacan's thought in periods, we can better judge Walter Davis's claim that Lacan refuses to make the tragic central to his conception of subjectivity. As Davis puts it, "Lacanian thought . . . constitutes a systematic attempt to displace a tragic understanding of the psyche." Walter A. Davis, *Death's Dream Kingdom: The American Psyche Since 9–11* (London: Pluto Press, 2006), 95. This verdict certainly has merit relative to Lacan's early and late periods. In these epochs, Lacan turns away theoretically from a confrontation with contradiction. But in the middle period, he propagates a tragic vision of the subject.

Chapter 2

Life

Lacan's life spanned a time when the most influential philosophical innovations in the world came from France. Structuralism, existentialism, and deconstruction all emerged out of the French intellectual world, while major developments occurred in this world in feminism, phenomenology, and Marxism. Lacan lived at the heart of these innovations and was himself responsible, at least indirectly, for the advancement of some of them. An important starting point for situating Lacan's intellectual contributions is to take stock of the large shadow that Jean-Paul Sartre cast in France during the middle of the twentieth century. Although Lacan, born in 1901, was a few years older than Sartre (who was born in 1905), he nonetheless belonged to the wave of thinkers who emerged after Sartre catapulted to universal renown.[1] Lacan felt himself to be caught in the wake of Sartre's philosophical achievements, which is why his references to Sartre are common but almost always implicit rather than explicit. This begins in his early essay on the mirror stage, "The Mirror Stage as Formative of the Function of the *I* as Revealed in Psychoanalytic Experience" (1949), which concludes with an explanation of how the mirror stage calls the supposedly free Sartrean subject into question. This explanation attempts to refute Sartre's philosophical position without ever mentioning his name. In this way, despite the chronological facts of Lacan's life and despite Lacan's philosophical distance from his contemporaries, it makes sense to classify him among the post-Sartrean thinkers of twentieth-century France.

Jacques Lacan was the first child of Alfred Lacan and Emilie Baudry, born on April 13, 1901, in Paris. His parents gave him a classical education, which allowed him to become acquainted with the thought of Baruch Spinoza and Friedrich Nietzsche as a teenager. Spinoza played an important role in the thinking of the young Lacan, but later, as he developed his own system, Lacan would exchange Spinoza's influence for Immanuel Kant's and G. W. F. Hegel's. After going to the university and then to medical school, Lacan became a psychiatrist. Gaëtan Giatan de Clérambault, whom Lacan called "my only master in psychiatry," was the decisive influence in this domain.[2]

Clérambault pushed Lacan in the direction of Freud and psychoanalysis. Lacan's interest in philosophy contributed to the merging of his work as a psychiatrist with his growing investment in psychoanalytic treatment in the late 1920s and early 1930s.

The background in psychiatry and the influence of Clérambault led Lacan to take a substantially different approach to psychoanalysis than Freud, its founder. Although Lacan would become famous for a reinterpretation of psychoanalytic thinking that he labeled a "return to Freud," Lacan's point of departure ran in an opposed direction. While Freud came to psychoanalytic theorizing through the treatment of neurotics – patients who suffered either from psychosomatic physical ailments or psychological symptoms such as hysteria, anxiety, or the tendency to repeat self-undermining patterns of behavior – Lacan did so through the analysis of paranoiacs. Paranoia is a form of psychosis. Psychosis (which entails a break in the patient's relationship to everyday reality) rather than neurosis was Lacan's starting point for psychoanalytic thinking, which means that he, even more than Freud, focused on those who had a skewed relationship to the social order.

In his doctoral thesis of 1931, he addressed the case of Aimée (Marguerite Pantaine). Aimée was Lacan's patient at Sainte Anne's Hospital, where she had been committed after attacking a well-known actress outside a theater. By linking the development of paranoia to the concrete material relations of the subject, Lacan forged a new path for the understanding of psychosis, one that emphasized material conditions instead of genetic explanations. For Lacan, what was important was the social and familial situation of the subject who became psychotic, a situation linked to the structure of a class-based society. Taking a clue from Clérambault, he linked psychosis to normality. Clérambault and Lacan worked together from 1928 to 1931. A break between them occurred in 1931 directly because of Lacan's claims in his thesis, which Clérambault saw as plagiarizing his ideas about the proximity between paranoia and normality. In 1932, Lacan published his thesis on Aimée under the title *On Paranoid Psychosis in Its Relations to the Personality* [*De la psychose paranoïaque dans ses rapports avec la personnalité*].[3]

After the publication of his thesis, Lacan sent a copy to Freud in Vienna, hoping to show Freud the power of psychoanalytic ideas in the field of forensic psychiatry. It is unclear whether Freud ever read Lacan's thesis. He responded with a return postcard that simply acknowledged receipt of the work. This undoubtedly disappointed Lacan, which is perhaps why it represents Lacan's sole attempt to contact Freud, despite basing so much of his project on Freud's.

The publication of this thesis did not immediately turn Lacan into an international celebrity, but it did garner him some positive attention from surrealist artists and poets. Surrealism had a major impact on Lacan's life during his thirties because it included others who valued insights into the unconscious. His relationships with surrealist artists played a formative role in Lacan's thinking and practice. Given the immense esteem that surrealists had for Freud and psychoanalysis, these relationships helped to direct Lacan on the path of becoming a practicing analyst.

One measure of Lacan's status – or lack of status – in the 1930s was the treatment that he received from Ernest Jones when Lacan delivered his paper on the concept of the mirror stage at the Marienbad conference of the International Psychoanalytical Association in August 1936. During Lacan's talk, Jones interrupted him and told Lacan that he had exceeded the time limit. This put an end to Lacan's attempt to communicate with the International Psychoanalytical Association, but more important, it revealed Lacan's position in the theoretical and psychoanalytic world of the 1930s. While he had admirers among surrealist artists, he was not a big name. He was not someone whom Jones might fear interrupting. Clearly miffed, Lacan did not even submit his paper to be part of the conference proceedings.[4]

In the same year that Lacan published his thesis on Aimée, he began himself to undergo psychoanalysis with Rudolf Loewenstein. This was known as a training analysis, which is the procedure through which a psychoanalyst becomes established as a practitioner. Rather than requiring a medical degree or some form of professional education, psychoanalytic practice demands one go through the analytic process oneself. This is done to aid in preventing the fledgling analyst's own unconscious desires from excessively impacting the future practice. For most aspiring analysts, the choice of a training analyst plays a decisive role in their future practice.

This was not the case for Lacan. He felt that Loewenstein was ill-suited to analyze him given Loewenstein's investment in strengthening the ego as the proper psychoanalytic procedure. Lacan vehemently opposed the ego psychology of Loewenstein, which he viewed as an insidious instrument of normalization designed to generate well-adapted, docile members of society. Given that Lacan knew Loewenstein's orientation before submitting to a training analysis with him, it appears that he wanted an analyst who would not serve as an intellectual or practical guidepost. Lacan devoted most of his early essays to eviscerating the ego psychology that provided the basis for Loewenstein's approach to psychoanalysis. Needless to say, his relationship to Loewenstein was not a close one. Nonetheless, the training analysis with

Loewenstein served its purpose by enabling Lacan to analyze patients as a member of the International Psychoanalytical Association. In 1938, he became a practicing analyst in addition to working as a psychiatrist.

Building on his analysis of Aimée, Lacan delved into another famous criminal case in France. In 1933, two sisters, Christine and Léa Papin, killed the wife and daughter of the man who employed them as servants. This case became an important synecdoche for class struggle in France, according to many leftist thinkers at the time, including Simone de Beauvoir and certain doctrinaire Marxists. This made the Papin sisters a *cause célèbre*. Lacan neither criticized nor celebrated the sisters but instead wanted to explain their actions. His explanation took the form of an article entitled "Motives of Paranoiac Crime: The Crime of the Papin Sisters," which appeared in a surrealist magazine entitled *Le Minotaure* in 1933. For Lacan, the sisters were caught up in an imaginary relation with each other from which they couldn't free themselves. Their attack on the family of their master was not so much a miniature class war as an expression of their own self-destructive drive that could not find its proper target. Lacan's psychiatric analysis here already began to show the signs of his turn to psychoanalytic theory. He cited Freud as an important point of reference and emphasized the role of the unconscious in the crime. The 1930s marked Lacan's birth as a psychoanalytic theorist and practitioner.

The 1930s was also the decade in which he started a family of his own. In January 1934, Lacan married Marie-Louise Blondin. They had three children together – Caroline, Thibault, and Sybille. Lacan was largely an absent father to these children. Although the first child from this marriage was not born until 1937, by 1941 he already had a child by another woman, Sylvia Bataille, the ex-spouse of philosopher and friend of Lacan, Georges Bataille. In fact, while Lacan's first spouse was pregnant with his daughter, his lover Sylvia Bataille also became pregnant. Lacan had moved in with her in 1939, but they did not marry until 1953. Their child, Judith, became the spouse of Lacan's disciple, Jacques-Alain Miller, and was a psychoanalytic thinker in her own right. She played an important role in advancing Lacan's legacy, whereas the children from his first marriage played no role at all and received little attention from him throughout their lives.

During World War II, Lacan retreated from public life in order to avoid becoming complicit with Nazism. Although he played no role in the resistance, he also avoided collaboration. This was a position that Sartre would rule out as an existential possibility. According to Sartre, under the occupation, one had a clear choice – resist or collaborate. Lacan rejected both the heroism of resistance and the capitulation of collaboration. Biographer Élisabeth

Roudinesco describes the complexity of Lacan's position under the occupation. She claims, "Though he was never a Petainist, he had little sympathy for the Resistance, either. He hated oppression but was scornful of heroism."[5] Trying to thread the needle between resistance and collaboration, Lacan found himself on a political island, as he often did. But during the war, he became increasingly acquainted with the French intellectual scene, including the existentialists Sartre, Beauvoir, Albert Camus, and Maurice Merleau-Ponty. While Lacan referred to each of them in his seminars, none of them ever referred to him in their works.

After the war, Beauvoir asked Lacan to meet a few times to discuss psychoanalysis in preparation for her book *The Second Sex*. From Lacan's perspective, a few sessions would be woefully inadequate to communicate what needed to be said, so he proposed five to six months of discussions, which did not fit Beauvoir's timetable.[6] This missed intellectual encounter damaged both the feminist implications that Lacan might have drawn out in his development of psychoanalysis and Beauvoir's take on psychoanalysis in *The Second Sex*, which wrongly, though understandably, saw it as hostile to the feminist project.

Along with his intervention in psychiatry with the thesis on Aimée and the beginning of his work as a psychoanalyst, Lacan began to attend Alexandre Kojève's seminars on Hegel and the *Phenomenology of Spirit*. This work had such a monumental importance for twentieth-century thought because it provided a way of making sense of the intractable contradictions that become especially prominent in modern society. It's one of the most difficult works in the history of philosophy, but Kojève's seminars made it approachable. Many significant figures of twentieth-century French thought attended these seminars, which ran from 1933 to 1939. One can posit, without any exaggeration, that the audience of Kojève's seminars consisted of a who's who of future French thought. Kojève not only shaped subsequent French philosophy. His unique amalgam of Hegel, Martin Heidegger, and Karl Marx was one of the most significant philosophical developments of the twentieth century.[7]

Kojève's ideas probably influenced Lacan more than any other thinker who attended the seminars. In addition to the time that he spent there, Lacan also met with Kojève on a weekly basis at his own home. From Kojève – whom Lacan once called his "master (truly the only)" – Lacan picked up an interpretation of Hegel's dialectic that would drive his thinking throughout much of his life.[8] This modern conception of dialectic, unlike Plato's ancient version, identified contradiction as the motor of thought and existence. Kojève provided Lacan with the tools to integrate Hegel's thinking about subjectivity as an entity always divided and at odds with itself into psychoanalytic thought. It is difficult to overstate the influence that Kojève's particular brand of Hegelian philosophy had on Lacan.

Lacan himself testified to this in an offhand statement that he made in his first seminar. While explaining the structure of the symbolic order, Lacan notes the importance of the master/slave dialectic for understanding how this order functions. He states, "at every turn, I take my bearings from the master-slave dialectic, and I re-explain it."[9] While at first blush this statement appears to indicate Lacan's embrace of Hegel rather than Kojève, when one understands the importance that Kojève gives to the master/slave relation, it is clear that this extraordinary claim bespeaks his outsized influence on Lacan. Kojève interprets the master/slave dialectic as the skeleton key for Hegel's entire philosophy. This dialectic shows how a struggle for recognition produces the master/slave relation and how this relation leads to an impasse in which no one experiences satisfying recognition. The failure of recognition drives the movement of history and ultimately, Kojève believes, puts an end to these two positions.

When Lacan asserts the priority of this dialectic for his own thinking, he implicitly embraces Kojève. Even the terms that Lacan uses here to describe this dialectic – *master* and *slave* [*maître* and *esclave*, in French] – are Kojève's, not Hegel's. Hegel's *Herr* and *Knecht* [in German] would be more accurately rendered as *lord* and *servant* (*seigneur* and *serviteur* in French), but Kojève popularized the opposition of *master* and *slave* to such an extent that these terms simply replaced Hegel's own, as Lacan's claim here illustrates, not just in France but around the world. Lacan continued to employ them throughout his intellectual trajectory.

Kojève's seminars did not just offer Lacan intellectual support. In addition, their form served as the paradigm for Lacan's own seminars nearly twenty years later. Lacan began his seminars in 1953, with a year devoted to Freud's essay on psychoanalytic technique and continued them almost until his death in 1981. He held these seminars at Sainte Anne Hospital, where he lectured mostly biweekly during the school year to analysts and other interested intellectuals. The list of attendees and guests at Lacan's seminars includes significant figures from French intellectual life, such as the Hegel scholar Jean Hyppolite, the literary theorist Paul Ricoeur, the linguist Émile Benveniste, the intellectual historian Alexandre Koyré, the radical leftist Félix Guattari, and others.

In addition to Kojève, the other key friend who played a crucial role in the development of Lacan's thought was the structuralist Claude Lévi-Strauss. The structuralism of Lacan's early period follows from that of Lévi-Strauss.[10] Although Lacan adds the subject while Lévi-Strauss rejects it, his concept of the symbolic order owes an immense debt to Lévi-Strauss's thinking about the structures that undergird kinship relations.[11] Lévi-Strauss played a determinative role in Lacan's thinking, but the reverse was not true. Lévi-Strauss did not find anything in Lacan's philosophy that he could bring to bear on his anthropology. This is a common theme among those whom Lacan cites in his own work. Typically, others that influence him don't perceive a reciprocal influence, even when it may exist.

In the 1960s, Lacan met Michel Foucault, Gilles Deleuze, and Jacques Derrida. Foucault participated in Lacan's thirteenth seminar devoted to *The Psychoanalytic Object, 1965–1966*. During this seminar, Lacan analyzes the painting *Las Meninas* (1656) by Diego Velázquez that Foucault interpreted in the opening chapter of *The Order of Things* (1966). Even though Lacan claimed that he was building on Foucault's interpretation, he actually departed significantly from it. While Foucault reduced the painting to being an expression of what he called the epoch of representation, Lacan emphasized the point of absence within the representation, a point that he identified with his own concept of the gaze. But Foucault did not even attend the session where Lacan brought forward his own interpretation of the painting. It was a completely missed encounter.

Similarly, Lacan's initial meeting with Derrida occurred at cross purposes. Although they both lived in Paris, they did not meet until Lacan visited the United States for the first time, where they were both speaking at a structuralism conference in Baltimore. In an essay that he wrote after Lacan's death, Derrida describes this initial meeting. He says, "when I met Lacan in Baltimore for the first time, in 1966 – we were introduced to each other by René Girard – his first words, uttered in a friendly sigh, were: 'So we had to wait to come here, and abroad, in order to meet each other!'"[12] While Derrida presents their encounter as a friendly one, he evinced a thoroughgoing theoretical opposition to Lacan. As with Foucault, Lacan found no theoretical comradery with Derrida, despite the absurd tendency to group all of them within the same intellectual camp.

In the 1950s, Lacan befriended the German philosopher Martin Heidegger. The two were close enough that Martin and his spouse Elfride came to visit Jacques and Sylvia in France when Heidegger came for a conference devoted to his ideas.[13] In her biography of Lacan, Élisabeth Roudinesco recounts an amusing anecdote about this visit that reveals Lacan's mischievousness. Jacques and Sylvia took Martin and Elfride out for a drive in the French countryside. Jacques sped up the car to a pace that frightened Elfride, who asked him to slow down. In response, he perversely increased the speed. During the entire drive, Martin practiced authentically keeping silent while his spouse complained. Although this event seems to bespeak tension between Lacan and Heidegger, Lacan later visited Heidegger in Freiburg when the latter was near death. The relation with Heidegger was amicable but philosophically skewed.[14]

It was yet another instance where the intellectual debt ran in one direction only. While Heidegger's influence on Lacan did not approach that of Kojève or Lévi-Strauss, Lacan did occasionally borrow Heidegger's vocabulary. In his discussion of Edgar Allan Poe's "The Purloined Letter," Lacan claims that at the end of the story, the minister who is stuck with a fake letter, may be called upon to "*Eat your Dasein!*"[15] This is a term that Heidegger popularizes in *Being and Time*, a term associated solely with Heidegger. Lacan intimates that this is the position in which one finds oneself at the end of analysis, when one is bereft of the condolences of a symbolic identity. What's more, in 1956, Lacan translated Heidegger's essay "Logos" into French. But in general, Heidegger didn't figure prominently in Lacan's theoretical development. This is because, influenced by Kant and Hegel, Lacan was a thinker of mediation and not a phenomenologist. In other words, Lacan's starting point was not what experience registers but the limiting and contradictory structure through which experience occurs. For his part, Heidegger never even attempted to work through Lacan's theory. When Lacan sent him a copy of his *Écrits* in 1966, Heidegger claimed in response, "It seems to me the psychiatrist needs a psychiatrist."[16] Like many of Lacan's readers, Heidegger couldn't make head nor tail of the written essays because he did not have the transcripts of the much more intelligible seminars to consult.

A rupture occurred in Lacan's seminar in 1963, when Sainte-Anne Hospital refused to continue to house the seminar due to Lacan being ostracized by the International Psychoanalytical Association. On November 20, 1963, Lacan had begun his yearly seminar at Sainte-Anne. He planned on devoting the eleventh seminar (1963–1964) to the *Names-of-the-Father*, for which this lecture would be the first session. Unfortunately, due to the expulsion from the International Psychoanalytical Association, it would also be the last, leaving this seminar aborted in its infancy. The expulsion occurred not primarily, as one might expect, because of a doctrinal dispute between Lacan and the psychoanalytic authorities, but because of Lacan's practice of what he called the short session. The short session is the trademark of Lacanian analysis and differentiates it from every other branch of psychoanalytic practice.

The short session was Lacan's own invention, a product of his belief in the importance of punctuation to determine significance. According to the doctrine of the short session, a psychoanalytic session should not necessarily last the standard fifty minutes. As Lacan saw it, the problem with this standard-length session was that the analysand could always try to run out the clock, spending a great deal of time babbling away on psychically unimportant matters while holding out on what might be really impactful. As a result, Lacan believed that it was better for the analyst to punctuate the session unpredictably by ending it abruptly at a point of significance for the analysand (a significance that remains for the analysand to interpret, thus requiring a more active engagement on the analysand's part). Due to this practice of the short session, Lacan was able to see many more analysands than more traditional psychoanalysts, who were confined to one analysand per hour. However, according to the International Psychoanalytical Association, the short session was not a theoretical advance but a self-interested money-grab on Lacan's part. The organization thus saw fit to banish Lacan from its ranks and to deny him the status of a training analyst, which meant that he could not officially train other analysts. The expulsion also seemed to announce the end of Lacan's teaching, since Sainte-Anne refused to allow him to give his seminars on the premises. He could no longer train analysts and had no place to instruct them in his approach.

Institutionally homeless, Lacan's seminar seemed to have reached an unplanned end point. But the intervention of Lacan's friend, Louis Althusser, saved the seminar and actually broadened its reach. Althusser appealed to the École Normale Supérieure, where he taught, to provide Lacan with a room to hold his seminar. The authorities granted permission, and Lacan began to offer his teaching to the public as well as psychoanalysts. Ironically, Lacan's expulsion from the International Psychoanalytical Association ended up giving him a much larger platform to advocate for his thought than he otherwise would have had, with the result that his influence on psychoanalytic thinking began to outstrip that of any other living analyst. From the standpoint of the International Psychoanalytical Association, his expulsion, which had been meant as a punishment for his deviation from the association's traditions, completely backfired. In 1964, Lacan even founded his own psychoanalytic school, L'École Freudienne de Paris. This organization didn't have the reach to compete with the established International Psychoanalytical Association, but it did have a sizeable impact on psychoanalysis in France.

Althusser was the only major thinker in Lacan's lifetime who avowed any influence from Lacan's work. Unlike other figures such as Lévi-Strauss and Hyppolite who knew Lacan well but never allowed his theory to have any impact on their own thinking, Althusser brought Lacan's thought into his Marxism. Lacan's conceptions of the imaginary and symbolic orders played a central role in Althusser's most famous work, the essay "Ideology and Ideological State Apparatuses." In addition, he wrote another essay, "Freud and Lacan," describing Lacan's importance alongside that of Freud.[17]

The first seminar that Lacan gave at the École Normale Supérieure was the eleventh and bore the title *The Four Fundamental Concepts of Psychoanalysis, 1963–1964*. This seminar marked a significant turning point in Lacan's life. Not only was it given to a larger audience than usual, but it also introduced Lacan to his future son-in-law and literary executor, Jacques-Alain Miller. Miller, a student of Althusser at the time of the seminar and a young Maoist, was immediately taken by Lacan. For his part, Lacan found himself drawn to Miller, who, despite his young age (nineteen at the time), posed the most challenging questions in the seminar. From this moment on, Miller became Lacan's primary intellectual guardian and inheritor. Miller began to act as the official mouthpiece for Lacan, even going so far as to edit the seminar on *The Four Fundamental Concepts of Psychoanalysis* for publication. Miller's growing importance alienated many of those who had been with Lacan from the early seminars.[18] He remains a divisive figure among Lacan's followers because his distinctive interpretation of Lacan's work determines not only the course of Lacan's posthumous intellectual trajectory but even the structure of his published seminars.[19]

When he took up the eleventh seminar again in January of 1964, newly housed at the École Normale Supérieure, Lacan did not simply resume the *Names-of-the-Father* seminar that his expulsion from the International Psychoanalytical Association had interrupted. Driven by the belief that every interruption is a punctuation, he decided to change course completely and take the opportunity to outline the basic concepts of psychoanalysis from his unique point of view. This turn ended up producing the most accessible seminar and the one that would do the most to disseminate Lacan's thought around the world. The interruption of the seminar drove Lacan to construct what is clearly his magnum opus (*Seminar XI: The Four Fundamental Concepts of Psychoanalysis, 1963–1964*), even if Lacan himself didn't see it as such.

The first session of this seminar addressed Lacan's expulsion from the International Psychoanalytical Association, which he linked to Baruch Spinoza's excommunication, his *cherem*, from the Jewish community of Amsterdam on July 27, 1656. The Jewish community exiled the young Spinoza from its midst with utmost severity due to his undoctrinaire thinking and the challenge that he posed to the religious hierarchy. By turning himself into the contemporary version of Spinoza suffering under a *cherem*, Lacan did not attempt to express any theoretical solidarity with Spinoza. Instead, he used this homology as a way of transforming himself into a hero of intellectual freedom, someone not afraid to risk excommunication for the sake of truth.

As part of his move to reach a wider audience, Lacan oversaw the publication of all his major writings (his written work outside the seminar) in 1966. In an enormous volume entitled simply *Écrits*, Lacan collected all the major essays that he had written up to that time. Along with Foucault's *The Order of Things* (*Les Mots et les choses*), published in the same year, the *Écrits* was a bestseller in France, despite the relative unintelligibility of Lacan's writing. Although certain thinkers (such as Jean-Claude Milner) insist on the primacy of the written work for Lacan's system, this position accounts for neither the needless difficulty of the essays nor their dogged concern with battles against other psychoanalytic orientations (such as, especially, ego psychology).[20] Nonetheless, the success of this publication buoyed Lacan, even though he expressed disdain for publication. The success of the *Écrits* led to a greater public attendance at Lacan's seminars, which prompted him to offer some of them, special closed sessions, to only a select group of students.

The seminars immediately before and after *Seminar XI* – the entire decade of the 1960s – mark the theoretical high point of Lacan's thinking. From the ninth seminar on identification (1961–1962) through the sixteenth on the big Other and little other (1968–1969), Lacan developed the form of his theory that has had the most lasting importance around the world. Though compelling ideas emerge later – such as the formulas of sexuation in *Seminar XX* (1972–1973) – it is in this middle period that Lacan articulates his most radical and far-reaching ideas, primarily through working out the idea of the *objet a* and recognizing the role of enjoyment in subjectivity.

In the last ten years of his life, Lacan became increasingly obsessed with Borromean knots. The Borromean knot holds together three pieces of string in such a way that if one were to be removed, the entire knot would collapse. This form of knot provided a way for Lacan to visualize the relationship between his three registers of experience – the symbolic, the imaginary, and the real. It was not a metaphor for the relationship but a topological enactment of it. As a result of this fascination with knots, the later seminars often lost the intelligibility of the earlier ones and descended into a cultist obscurantism designed to appeal only to initiates. No contemporary Lacanian thinkers refer to the Borromean knots to make sense of subjectivity or the social order. This itself is the definitive verdict on Lacan's turn to the Borromean knot.

Lacan's last major act before his death in 1981 was to dissolve his École Freudienne de Paris. At the time, it was not clear that he had the right to do so, since the set-up of the school was not that of a dictatorship, even though he might have imagined it to be so. Althusser, for one, claimed that Lacan did not have the authority to issue a statement of dissolution for the school. Regardless, Lacan's act effectively ended the school. This dissolution allowed Jacques-Alain Miller to take over a new Lacanian school soon after Lacan's death, named the École de la cause freudienne. Since he also oversaw the gradual release of Lacan's seminars for publication (a process that is, amazingly, still ongoing), Miller had enormous control over Lacan's legacy. Nonetheless, a great deal of splintering among Lacanian-oriented groups took place after Lacan's death.

Lacan died on September 9, 1981, at the age of 80. According to biographer Élisabeth Roudinesco, his final words were, "I am stubborn . . . I am disappearing."[21] While the person disappeared, the thought did not. One might even say that Lacan's death caused his star to rise in the theoretical firmament. After he was gone, diverse thinkers could employ Lacan's thought in directions that he himself would have vigorously resisted, including the direction of leftist politics.

Despite his contemporary position as a central figure in the theorization of leftist politics, Lacan himself was not a figure of the Left. He was a political conservative. While many of his students and trainees (including Miller and Lacan's daughter Judith Miller) were Maoists, this political orientation never tempted him. He saw psychoanalysis as a way of dismantling the myth of progress that underwrites most leftist politics. Lacan's personal investment in the accumulation of wealth also militated against any commitment toward egalitarianism. But this hasn't prevented many radical leftists – Alain Badiou and Slavoj Žižek, to name just two – from discovering the emancipatory political fecundity of his thought.

Since one of Lacan's contributions to psychoanalytic theorizing was to deal a death blow to psychobiographical criticism, one should probably have skipped this section of the book if one wanted to be true to Lacan. However, the point of understanding Lacan's biography is not to explain his thought as an expression of its context but rather to see how this thought transcended and deformed the context out of which it emerged. For instance, Kojève's influence did not lead Lacan to insist on the primacy of the subject's desire for recognition as Kojève did. Instead, Lacan transformed Kojève's conception of desire to make it his own. This is just one instance of how Lacan transcended his milieu.

Lacan's life reveals a person engaged with his intellectual world while also struggling to conceptualize what challenges the givens of that world. In this sense, his biography is in keeping with the psychoanalytic project itself, which emphasizes what does not fit in the prevailing order of things. As Lacan himself insisted, thinkers are not reducible to their biographies but constantly think what should be impossible for them to think; they break through with ideas that defy everything that constitutes them. This is what makes a thinker such as Lacan worth reading in the first place.

Notes

1 Sartre and Lacan knew each other and had several friends in common but were not themselves close friends.

2 Jacques Lacan, "On My Antecedents," in *Écrits: The First Complete Edition in English*, trans. Bruce Fink (New York: Norton, 2006), 51.

3 An English translation of Lacan's thesis on Aimée has never been published as a book.

4 Even though Lacan's essay on the mirror stage would become his most famous written work, his original talk from 1936, which was quite different from the written text eventually published in 1949, did not survive. For an account of this lost artifact, see Élisabeth Roudinesco, "The Mirror Stage: An Obliterated Archive," trans. Barbara Bray, in *The Cambridge Companion to Lacan*, ed. Jean-Michel Rabaté (Cambridge: Cambridge University Press, 2003), 25–34.

5 Élisabeth Roudinesco, *Jacques Lacan*, trans. Barbara Bray (New York: Columbia University Press, 1997 [1993]), 158.

6 Roudinesco recounts this missed encounter in Roudinesco, *Jacques Lacan*.

7 See Alexandre Kojève, *Introduction à la lecture de Hegel*, ed. Raymond Queneau (Paris: Gallimard, 1947). Unfortunately, the English translation of this work excludes several important sessions from the French original.

8 Jacques Lacan, "Five Letters from Jacques Lacan to Alexandre Kojève," ed. Juan Pablo Lucchelli, trans. Todd McGowan, *American Imago* 73.3 (2016): 341. Juan Pablo Lucchelli discovered this dedication that Lacan wrote to Kojève on the first issue of the journal *La Psychanalyse* in Kojève's private library that had been donated to the Bibliothèque Nationale de France.

9 Jacques Lacan, *The Seminar, Book I: Freud's Papers on Technique, 1953–1954*, ed. Jacques-Alain Miller, trans. John Forrester (New York: Norton, 1988 [1975]), 222.

10 Lucchelli contends that Lacan borrows many of his early claims from Lévi-Strauss, including the idea that the signifier has structural priority over the signified. According to Lucchelli, "It seems clear that Lévi-Strauss postulates the supremacy of the signifier over the world (and thus over the signified)." Juan-Pablo Lucchelli, *Lacan avec et sans Lévi-Strauss* (Paris: Éditions Nouvelles Cécille Defaut, 2014), 62. While Lacan acknowledges the importance of Lévi-Strauss at certain points, he doesn't credit him for several major ideas, although Lucchelli identifies an intellectual debt. See also Markos Zafiropoulos, *Lacan et Lévi-Strauss, ou le retour à Freud, 1951–1957* (Paris: Presses Universitaires de France, 2003).

11 See Claude Lévi-Strauss, *The Elementary Structures of Kinship*, trans. James Harle Bell, John Richard von Sturmer, and Rodney Needham (Boston: Beacon Press, 1969 [1949]).

12 Jacques Derrida, "For the Love of Lacan," in *Resistances of Psychoanalysis*, trans. Peggy Kamuf, Pascale-Ann Brault, and Michael Naas (Stanford: Stanford University Press, 1998 [1996]), 50.

13 Sartre and Merleau-Ponty, though more intellectually proximate to Heidegger than Lacan, boycotted the conference due to Heidegger's Nazism. Lacan had no qualms about going to the conference and even entertaining Heidegger at his home.

14 For the complete version of this anecdote, see Élisabeth Roudinesco, *Jacques Lacan & Co.: A History of Psychoanalysis in France, 1925–1985*, trans. Jeffrey Mehlman (Chicago: University of Chicago Press, 1990 [1986]), 299.

15 Jacques Lacan, *The Seminar of Jacques Lacan, Book II: The Ego in Freud's Theory and in the Technique of Psychoanalysis, 1954–1955*, ed. Jacques-Alain Miller, trans. Sylvana Tomaselli (New York: Norton, 1991 [1978]), 205.

16 Quoted in Roudinesco, *Jacques Lacan*, 231.

17 According to Althusser, Lacan reveals the ultimate radicality of the unconscious as completely irreducible to consciousness. Althusser contends that Lacan enables us to see that "philosophico-idealist interpretations of the unconscious as a second consciousness, of the unconscious as bad faith (Sartre), of the unconscious as the cankerous survival of a non-current structure or non-sense (Merleau-Ponty), all the interpretations of the unconscious as a biologico-archetypical 'id' (Jung) became what they were: not the beginnings of a theory but null 'theories,' ideological misunderstandings." Louis Althusser, "Freud and Lacan" (1964), in *Lenin and Philosophy and Other Essays*, trans. Ben Brewster (New York: Monthly Review Press, 1971), 208. After Lacan's contribution, there can be no more doubt about the unconscious as a break from both biology and culture.

18 Miller himself offers an explanation for the rift that he created among Lacan's followers. He says, "This conflict goes back to 1964 when I first met Lacan, before I had met his daughter. The two of us got along from the very first, and this itself has always displeased certain of his other students. It was me, still a student at the time, that he invited for weekends at his country house! It was me to whom he gave the mission of transcribing [the seminars]. He had always refused to have the seminar published, that is, until I established the text of the 'Fundamental Concepts' in a way that won his approval because he recognized himself in it. He put his hand on my shoulder; we made a pact. He gave me this task, he didn't give it to the others. And he chose me from the crowd to make me promise that I would take on all of the seminars ... It is this that they cannot tolerate: they dream to get from me that which they lost of the Freudian field because of their conflict with Lacan. I symbolize the living signifier of their castration!" Quoted in Sherry Turkle, *Psychoanalytic Politics: Jacques Lacan and Freud's French Revolution*, 2nd ed. (New York: Guilford Press, 1992), 292–293. From this account, it is evident that Miller doesn't suffer from an excess of humility, although his analysis is certainly plausible.

19 While editing each seminar, Miller inserts titles for every session and heading for the subsections in the sessions that he himself creates. The reach and visibility of his editorial hand chafe certain Lacanian thinkers. When Miller initially published *Le Séminaire, livre VIII: Le transfert, 1960–1961*, his version contained so many errors that a group of psychoanalytic theorists got together and published their own book – *Le transfert dans tous ses errata* [*The Transference in All Its Errors*] – about the gravity of the mistakes in the text that Miller produced. After the appearance of this critique, Miller reedited the seminar and published a corrected translation, which is the one now available (and was the basis for Bruce Fink's English translation).

20 Milner is up front about this preference for the writing over the seminars in *A Search for Clarity*. He writes, "whoever is interested in knowledge always has the right, but not the duty, to neglect the seminars." Jean-Claude Milner, *A Search for Clarity: Science and Philosophy in Lacan's Oeuvre*, trans. Ed Pluth (Evanston, IL: Northwestern University Press, 2021 [1995]), 15. To be fair, when Milner wrote this in 1995, only a few of the seminars had appeared in print. As a result, it made sense not to give the seminars a prominent role in the structure of Lacan's thought. Otherwise, one risked giving the esoteric form of his thought, the seminars available only for the few, an absolute priority. But today, after all the seminars are publicly available and most of them are published, it is clear that they represent a form of Lacan's thought that one cannot neglect.

21 Quoted in Roudinesco, *Jacques Lacan & Co.*, 679.

Chapter 3

Reception

By and large, readers have not struggled with Lacan's ideas. Because of the unapproachable quality of his written work, they either dismissed him out of hand as a charlatan or completely misinterpreted his fundamental project. Linguist and political philosopher Noam Chomsky was perhaps the most outspoken proponent of the first position, but he had many fellow travelers. Confronted with what he perceived as Lacan's inaccessible style, Chomsky proclaimed, "my frank opinion was that he was a conscious charlatan."[1] Chomsky's dismissive judgment had many echoes around the world, so much so that one defender of Lacan, Peter Mathews, felt the need to write *Lacan the Charlatan* to respond to all the intellectual dismissals of his status as a serious thinker.[2]

It was easy for people to classify Lacan as a charlatan because all the public formulations of his ideas – lectures, publications, and even television appearances – strove for opacity. Lacan presented his ideas in an almost indecipherable way to force those interacting with him to abandon their preconceptions. He didn't want to put out a line of thinking that people could easily assimilate to what they already thought. It turns out that this is basically a program for being seen by most as a spouter of nonsense.

But those who dedicated themselves to finding something valuable in this appearance of nonsense often fared no better with it than those who were simply dismissive. Embracing Lacan – at least before 1989 – typically meant twisting his thought into a misshapen monstrosity that bore little resemblance to the thought itself. The works of Lacan that achieved a wide dissemination and that theorists eagerly took up led to comprehensive misunderstandings of Lacan's entire philosophical project.

The number one culprit in promulgating the misunderstanding of Lacan's thought is unsurprisingly his most influential and well-known piece of writing – "The Mirror Stage as Formative of the *I* Function as Revealed in Psychoanalytic Experience." No single work from Lacan has had more influence than his brief essay on the mirror stage that articulates his theory of how the ego forms in the subject. If Lacan had not written it, the widespread grasp of his philosophy would have advanced by decades, even though the brief essay brought him considerable acclaim. It was an idea that Lacan might have better honored in the breach than in writing it out. This essay was almost singlehandedly responsible for the mistaken association of Lacan with those who called subjectivity into question, even though seeing it this way derives from a misreading of the essay. For the sake of advancing the understanding of Lacan in the world, if we could destroy every copy of "The Mirror Stage" essay, we should do so.

"The Mirror Stage" essay aims at revealing how the subject's ego forms and proving how the ego serves as the source of an illusory mastery over the body. Lacan contends that between the ages of six and eighteen months old, the child lacks mastery over its body. Its body is a fragmentary entity, not a whole that it can control. But when the child looks in the mirror, it sees – or imagines – a wholeness that doesn't exist. The mirror image offers the illusion of wholeness and control that the child fails to have with its real body. Through the effect of this mirror stage, an imaginary ego develops, and the imaginary coherence of the ego obscures the real fragmentation of the body. "The Mirror Stage" reveals the imaginary source of the ego – it has its basis in the image, not in the actual capacities of the subject itself – and thus denounces the ego and its sense of mastery as illusory. The ego's illusion of mastery, Lacan argues at the end of the essay, leads to a misconception of freedom. When the philosophy of freedom bases itself on the illusion of the individual's autonomy, it fails to account for how the unconscious incessantly undermines the ego's mastery. Rather than being autonomous, the ego masks a bodily fragmentation that cannot serve as the foundation for freedom.

In "The Mirror Stage" essay, Lacan takes aim at Jean-Paul Sartre's existentialism that conceives of the subject as condemned to freedom. Lacan aims at preserving the lacking subject, the subject of desire, whose freedom becomes complicated but not at all eliminated by the determinations of the unconscious. Although he doesn't mention Sartre by name, he does identify existentialism and its failures as his target at the end of the essay. He claims that existentialism's investment in a purported "self-sufficiency of consciousness . . . ties the illusion of autonomy in which it puts its faith to the ego's constitutive misrecognitions."[3] Sartrean existentialism links freedom to the independence of consciousness, but the role of the mirror stage in forming the ego reveals that this independence is not so independent at all. Lacan's critique here sets the stage for a conception of subjectivity that locates its freedom in the irreducibility of subject to the ego or the irreducibility of the unconscious to its symbolic determinations.

Lacan's critique in this essay is a critique of the ego, not the subject, but this is a distinction that almost every reader failed to register. The ego is an illusion of mastery and wholeness, while subjectivity is a self-divided failure of mastery. "The Mirror Stage" became the emblem for Lacan's supposed critique of the subject, a critique that he never actually advanced. Almost all of Lacan's readers just missed what was at stake in this essay. This included Lacan's friend Louis Althusser. While Althusser did much to propagate Lacan's philosophy (including giving him space to teach at the École Normale Superieure), he also prioritized the mirror stage essay in his theory of ideological interpellation, a theory that came to dominate most thinking about how ideology works, especially within Marxism and film studies.

Althusser conceives of ideology as a system that hails individuals into it by leading them into recognizing themselves as subjects. In this way of thinking, the subject is not what doesn't fit in the social order but what does. For Althusser, the subject misrecognizes itself as the addressee of an ideological hail, just as the child looking in the mirror misrecognizes its mirror image as itself. In "Ideology and Ideological State Apparatuses," he states, "*all ideology hails or interpellates concrete individuals as concrete subjects*, by the functioning of the category of the subject."[4] One can see the slippage at work in Althusser's appropriation of Lacan's analysis of the mirror stage: Where Lacan identifies the ego as an effect of imaginary misrecognition, Althusser defines the subject as the result of this misrecognition. A confusion between ego and subject or between imaginary and symbolic takes place in the turn from Lacan to Althusser. What results is a massive diffusion of the image of Lacan as a critic of the subject in myriad fields. This seemingly innocent misreading on the part of Althusser transforms the great defender of the subject into its vehement opponent. Thanks to the initial inflated importance of the "Mirror Stage" essay and to Althusser's subsequent distortion of it, Lacan became philosophically unrecognizable for nearly twenty years in larger theoretical circles.

This interpretation of Lacan appeared across disciplines, but it infected none worse than that of film theory. For the most part, film theory in the 1970s and 1980s became a horrible amalgam of thinkers diametrically opposed to each other, and it constituted this amalgam through the critique of the subject, which was, in the idiom of the time (and following Althusser), an imaginary effect of the cinematic apparatus.[5] The interpretation of Lacan as a thinker reducing the subject to an imaginary effect was not idiosyncratic. It spread throughout the English-speaking world and made inroads everywhere, even in France, despite relying on a fundamental misreading of Lacan's theoretical project.

Armed with this misunderstanding of Lacan, a theorist might examine a classic Hollywood film, say Billy Wilder's *Double Indemnity* (1944), as a work that enacts the process of ideological interpellation. *Double Indemnity* depicts an insurance salesperson, Walter Neff (Fred MacMurray), conspiring with a woman, Phyllis Dietrichson (Barbara Stanwick), to kill her husband and collect his life insurance. While the film's narrative and its look reveal the tawdry underside of capitalist society, the structure of spectatorship – looking at a distance on a fantasized reality – has an ideological effect. One watches the film and imagines oneself with mastery over the filmic reality, a reality that appears seamless and impervious to radical change. According to the film theory of the 1970s and 1980s, spectators are concrete individuals who take themselves as subjects, thanks to the ideological deception that occurs when watching a film. This is the end point of the distortion of Lacan's thought, a distortion that made him appear to be a social constructionist.

The abstruse quality of the mirror stage essay undoubtedly contributed to this misreading. But it had the outsized importance that it had because Lacan published so few written works. For many critics looking to gain an entrée into Lacan's thought, "The Mirror Stage" functioned as a portal, especially in cinema studies. It also has the virtue of being short, so editors can stick it in an anthology for students. We now can see how deleterious the results of the infatuation with this essay were. The cinematic experience became reduced to the structure of ideological interpellation. From this theoretical viewpoint, narrative cinema was just the propagation of capitalist ideology in its most banal form. As a result, theorists completely missed the possible aesthetic radicality residing in even cinema's most common forms. These theorists were so anticapitalist that they could not recognize any mainstream critiques of capitalism. Thanks to the bastardized reading of Lacan, theory became too radical to notice any radicality in its objects.

A corrective was desperately needed, and it arrived dramatically in the form of Joan Copjec and Slavoj Žižek in the late 1980s and early 1990s. They were friends and theoretical comrades unafraid to write scathing criticisms of previous interpretations of Lacan's work. Copjec and Žižek, an American and a Slovene, theorized Lacan as a defender of subjectivity rather than a critic. They emphasized the link between Lacan and the tradition of German Idealism, a link that Lacan himself often disingenuously downplayed or even disavowed.[6] Appropriately, Copjec and Žižek's major contributions began in the same year – 1989.

In this year, Copjec published "The Orthopsychic Subject," which was a critique of the prevailing misinterpretation of Lacan that dominated film theory. This essay later became the lead chapter in her landmark first book, *Read My Desire: Lacan Against the Historicists*. Here, Copjec is at pains to distinguish Lacan's theory from all philosophies that reduce the subject to its historical context – hence the book's title. The problem with film theory, as Copjec sees it, is that it theorized away the possibility for cinematic radicality through its emphasis on how the filmic experience produces the subject as an imaginary effect of the apparatus.

Where earlier theorists seemingly inspired by Lacan took the subject as nothing but the effect of its signifying situation, Copjec advances a much more theoretically astute proposition – and one more in tune with Lacan's own thinking. "The Orthopsychic Subject" defends the subject as the result of a breach in signification, a response to the necessary failure of the symbolic order. Copjec writes, "the subject instituted by the Lacanian gaze does not come into being as the realization of a possibility opened up by the law of the Other. It is rather an impossibility that is crucial to the constitution of the subject – the impossibility, precisely, of any ultimate confirmation from the Other."[7] Copjec's claim here is not the naïve insistence that the subject exists prior to its symbolic context or transcends this context. She sees instead that the symbolic field – what Copjec refers to here as the Other – is riven with impossibility, an impossibility that constitutes the subject while giving birth to its desire. Through Copjec's interpretation of Lacan, the subject becomes a site that challenges the ruling ideology's dominance rather than confirming it, as so many earlier theorists believed. The breakthrough that this essay and book chapter represented is itself almost impossible to overstate, so thoroughly did it overturn the prevailing common sense about Lacan in relation to other theorists of the subject.

To measure the distance that separates Copjec's theoretical position from the prevailing one based on "The Mirror Stage" and Althusser, let's return to *Double Indemnity*. Armed with Copjec's insights, we could see how the film articulates a critique of ideology, not just how it performs an ideological interpellation. In her own analysis of the film, Copjec focuses on how *Double Indemnity* shows the breakdown of public space in capitalist society. Neff and Dietrichson don't get away with the crime because they fail at every point to use public space as a cover for their activities. Their retreat into privacy leads to their crime and also their inability to get away with it. By depicting this through the visual field, *Double Indemnity* avoids being the kind of ideological trap that traditional Lacanian film theory would make of it. The film functions as a critique of the ubiquity of private space in the capitalist universe. By revealing this, Copjec enables theorists to see the disruptiveness at work even in Hollywood cinema.

Copjec's essay not only challenged the Anglo-American reception of Lacan's thought. It even disturbed those in France who saw themselves as Lacan's direct inheritors and the guardians of his legacy. She presented the ideas that became "The Orthopsychic Subject" in 1988 at a Paris cinema conference called *Théorie du Cinéma et Crise dans la Théorie* [*Theory of Cinema and Crisis in Theory*]. The respondents to Copjec's paper were established Lacanian film theorists Christian Metz and Raymond Bellour, two thinkers invested in the traditional Lacanian film theory based on Althusser's reading of Lacan. Both verbalized their complete disagreement after the talk, but then Bellour went so far as to refuse to write the essay response to Copjec's essay that he had promised for the journal issue dedicated to the conference.

In lieu of an essay, Bellour wrote a letter to the journal detailing why a written response would be out of the question. Clearly, Copjec's talk touched a nerve with Bellour because it upended his previous certainty about the link between the cinematic apparatus and the mirror stage. This is why he could not just respond through the normal channels and had to express his outrage through a special letter. By introducing the gaze as an object that disturbs the visual field in the cinema and challenges mastery over this field, Copjec threw the accepted position into disarray. Bellour's letter claimed that Copjec "lets one believe that they [the French followers of Lacan] would all be incorrect in relation to a hypothetical truth of Lacan of which it [Copjec's essay] would be the possessor."[8] What Bellour could not admit – and what prevented him from writing his promised response essay to Copjec – was that she totally shifted the ground for understanding Lacan's philosophical project. Copjec returned film theory to a Lacanian position by challenging the misunderstanding rooted in Althusser's theory of ideological interpellation. This holds not just for cinema studies but for thinking about the gaze at work throughout the social order. Bellour's lack of response and subsequent excessive response revealed how Copjec's interpretation touched the unconscious. Bellour called her essay "an extreme and personal reaction" to obscure his own extreme defensiveness.[9] Copjec's essay revolutionized the Lacanian approach to film to such an extent that most following in her wake simply could not avow what she had done, except a small coterie of people devoted specifically to Lacan. Like Bellour, most film theorists in the decades following her work have avoided any substantive response. As Lacanian psychoanalysis has gone out of vogue in film studies, people in the field simply pretend that Joan Copjec didn't exist. They can dismiss Lacanian film theory because they know only of its traditional (and misconceived) version. Silence about Copjec's work extends beyond the first chapter of *Read My Desire*, however.

The book's final chapter matches the breakthrough of the first. This chapter challenges Judith Butler's constructivist notion of sex, a notion that was and remains the theoretical doxa. According to Butler, sex is not a substantial biological given but the result of the construction of gender. Gender construction leads us to assume the solidity of sex, but no such solidity exists. In Copjec's final chapter, provocatively titled "Sex and the Euthanasia of Reason," she shows that far from being a construction, sex is what interrupts all constructivist narratives. Sex, for Copjec, is the failure of sense that prevents construction from ever becoming complete. Copjec reveals that psychoanalytic theory stakes out an anti-constructivism that refuses all substantialism about sex since it recognizes sex as what blocks all social and symbolic structures.

In one of the most ingenious and audacious theoretical gestures ever put forward, Copjec links Lacan's formulas of sexuation to Immanuel Kant's antinomies of reason articulated in the *Critique of Pure Reason*. After beginning the chapter by dismantling Butler's constructivist conception of sex, Copjec demonstrates how Lacan's formulas of sexuation detail sex as a fundamental impasse within the structure of signification, just as the Kantian antinomies mark the points at which reason necessarily fails. By connecting feminine sexuation to the mathematical antinomies and masculine sexuation to the dynamical antinomies, this chapter lays out the priority of feminine subjectivity. The feminine side articulates a structural impossibility, while the male form responds to that impossibility with prohibition.[10] Feminine subjectivity marks the impossibility of attaining complete enjoyment, while masculine subjectivity confronts the prohibition against it. In this way, masculinity suffers from a deception: the prohibition makes a full enjoyment seem possible, otherwise it wouldn't be prohibited. Femininity, in contrast, has its basis in the structural impossibility of complete enjoyment. By theorizing the priority of feminine sexuation, Copjec considers Lacan and psychoanalytic theory as integral to the project of feminism. This both distinguished Copjec from the feminists that preceded her and paved a path for those who followed in her wake.

Copjec unleashed a tidal wave of psychoanalytic feminist theory that took Lacan as a central point of departure. Thanks in no small part to Copjec's interpretation of Lacan, feminist theorists began to see psychoanalysis as not just a weapon in the feminist arsenal but as itself feminist. These feminist contributions came from Renata Salecl in *(Per)versions of Love and Hate* (1998), Jean Wyatt in *Risking Difference* (2004), Hilary Neroni in *The Violent Woman* (2005), Alenka Zupančič in *The Odd One In* (2008), Jennifer Friedlander in *The Feminine Look* (2009), Hyon Joo Yoo in

Cinema at the Crossroads (2012), Frances Restuccia in *The Blue Box* (2012), and Mari Ruti in *Penis Envy and Other Bad Feelings* (2018), among many others.[11] In each case, it was Lacan's insistence on the real as the point where symbolization breaks down that enabled the feminist intervention that challenged the presuppositions of a sexist ideology.

These feminists writing in Copjec's wake came to a dramatically different verdict on the relationship between psychoanalysis and feminism than the feminists of the previous generation. Even those of the previous generation relatively friendly to psychoanalysis and Lacan nonetheless shared a basic suspicion that psychoanalytic theory was, at least on some level, invested in the promulgation of the phallus as a site of social authority. We can see this proclivity in the argument of Toril Moi's *Sexual/Textual Politics*. While she is not hostile to Lacan's thought and recognizes its uses for feminism, Moi believes that his thought demands that everyone accept the authority of the phallus. The problem lies in the position that Lacan grants to the phallus in the symbolic order, which everyone must occupy. Moi writes, "To enter into the Symbolic Order means to accept the phallus as the representation of the Law of the Father. All human culture and all life in society is dominated by the Symbolic Order, and thus by the phallus as the sign of lack."[12] While Moi sees that Lacan distinguishes the phallus as a signifier from the penis as a body part, his thinking does not go far enough, in her view, in the effort to distinguish them. Moi's feminism, along with that of others in her generation, such as Laura Mulvey, E. Ann Kaplan, and Elisabeth Grosz, turned to psychoanalysis for its theoretical resources but always did so warily.

It is important to mention one exception to this general trend – Jacqueline Rose. Rose was an unabashed feminist who embraced Lacan's thought without reservations. In *Sexuality and the Field of Vision*, Rose articulated a feminist vision of psychoanalytic theory, a vision that recognized this theory as itself intrinsically feminist. Three years before the publication of Copjec's "The Orthopsychic Subject," her book advanced the idea that Freud and Lacan's invocation of the phallus was an attempt to deflate rather than inflate its social and political position. Rose states that for psychoanalysis, "the status of the phallus is a fraud."[13] This distance between Rose's claim about the Lacanian conception of the phallus and Moi's is decisive. It mirrors the distance between a psychoanalytic feminism and a feminism that just employs certain psychoanalytic tropes. Rose stands next to Joan Copjec as a fundamental exemplar of the former position.

Just as Copjec ushered in a radical transformation in the reception of Lacan's thought in 1989, so did Slavoj Žižek. His book *The Sublime Object of Ideology* upended the theoretical world. Like Copjec, Žižek dissociated Lacan from the thinkers misleadingly associated with him – Gilles Deleuze, Jacques Derrida, Michel Foucault, and other French theorists. As Žižek shows, far from distancing himself from subjectivity in the manner of these other thinkers, Lacan takes the Cartesian cogito – subjectivity – as the basis for his theorizing. For Lacan, the lacking subject is not an illusion to be overcome but a fact to be embraced and even enjoyed.

Beginning in *The Sublime Object of Ideology* and following it up in over fifty subsequent books, Žižek works out a heretofore unremarked connection between Lacanian psychoanalysis, Hegelian dialectics, and the Marxist critique of capitalism. This connection consists in the recognition of a negativity that traverses the subject in both Lacan's psychoanalytic theory and Hegel's dialectics. For both Hegel and Lacan, subjectivity names a failure that cannot be integrated into the symbolic order. Bringing together Hegel and Lacan in this way reveals their implicit political project that augments the Marxist one in Žižek's eyes. Although he pronounces himself a Marxist, he also sees in Hegel and Lacan a political vision beyond that of Marx, a vision in which an irreducible contradiction plays the central role. The marriage of Hegel, Lacan, and Marx remains Žižek's most important legacy and has become the most fertile terrain of Lacanian theorizing. It helped to spawn a series of important books, from Rebecca Comay's *Mourning Sickness* (2010) to Adrian Johnston's *Adventures in Transcendental Materialism* (2014) to Dominik Finkelde's *Excessive Subjectivity* (2017).

Žižek's focus on negativity in Lacan's thought allows him to create a new theory of ideology that stretches this thought in a direction that Lacan himself could not have anticipated. This theory advances a direct challenge to Althusser by taking Lacan's subject as what resists ideological interpellation rather than the result that ideological interpellation produces. Žižek's Lacan is a politically radical thinker who allows us to understand why ideology works so well to keep capitalist subjects quiescent. Ideology, as Žižek understands it, delivers subjects from what Lacan calls the traumatic real. This is why they invest themselves so heartily in it. In the *Sublime Object of Ideology*, he writes, "The function of ideology is not to offer us a point of escape from our reality but to offer us the social reality itself as some escape from some traumatic, real kernel."[14] According to Žižek, Lacan's conception of the real offers an explanation for why ideology develops in the first place. It provides respite from a traumatic encounter with the real by giving the subject a social reality free from the real's disruptiveness.

While Copjec and Žižek are committed allies in advancing the cause of Lacanian theory, their take on it actually contains a crucial difference that manifests itself in the figure from German Idealism with which they associate Lacan's thought. While neither of them ever openly mentions this difference, it becomes almost self-evident with a cursory overview of their particular ways of commenting on Lacan's work. According to Copjec, Lacan is a Kantian committed to exposing the impasses of the symbolic order. As a result of this emphasis, she demonstrates a preference for Lacan's later thinking on sexuation in which these impasses come to the fore. The Lacanian subject for Copjec is one that constantly comes up against its unsurpassable limits, just like the Kantian subject.

For his part, Žižek invests himself in the idea of Lacan as a closet Hegelian. This necessitates Žižek privileging the Lacan of the middle seminars where he theorizes the importance of the real as the point of impossibility within the symbolic order. From Žižek's perspective, the real drives the subject forward through successive failures, just like the movement of the Hegelian dialectic. Contradiction is not an external barrier as it is for Kant but an internal split that animates subjectivity. Žižek latches on to the Lacan of the middle period, the Lacan who theorizes how what seems impossible can actually happen. This is a Hegelian version of Lacan.

While Žižek saw Lacan's theory as a way to move beyond certain limitations of Marxism, other theorists attempted to integrate the two movements together more closely. This process began with Marxist Louis Althusser, who took the mirror stage essay as paradigmatic, saw the subject as a problem to criticize, and, most damningly, failed to recognize the importance of the Lacanian real as the site for radical politics. These were failings that subsequent Lacanian Marxists would correct.

Three are especially worthy of mention – Fredric Jameson, Alain Badiou, and Anna Kornbluh. Jameson took Lacan's thinking as a path for reimagining the act of Marxist literary interpretation in *The Political Unconscious* (1982). This work employed Lacan's categories of the real, symbolic, and imaginary to illustrate how literary works might formally envision a resolution of the contradictions of their historical epoch. In *Being and Event* (1988), Badiou modeled his conception of the event as a radical break from the prevailing situation on Lacan's real. The event is what doesn't fit within the situation, just as the real is what interrupts the smooth functioning of the symbolic order. The event is also the site of political upheaval. Kornbluh, for her part, relied on Lacanian psychoanalysis to draw out the importance of symbolic forms for ushering in political change. This is her primary effort in *The Order of Forms* (2019). These Lacanian-inspired Marxists have produced works adjacent to those of Slavoj Žižek. All share with Žižek a commitment to recognizing the primacy of form over content.

A related political development that took place during the early 2000s was the adoption of Lacanian theory – this time, of the Lacan of the real – by Lee Edelman, who became one of the most influential queer theorists of his time. Edelman, who focused on the destructive potential of the Lacanian real and of enjoyment or jouissance, agitated for the disruption of the heteronormative symbolic order. Edelman's magnum opus, *No Future: Queer Theory and the Death Drive*, presents Lacan as a queer thinker, one who captures the fissures within heteronormativity. For Edelman, Lacan's thought fits queer theory perfectly because it distances sexuality from reproduction. Lacan denaturalizes sexuality and associates it with a self-annihilating drive. This was what Edelman picked up and made central in his Lacanian queer theory, which gained a number of adherents. In the aftermath of Edelman's work, debates between queer theory's Lacanians and anti-Lacanians became commonplace.

Lacanian theory belatedly moved to the question of racism. A recent major intervention in this area came from Sheldon George with the publication of *Trauma and Race: A Lacanian Study of African American Racial Identity* (2021). Many others have picked up on George's lead in the early 2020s. According to George, racism is not just the result of symbolic exclusions and imaginary hatreds. It partakes of the real in the way that prevailing conceptions of racism don't fully theorize. The racist desires through the suffering of the racialized other. This desire stems not from the symbolic structures of racism but from the realm of the real that these structures do not reach. This is why extralegal activity such as lynching plays such an important role in racist society, beyond the legal sanctions against racism. It also explains why legal and educational efforts to eradicate racism that remain on the level of the symbolic order, no matter how well intentioned, are not enough to eradicate racism in our society.

The turn to a Lacanian interpretation of racism is a welcome development and bespeaks the continued vitality of Lacan's thought today. It also signals that the political domain represents a privileged site for contemporary Lacanian theorizing. The fact that a massive volume on psychoanalytic political thinking entitled the *Routledge Handbook of Psychoanalytic Political Theory*, with almost half of its essays devoted to Lacanian theory, was published in 2020 testifies to Lacan's enduring significance as a theorist with something to communicate about our political arrangements.[15] This is where we should see Lacan's importance, not only in the number of clinicians who continue to practice under his banner.

On a global scale, Lacan's theoretical contributions have reverberated far beyond his clinical ones. In many parts of the world, Lacan's theoretical impact is tremendous, even where there exists a great deal of resistance to his clinical approach. To be sure, there are significant Lacanian clinical movements in France, South America (especially Argentina), and Australia, but there are large regions of the world, such as North America, where only a smattering of Lacanian practitioners exists, usually in big cities such as New York, Boston, and San Francisco.

In addition, among clinicians, doctrinal battles constantly arise over the proper interpretation of Lacanian theory and practice. Many of these battles center around the figure of Jacques-Alain Miller, Lacan's son-in-law and literary executor who controls the publication of all Lacan's materials. One such split involved a divide between analysts devoted to Miller and those devoted to Colette Soler. This and other clinical battles have had an impact on Lacan's reception, especially in France. But it is outside the reach of Miller – outside the clinic – that Lacan's impact on the world resounds the loudest.

There are many Lacanian clinicians who themselves have worked to bridge the gap between the analytic clinic and cultural theorizing. Works from these clinicians include Molly Rothenberg's *The Excessive Subject* (2010), Tracy McNulty's *Wrestling with the Angel* (2014), and Carol Owens and Stephanie Swales' *Psychoanalyzing Ambivalence with Freud and Lacan* (2019). These works move beyond the case study and the explanation of clinical practice to trace the implications of clinical insights for social processes and cultural objects.

The most important Lacan is the Lacan of the real, the version that emerges in the middle period. This version of Lacan has become the predominant psychoanalytic approach within cultural theory and continental philosophy today. Here, Lacan's impact is the equal of thinkers such as Kant, Hegel, Marx, Freud, and Frantz Fanon. This is because the Lacan of the real, the Lacan who sees a gap within every symbolic structure, is an inherently political Lacan. A whole stream of emancipatory political theorists has emerged out of Lacan's conception of the real as the rupture within the symbolic. This priority of the real has only become a viable interpretation of Lacan after the publication of his seminars in the last few decades. All the seminars are now available for the public online. No longer stuck with just the *Écrits*, theorists can now recognize the extent of Lacan's contribution. The darkness of the 1970s and 1980s dominated by the imaginary has given way to the real starting in the 1990s and continuing through today. The understanding of Lacan has finally broken the mirror that kept it trapped. The real Lacan has much more value for us than the imaginary one.

Notes

1 Noam Chomsky, "An Interview," *Radical Philosophy* 53 (1989): 32.
2 See Peter D. Mathews, *Lacan the Charlatan* (London: Palgrave, 2020).
3 Jacques Lacan, "The Mirror Stage as Formative of the *I* Function as Revealed in Psychoanalytic Experience," *Écrits: The First Complete Edition in English*, trans. Bruce Fink (New York: Norton, 2006 [1966]), 80.
4 Louis Althusser, "Ideology and Ideological State Apparatuses," in *Lenin and Philosophy and Other Essays*, trans. Ben Brewster (New York: Monthly Review Press, 1971 [1969]), 173.
5 Daniel Dayan takes up this line of thinking in his influential essay "The Tutor-Code of Classical Cinema," which interprets Lacan's mirror stage article as a critique of subjectivity as imaginary. Dayan writes, "Lacan … operates a radical desacralization of the subject: the 'I,' the 'ego,' the 'subject' are nothing but images, reflections. The imaginary constitutes the subject through a 'speculary' effect common to the constitution of all images. A mirror on a wall organizes the various objects of a room into a unified, finite image. So also the subject is no more than a unifying reflection." Daniel Dayan, "The Tutor-Code of Classical Cinema," *Film Quarterly* 28.1 (1974): 24. The parent text of Dayan's critique of the cinematic production of the subject is Jean-Louis Baudry, "Ideological Effects of the Basic Cinematic Apparatus," trans. Alan Williams, *Film Quarterly* 28.2 (1974–1975): 39–47. One can see in Dayan's essay the influence of Althusser's reduction of the subject to the ego and the symbolic to the imaginary.
6 Lacan's attempt to distance himself from Kant becomes clear when Lacan associates the Kantian moral law with the Marquis de Sade's will to enjoy, and his effort to distinguish himself from Hegel becomes evident in *Seminar XI*, where he specifically opposes his thinking about alienation to Hegel's.
7 Joan Copjec, *Read My Desire: Lacan Against the Historicists* (Cambridge, MA: MIT Press, 1994), 36.
8 Raymond Bellour, "Cher amis de *Hors Cadre* … ," *Hors Cadre* 7 (1989): 52.
9 Bellour, "Cher amis de *Hors Cadre* … ," 52.
10 Copjec provides perhaps the most cogent account of the contrast between masculine and feminine sexuation. She writes, "Rather than defining a universe of men that is complemented by a universe of women, Lacan defines man as the prohibition against constructing a universe and woman as the impossibility of doing so." Joan Copjec, *Read My Desire*, 235. As Copjec recognizes, the masculine investment in prohibition marks a decided retreat from feminine impossibility.
11 See also the many other works of Mari Ruti, including Mari Ruti, *The Age of Scientific Sexism* (New York: Bloomsbury, 2015), and Mari Ruti, *The Ethics of Opting Out: Queer Theory's Defiant Subjects* (New York: Columbia, 2017).
12 Toril Moi, *Sexual/Textual Politics: Feminist Literary Theory* (London: Routledge, 1985), 100.
13 Jacqueline Rose, *Sexuality in the Field of Vision* (London: Verso, 1986), 64.
14 Slavoj Žižek, *The Sublime Object of Ideology* (London: Verso, 1989), 45.
15 See Yannis Stavrakakis, ed., *Routledge Handbook of Psychoanalytic Political Theory* (London: Routledge, 2019).

Chapter 4

Concepts

Symbolic Order

Lacan's importance as a thinker begins with the emphasis that he places on the symbolic order, which is the structure that lies behind all our actions and gives them significance. Even though the critique of the imaginary dominates his earliest psychoanalytic thinking, the stress that he places on the signifier in the formation and continual mediation of subjectivity propels him onto the theoretical scene and carves out a singular place for him among psychoanalysts. Lacan's conception of the symbolic marks a significant advance on Freud's thinking – and that of other psychoanalysts.

Lacan is the first psychoanalytic thinker to include the fundamental role that mediation plays in constituting the social reality in his theory. The symbolic order provides the connective tissue between people that mediates their interactions and gives them a path to relate to each other. For Lacan, reality is not immediately present for us and accessible. It becomes available only through the mediating power of language, which provides signifiers that designate the make-up of this reality. The symbolic order is language and everything that we use to create significance in the world. It includes laws, social structures, and all the ways that we designate ourselves and what's around us. The symbolic order doesn't bring objects into being, but it does provide access to them.[1]

Without the symbolic order, we would have no means for signifying anything at all. We would have no capacity for interacting with each other or with the world of objects. The significance that we find in our existence stems from our initial subjection to the symbolic order and its determinations. It provides the starting point for everything that we concern ourselves with. The subject cannot opt out of the symbolic order. It provides the necessary background against which subjectivity can emerge.[2]

Lacan's emphasis on the priority of the symbolic order links him with structuralism. For the structuralist (such as the Swiss linguist Ferdinand de Saussure and the French anthropologist Claude Lévi-Strauss), a social structure determines our existence, even when we believe that we are acting freely.[3]

Rather than considering people as isolated individuals acting on their own, structuralists grant the form of the social structure a constitutive role relative to the individuals within it. The structure regulates what we say, what we eat, and whom we marry. Every structuralist envisions something akin to Lacan's symbolic order at work in society. But what separates Lacan from structuralism is his concern, which traces back to Kant and Hegel, with the subject. Structuralists on the whole reject the subject, but Lacan gives the subject pride of position within his philosophy.[4]

The symbolic order lays out a fiction that establishes a way for subjects to orient themselves. This fiction emerges without any grounding in the actual order of things. One symbolic fiction doesn't prevail over another because it better corresponds to the world outside it. It prevails because it better accommodates itself to the psyches of those existing within it.

Although the symbolic order orients our entire existence, no one can see it directly. This order makes itself manifest indirectly, through the significance that it assigns to various signifiers. Its invisibility contrasts the symbolic with the imaginary, which is the order of the visible. As a result of its invisibility, the symbolic order is much more difficult to apprehend than the imaginary. We can only experience it through its effects, not within the field of perception. In *Freud as Philosopher*, Richard Boothby explains that "the symbolic is always conditioned by its relation to a network of signifiers that is not and in fact *cannot* be made an object of perception. We perceive speech and writing but not the symbol system that makes them possible."[5] One can register the presence of individual signifiers but not the overall structure of signification. The power of the symbolic order resides in its complete imperceptibility. Of course, we can see words written on a paper, but what we can't see is the actual working of the symbolic order – the act of signification as it takes place. Lacan believes that he can make us aware of it, but we still cannot perceive it directly. Under the cover of this imperceptibility, it weaves a destiny with which each subject must wrestle.

One might think of the symbolic order as the first map that one places on a terrain. Prior to the introduction of the map, there are differences on the terrain but none that matter for people. The map lays out the borders that separate one province from another, as well as the routes that allow one to navigate within and between the various provinces. All distinctions that we make between places become possible thanks to the map. An initial map of the territory generates the differences between various places that allow us to make distinctions. We get our bearings through the symbolic map.

The map makes evident the point that divides one province from another, and it becomes possible to chart a path leading from one to the other.

Without the map, the distinction between these two provinces would not exist. The territories now known as distinct would be indistinct and bleed into each other, even though the land that both occupy wouldn't change. Natural obstructions such as bodies of water and mountains appear on the map, but they also acquire a signification – such as the *Amazon* or the *Andes* – that distorts and fundamentally transforms their natural being. The symbolic order gives the terrain of our entire existence its coordinates. In this sense, it is akin to an initial map of everything.

What's misleading about the map as a way of thinking about the symbolic order is that one can imagine a world prior to the introduction of the map. One maps a territory that already exists. This is not what happens with the symbolic order. It generates the condition of possibility for relating to the terrain that it maps. Unlike the map, the symbolic order is not a secondary phenomenon. Lacan contends that it has primacy relative to our perception of what it signifies.

To arrive at this position, Lacan must modify the understanding of signification that he inherits from Saussure, even though he remains indebted to Saussure theoretically. Saussure challenges the everyday view of language that links words with the objects to which the words refer. According to Saussure, language doesn't directly refer to objects in the external world. It is a system that creates significance through negation, not through any positive assertion of identity between words and things. The relationship between a signifier and other signifiers determines the signifier's significance.

We know what a chair is because we contrast it with a table, not because the signifier *chair* refers to an actual object that is a chair. Similarly, the understanding of the signifier *child* stems from the contrast between the child and the adult, and so on. In his *Course on General Linguistics*, Saussure constructs a system of signification that doesn't require reference to objects in order to function. It has signifiers and what they signify – their signifieds – without recourse to any referents or objects. The signified is the signification, not the object being referred to. For Lacan, so far, so good.

But whereas Saussure contends that the signified has priority over the signifier, Lacan reverses this. In the working out of signification, the signifier matters more than the signified. Or: what we say matters more than what we mean. Lacan's position concerning the signifier's relationship to the signified derives from a psychoanalytic understanding of the unconscious and how the unconscious appears in language.

This is clearest in the case of the slip of the tongue. Freud's interpretation of slips and other errors implicitly indicates the priority that Lacan grants to the signifier. Let's say that I am telling someone how much I love my romantic partner named *Jeffrey*. But when speaking, I slip and say *Frank* instead of *Jeffrey*. Realizing my mistake, I quickly recover and correct myself, explaining, "Of course, I meant *Jeffrey*, not *Frank*." The problem with this correction is that it assumes that what I meant, the signified, corresponds with my desire. Freud contends that the slip reveals that my unconscious desire lies elsewhere – for *Frank* (perhaps my former romantic partner) rather than *Jeffrey*. Unfortunately for me, Jeffrey would surely come to the same conclusion as Freud when I constantly called him *Frank*.

The logic behind Freud's theory of the slip also manifests itself in the psychoanalytic session. Analysts pay attention to what patients say, not what they mean to say. Because psychoanalysis focuses on the unconscious, it enables Lacan to grasp how the signifier determines the signified and not vice versa. The symbolic order is a system of signifiers. The role of the signified is always secondary because the signifier allows for the expression of unconscious desire that remains repressed in consciousness. The signifier expresses the unconscious, while what we mean to say remains on the level of consciousness. Grasping the priority of the signifier over the signified in this way enables Lacan to see, in a way that Saussure does not, the power of the symbolic order over the signification of our reality. The signifier has this power because it is the site where unconscious desire can indirectly emerge.[6]

Nowhere is the transformative power of the signifier more evident than in the case of Mount Everest. As a natural feature of the earth, Mount Everest is just another mountain on the planet's largest land mass. Other than being the point where the land reaches highest above sea level, there is nothing special about it. But as a result of the signifier, Mount Everest garners more attention than any other mountain on the planet. People invest their desire in this place and come to climb it rather than just staying put in the comfort of their own homes. It stands out through the role that the signifier plays in differentiating it from the rest of the natural world.

The signifier *Mount Everest* doesn't just signify some ordinary mountain in Nepal. It stands out because it signifies the tallest mountain in the world. This gives Mount Everest a symbolic status that no other mountain has. This distinction wouldn't be apparent to us if we didn't have the signifier to make it so. Absent a signifier for the tallest mountain, we would not be able to think in these terms and would likely view Mount Everest as just a forbidding place that gets very cold. We would do our best to avoid getting up too high on it lest we end up dead. But the availability of this signifier has a radical effect on people's behavior. The symbolic status that a specific signifier has pulls people toward it. Despite the danger associated with climbing Mount Everest, people flock to it to associate themselves with the signifier *Mount Everest*. After climbing it, one can use the signifier to tell others about what one has done. To climb this mountain is to partake in the status that this particular signifier has. For almost everyone on earth, *Mount Everest* means something significant.

Although people come to Mount Everest for the sake of the signifier, no one who comes there recognizes this. People want to climb *Mount Everest*, the signifier that has an impressive symbolic status attached to it, but they tell themselves that they want to climb Mount Everest, the actual mountain that protrudes into the sky. This mountain draws them in because of its status as a signifier, but it appears to have an entirely natural significance. It appears to transcend the human world altogether. Climbers seek to transcend the signifier on Mount Everest, but they inevitably find themselves on *Mount Everest*, no matter how high they go.

In this way, Mount Everest reveals the basic deception that occurs in the symbolic order, as Lacan conceives it. We look at signifiers as if they point beyond the symbolic order to a transcendent world. But signifiers don't relate to what lies beyond them.[7] They relate to each other and generate significance through their interrelation. *Mount Everest* attracts so many climbers because of its relationship to other signifiers. It signifies more height than *K2* or *Kilimanjaro*. These other signifiers give it the appeal that draws in so many climbers because the contrast generates the symbolic status associated with *Mount Everest*.

One can easily imagine a world in which we didn't name mountains at all, just as we don't name most hills today. Such a world would have various high places but no highest place, nowhere with a special signification attached to it. Were this the case, many people who died on Mount Everest would have been spared. If *Mount Everest* were just an anonymous peak in Nepal, adventurers from around the would not risk their lives to climb it.

All the attention that Mount Everest garners does not leave it as it is. The symbolic order transforms what it signifies. The enormous number of climbers attracted to the tallest mountain in the world reshape this mountain as they climb it. To facilitate climbing, a system of ladders now changes the face of the mountain. Even more significantly, massive quantities of waste from the climbers have turned the mountain into a thoroughly human space. While climbing the mountain, one cannot avoid constant reminders of the signifier in the form of the garbage that one encounters. Although the protrusion of earth doesn't disappear, the signifier turns it into a monument to humanity.[8]

As Mount Everest shows, the symbolic order doesn't just determine significance. It determines worth as well. Certain signifiers evoke more value than others, which is why people want to have these signifiers attached to them. Other signifiers indicate a lack of value, which leads people to avoid them. People readily take up signifiers such as *executive* or *judge*, while they seek to dissociate themselves from those like *homeless* or *criminal.*[9] Signifiers don't just remain in a purely external relationship to the people who bear them. They shape the psyche, so that those constantly bombarded with the signifier *criminal* begin to see themselves as criminals. Conversely, those addressed with the signifier *judge* start to conceive of themselves as judges, even though *judge* is just a symbolic position that they occupy and cannot be a source of real subjectivity.

In addition to assigning signification and value, the signifier has a political bearing, which is something that Lacan himself never stresses, even though his philosophy makes it apparent. The signifier can give one an elevated position in society, or it can consign one to a marginal one. Think about the power of the signifier *communism* in the West after the rise of the Soviet Union. This signifier did not just denote the ruling regime in the Soviet Union but also shaped the lives of millions who never set foot there. Hitler's rise to power in Germany would have been unthinkable without his demonization of everything associated with the signifier *communism.* He made it clear that Germans needed to embrace National Socialism if they were to escape the communist menace. Although the actual threat of communists taking over Germany was minimal, the signifier *communism* evoked such horror that Hitler was able to persuade many – including traditional conservatives – who were otherwise skeptical of him. But the power of this signifier was not confined to Europe.

In the United States, the signifier *communism* changed lives, wrecked careers, and dramatically altered the political landscape. The Red Scare turned *communism* into the portent of doom. During this period, whether one was an actual communist ceased to matter. What counted for one's position in American society was one's relationship to the signifier *communist.* If this signifier attached itself to a person, that person's status within the society suffered a precipitous downturn. Once judged a *communist,* one could not work in many industries or even keep one's circle of friends. Association with this signifier made people into social pariahs, even if they had no relationship at all to communism as a political movement. Even people who weren't communists had to live in constant fear of having this signifier attached to them. The end of the Red Scare didn't bring the politically nefarious power of the symbolic order to a close. It continues to shape our political possibilities in ways that aren't always immediately evident.

But the politics of the symbolic order is not simply oppressive. An understanding of the role that the symbolic order plays in assigning value has also led to various forms of political activity focused on signifiers.[10] While Lacan himself didn't engage in this political activity, his conception of the symbolic order points toward it. We can see this understanding informing the feminist movement around the world in the 1970s. Feminists fought for material equality – fairness in pay, access to abortion, representation in leadership positions – but they also tried to change language itself.

Many assumptions that governed how people spoke became questionable thanks to the feminist struggle. Feminists pointed out that one could not simply use the pronoun *he* to refer to everyone, just as one could not generalize about men and women with the term *man*. The names for occupations also needed to change for the sake of achieving equality. Feminists championed *firefighter* in lieu of *fireman*, *police officer* instead of *policeman*, and *postal worker* rather than *mailman*.[11] In each case, they attempted to eliminate the priority of the masculine within the symbolic order. Their premise was that the symbolic dominance of the masculine was just a contingent result of historical forces that they could change – a position in keeping with Lacan's understanding of the symbolic order.

For feminism, the point was changing the words that people used. If people began to use nongendered words to refer to occupations, it would become easier for women to enter these occupations. People could envision hiring a woman to be a *journalist* more easily than they could a *newspaperman*. The struggle on the level of the signifier didn't just remain on this level. It had clear material ramifications due to the power that the symbolic order has in shaping the social reality that it signifies. We can engage in struggle concerning signification because the symbolic order is always contradictory.

As Lacan's thought moves forward into the 1960s – what I am calling his middle period – the contradictory status of the symbolic order becomes more pronounced. This places him increasingly proximate to Hegel, whose dialectical philosophy focuses on contradiction as the irreducible ontological fact. The subject emerges through the contradictions of the symbolic order, but it doesn't exist beyond this order.

The ultimate difficulty in our relationship with the symbolic order is that the analysis of it necessarily takes place from within it. As subjects, we are inside, even though the symbolic order cannot signify subjectivity itself. The external perspective is denied to us as speaking beings. As Lacan says in his *Seminar XIV: The Logic of Fantasy, 1966–1967*, "there is no metalanguage."[12] We can never look at the symbolic order from the outside. Once introduced into the symbolic order, we're stuck within it. We can't look at things separated from the lens that the signifier gives us to look at them.

A quick thought experiment will confirm this. If we try to imagine how to describe ourselves without using any signifiers, the futility of trying to escape the symbolic order becomes evident. I would have to use signifiers to get beyond the signifier, which leaves me in a vicious circle.

The absence of an external perspective on the symbolic order limits how we challenge this order. Rather than looking at the symbolic order from an Archimedean position outside it, we must examine it through its internal contradictions. By paying attention to the contradictions that rupture the symbolic structure from within, we access the real. Despite the attention that Lacan gives to the symbolic order, the real is where the action is.

Imaginary

Subjectivity occurs through the interaction of three registers – the imaginary, the symbolic, and the real. Despite all the changes that occur from the time Lacan starts thinking about psychoanalysis to the day that he dies, his investment in the imaginary, the symbolic, and the real as what constitutes the subject's experience never wavers. While the real has a more marginal position early in Lacan's thinking and the imaginary recedes a bit during the middle period, none of the three ever fully disappears.

Lacan emerges as a thinker through an explanation and critique of the imaginary, which he theorizes during his discussion of the mirror stage. In a version that has since disappeared, Lacan gave a talk about the mirror stage at the 1936 conference of the International Psychoanalytical Association. In 1949, Lacan delivered a much-revised rendering of this talk as "The Mirror Stage as Formative of the Function of the *I* as Revealed in Psychoanalytic Experience," which he published in the *Écrits* in 1966. "The Mirror Stage" essay points out the deception that occurs when the young child looks in the mirror and recognizes its own body. It's a necessary deception for the formation of the ego, but it's a deception all the same. The image lures the child into a belief in its own mastery over its body – a mastery that it lacks in reality.[13]

When Lacan uses the term *imaginary* (*imaginaire* in French), he invokes two distinct senses of the word. It is the order of the image – what we can see – and it is illusory. Like the sensibility in Kant's philosophy, the imaginary is the field of perception, not just what we see but also what we hear, smell, taste, and touch. The scene I see when walking down the street, the screen I look at on my computer, and the neighborhood I observe out my window – all these constitute the field of the imaginary. It is made up of the images that I encounter all the time.

But at the same time, the imaginary names the fundamental deception that occurs in the subject's experience. As Lacan's analysis of the mirror stage shows, the imaginary misleads us into viewing wholeness where there is division and mastery where there is an absence of it. If I just pay attention to images, my world seems full. It seems to exist without a symbolic framework underwriting it and without any gaps within it. To adhere to the imaginary is to find oneself caught up in an illusion of completeness. This is why Lacan in the early and middle periods challenges the predominance of this register.

The imaginary can present an illusion of completeness because it appears to involve just two parties – someone looking and what is seen. The imaginary relationship is a dualistic one that fails to account for the influence of a third party on this dualistic interaction. From within the imaginary perspective, I consider only what's on my computer screen, not the structure that makes it possible for me to view this screen, including the labor that produced my computer in the first place and the coding that mediates my encounter. Seeing a direct, one-on-one relationship with the image amounts to falling for an imaginary lure. Lacan wants to bring the symbolic and real to light to counter the blinding power of this lure.

Nowhere is the imaginary deception more pronounced than with the ego. While Freud doesn't praise the ego, neither does he go out of his way to deride it. Lacan, in contrast, targets the ego critically from his entrance onto the psychoanalytic scene. The critique of the ego is a constant throughout Lacan's trajectory as a thinker. As Lacan sees it, the ego is imaginary: It is a bodily image that forms through looking at the other (and oneself in the mirror) that pretends to an agency that it doesn't have. The imaginary ego deceives the subject about its constitutive lacking status. Subjects that think of themselves in terms of their egos fail to recognize themselves as divided subjects. The ego hides lacking subjectivity, which is why Lacan views the ego as essentially deceptive.[14]

We can't do without the imaginary order, nor without the ego. But the task of psychoanalysis, at least early on in Lacan's career, involves the analyst assisting the subject in working through imaginary self-deception – the belief that the subject is its ego. While looking at the image, no one grasps the structuring role that the symbolic order plays in constituting this image or the real gaps that populate this symbolic order. As a result, the imaginary appears to present an unvarnished truth while obscuring the fictional symbolic order that underlies it. Enthralled by the imaginary, we can't see what we can't see. We can't see that we can't see everything. While the subject allows itself to be captivated by images, absence disappears in the surfeit of presence. The problem with the imaginary is that it is too visible: We see the imaginary as a whole and never see what it's missing – namely, the symbolic order and the real.

When we become caught up in the imaginary and taken in by what we perceive, we miss the primacy of the symbolic order relative to the imaginary. The symbolic order dictates what has significance in the field of the imaginary – what we value in what we see. Let's take the example of a diamond. We look at a diamond and imagine that it has the value it does because of its great beauty. It sparkles and reflects bright colors. It's smooth to the touch. If we approach the diamond through the register of the imaginary, the value appears to derive from its appearance.

Once we take the symbolic order into account, the situation changes dramatically. It becomes clear that the framework that the symbolic order provides gives the diamond the value it has. The diamond appears more beautiful to us than quartz because our symbolic framing assigns it much more value. The symbolic order gives the diamond and quartz different positions within its structure, and this affects how we see these objects. The imaginary qualities exist, but they aren't determinative in the way the symbolic is, according to Lacan.[15]

A joke about a defendant facing burglary charges captures nicely the relative weight of the imaginary and the symbolic. The judge asks him, "How do you plead to the charges against you?" The defendant says, "I don't recognize this court." The puzzled judge inquires, "Why not?" The defendant explains, "It's been redecorated since the last time I was here." The joke here relies on the defendant talking about the imaginary – how the court looks – and the judge believing that he's talking about the court's symbolic status. The authority of the court resides in its symbolic status, not its image. The redecoration doesn't affect the symbolic status at all but is merely an imaginary change. The joke plays on the distinction between the imaginary and the symbolic, our ability to move from one order to the other. Confusion between these two orders can create comedy, but it also can play a crucial role in sustaining oppressive situations.

When understood in this way, the political weight of Lacan's theory becomes clearer. The predominance of the imaginary over the symbolic blinds us to the political structure that determines what appears as visible to us. For instance, the subject sees images that indicate the existence of racial difference. For people in most contemporary societies, racial difference appears as a natural fact like the sun rising in the east. But skin color exists within the imaginary order. Its visibility for people stems not from how it looks. The images of difference in skin color become visible due only to the racist symbolic order that gives racial difference a significance that it otherwise would not have. In thrall to the imaginary realm of visible distinctions, we miss the symbolic order that causes us to register these distinctions.

Lacan's insistence on the structural priority of the symbolic order relative to the imaginary works against the obviousness of the imaginary and the hiddenness of the symbolic. Psychoanalysis, as Lacan understands it in his early period, is a struggle to reveal the imaginary illusion that predominates within our experience of things.

The Matrix (Lana and Lilly Wachowski, 1999) is undoubtedly the most important film about the politics of imaginary deception – the film most coincident with Lacan's early period. The film depicts a world in which people live out their lives according to a symbolic code, the eponymous Matrix. No one within the social reality of the film recognizes the dominance of the Matrix over their lives because they remain caught up in an imaginary deception: They experience a full world replete with meaning, not the meaningless symbolic order that actually controls their reality. The film ends with the hero Neo (Keanu Reeves) undergoing a version of Lacanian psychoanalysis and seeing the symbolic code where everyone else sees images. This gives him the ability to act against the dominance of the Matrix. At the end of the film, Neo is a subject no longer duped by the imaginary, which allows the spectator to awaken to this possibility as well. Without the imaginary deception, the symbolic order loses its absolute power over the subject in both *The Matrix* and in Lacan's early period.

The problem is that we cannot avoid the imaginary illusion. Our desire takes its bearings from the imaginary register, which provides an image through which we can situate what we desire.[16] Without the imaginary, we would have nothing to lure desire and move it forward. Although in his early thinking Lacan views psychoanalysis as a way of dissipating the lure of the imaginary, the imaginary remains a necessary deception. We need a field of images, just as we need an ego, to avoid having no sense of a world or sense of a self at all. This is why, more and more as Lacan goes along, he ceases to theorize imaginary deception as the central problem that psychoanalysis confronts.

The weight that the imaginary has in Lacan's thinking changed drastically from the 1950s to the 1970s. His theory in the early period responded to the dominance of ego psychology, and the critique of the imaginary was his way of countering this trend. As an alternative, Lacan argues that moving past the imaginary illusion is the primary aim of psychoanalysis. The imaginary deception begins in the mirror stage but continues as long as the subject invests itself in the development of its ego. Lacan inveighs against psychoanalytic efforts to foster a healthy ego because he recognizes that the ego is always an illusion, not an ally in the analytic process, as some analysts would have it.[17] Later, he becomes less concerned with the imaginary obscuring the symbolic order and more focused on the inability to see the real disruption of the symbolic.

But in the 1950s, the imaginary marks a deviation from the operations of the symbolic order. In the thinking of Lacan's first two seminars, psychoanalysis intervenes to clear away the imaginary detour. As he says in *Seminar II*, "It is precisely the exercise of the dialectic of analysis which should dissipate . . . imaginary confusion."[18] Psychoanalysis helps one clear up the imaginary hiccup within the symbolic structure. By doing this, it allows the subject to recognize the symbolic forces acting on it. Although no one can escape the imaginary, one can work through its illusions to arrive at the symbolic structure that underlies them.

Lacan's early emphasis on imaginary deception has a distinctly Kantian ring to it. According to Kant, our common sense fails to recognize the categories of the understanding that govern what appears in our reality. We wrongly believe that we perceive things in themselves and miss how the understanding shapes all appearances. In Lacan's terms, one could say that we don't see the symbolic order that gives significance to everything that we perceive. Lacan's early emphasis on curing the deceptiveness of the imaginary reveals his status as a Kantian philosopher. This becomes even more pronounced as the early period advances.

By the time of *Seminar III: Psychoses, 1955–1956*, Lacan places the imaginary deviation at the center of his theory of psychosis. One becomes a psychotic – one falls into, say, paranoia – because one loses anchoring within the symbolic order. The imaginary comes to predominate over one's entire experience. Unlike the neurotic, the psychotic cannot gain any symbolic purchase on the imaginary plenitude that surrounds it. Although the psychotic has access to signifiers, it lacks the stabilizing signifier that would allow it to recognize the workings of the symbolic order. To be psychotic is to be stuck in the imaginary, to relate to words as if they were images.

The imaginary never drops completely out of Lacan's thinking, although during the middle period of the 1960s it takes a backseat to the relationship of the symbolic order and the real. While *Seminar VI: Desire and Its Interpretation, 1958–1959* still centers desire around the imaginary lure, a significant change takes place the following year, with *Seminar VII: The Ethics of Psychoanalysis, 1959–1960*. References to the imaginary disappear almost completely in this seminar, and desire begins to take the real as its starting point. Even though Lacan quickly moves away from the claims that he makes in *Seminar VII*, the association of desire with the real rather than the imaginary would remain in subsequent years. In the years up to *Seminar VII*, the object at work in desire was imaginary. Beginning in

Seminar IX: Identification, 1961–1962, the object that drives our desire ceases to be just an imaginary object.

Instead of the image being what kickstarts desire, the driving force of desire becomes what is lacking in the image – what cannot be represented on the imaginary level. With this new theorization of the force behind our desire, Lacan shifts the emphasis from the contrast between the symbolic and the imaginary to that between the symbolic and the real. Whereas the imaginary is visible, the real remains irreducible to the visual field. It is what can't be seen but nonetheless structures the visual field as a disruptive absence.

The imaginary continues to play a minor role in Lacan's middle period of the 1960s. At this point, imaginary wholeness obscures the gap of the real within the symbolic order. When we focus on the imaginary, we miss the real. Subsequent thinkers who emphasize Lacan's middle period (the 1960s) as the most important tend to downplay or even ignore the imaginary in their theoretical approach.[19]

In the later seminars of the 1970s, the imaginary's importance returns, albeit with an entirely new twist. The imaginary becomes one strand of a structure – the Borromean knot – that holds together our subjectivity. The deceptive quality of the imaginary ceases to be important for Lacan in this period because his concern is with its role in safeguarding the coherence of the subject's experience, a coherence that requires the interaction of all three registers. If one drops out, the whole apparatus falls apart. The status of the imaginary at this point becomes equal to that of the symbolic and the real. All three work together to structure subjectivity.

One of the key mistakes that people make when thinking about the relationship between the imaginary and the symbolic order is to consider this relationship a chronological one, as if one starts out in the real, moves into the imaginary as a child, and finally ascends into the symbolic. This error stems from thinking about Lacan's theory as a model of development through stages, which is a direction in psychoanalytic thinking that Lacan tries to counter. There is no path that one follows as one develops. The three registers are not stages on life's way. Understanding the imaginary, symbolic, and real as developmental stages leads one completely astray. Instead, one should view them as the basis for our experience.

Despite how the chronological reading of the registers would have it, the imaginary is not something to be transcended in order to accede to the symbolic. It is a matter of grasping its limitations – the way that the symbolic order and the real undermine the imaginary illusion of wholeness. No one leaves the ego behind or stops looking out at the world. The imaginary register endures for everyone because no one can exist solely in any of the registers. The idea that runs throughout Lacan's trajectory – throughout each period – is that there is no symbolic or real without the imaginary, just as there is no imaginary prior to the symbolic and the real. The subject must relate to the different registers by recognizing how each works with the others. One can only avoid being seduced by the image when one properly situates it.

Real

More than either the imaginary or the symbolic order, the real as a category undergoes significant transformations as Lacan's philosophy unfolds. This is one of the central ironies in Lacan's thinking because he initially theorizes the real as what doesn't change amid the reordering of the symbolic order. When he describes the real in *Seminar II: The Ego in Freud's Theory and in the Technique of Psychoanalysis, 1954–1955*, Lacan claims, the real "is something one always finds in the same place, whether or not one has been there."[20] There is a constancy to the real that both the imaginary and the symbolic lack. One can change one's symbolic perspective, but the real is what stays put. At least for the early Lacan.

In the middle and late periods, the idea that the real returns to the same place gives way to the real as a point of symbolic impossibility. The real is symbolically impossible but nonetheless occurs. As the concept of the real evolves, so does its importance in Lacan's theory. The real goes from being almost an afterthought in the early period to being the most impactful of the three registers in the late one. Mapping the trajectory that the real takes as a concept thus offers unique insight into how Lacan's philosophy changes. There is an early real, a middle real, and a late real.

The term *real* seems an odd choice to begin with on Lacan's part. When we think of what's real, we imagine the banal facts of our daily lives. We classify as real the objects that we encounter all the time – sidewalks, trees, cars, and the like. But in Lacan's theory, the real doesn't refer to the everyday reality with which we constantly interact. It is what disrupts our everydayness, the point in our experience that doesn't fit with everything else. We encounter the real when we lose our sense of reality, not when all feels real to us. In this sense, Lacan's real might be better called the *irreal* or the *unreal*. The real is what doesn't fit smoothly in the symbolic order and resists having any signification. But the terminological choice is not simply a blunder on Lacan's part. The inaptness of Lacan's basic terminology stems from the transformation that his thinking undergoes from the 1950s to the 1970s.

His ideas evolve while his language often stays the same. As a result, in order to know what Lacan means, one must ask oneself when he was speaking.

In Lacan's early period of the 1950s, the *real* indicates the terrain outside of symbolization. The signifier lays itself over the real, but not to such an extent that we cannot grasp the existence of this other realm. It exists prior to the advent of the signifier and continues to exist beyond the symbolic order. For the early Lacan, the real is a layer beyond the symbolic one. This first definition of the real doesn't so much defy our usual modes of thinking. One can understand why Lacan initially employs the term *real* in the way that he does.[21]

The relationship between the real and the symbolic order in the early period of the 1950s is dualistic rather than dialectical.[22] That is to say, the real has an external status to the symbolic order and exists outside it, in opposition to it. The symbolic order is on one side while the real is on the other. There would be a real even if the signifier never came along to allow someone to talk about it. Although the symbolic order makes a discussion of the real possible, both registers exist on separate planes.

It is easy to recognize the parallel here between the early Lacan and Kant. Just as Lacan theorizes the symbolic order and the real existing outside each other in a dualistic relation, Kant argues that the appearances that we can access are distinct from the things in themselves that we can't. The appearance doesn't reveal the thing in itself when it breaks down, but instead the thing in itself remains inaccessible for us, just like the real in Lacan's early period. Kant's dualism between the appearance and the thing in itself mirrors Lacan's dualism between the symbolic and the real.

The dualism of the symbolic order and the real results from Lacan's insistence early on that the real doesn't emerge internally in the symbolic but preexists it. Lacan's sense of the priority of the real is evident in the early seminars, but nowhere as clearly as in *Seminar I: Freud's Papers on Technique, 1953–1954*. In this seminar, Lacan states, "One can only think of language as a network, a net over the entirety of things, over the totality of the real. It inscribes on the plane of the real this other plane, which we here call the plane of the symbolic."[23] The two planes are entirely separate. The symbolic order lets us reach the real by talking about it, but the real is not internal to the symbolic.

The real simply is what it is. There is no possibility for negation or contradiction in the real – just as Kant doesn't allow for contradictions in the thing in itself – because everything about it is self-identical. This self-identity leaves no space for deception or lying. It is only when we introduce the signifier that deception becomes possible. One can be wrong about a symbolized truth, but not about the real. The real remains completely outside of the signifiers that we use to approach it.[24]

In this dualistic conception, the real always stays the same regardless of how we attempt to symbolize it. That is why it is what returns to the same place. For much of human history, the position of the stars in the sky was real in the sense of the early Lacan. People could come up with different ways of symbolizing their positions – from the geocentric systems of Aristotle and Ptolemy to the heliocentrism of Copernicus and Galileo – but the stars themselves were constant. Their movement in the sky followed a predictable path even when one used a competing symbolic order to make sense of this movement. In Lacan's early period, he believes that this constancy amid different symbolizations lets us know everything is not simply reducible to the signifier. We know that there is something behind our signifiers because something stays the same when the symbolic order changes.[25]

For the early Lacan, the symbolic order is how we arrange or group the real. The real provides the raw material for the symbolic – whether a coin comes up heads or tails when we flip it – and the symbolic orders it. The symbolic order doesn't determine what will come up on the coin, but it does determine that this result is important. The symbolic makes certain determinations about this real, precluding some things and mandating others. Symbolic determinations affect the real through the act of ordering it.

The exact moment when the definition of the real changes in Lacan's thought is difficult to pin down. But it is definitely apparent in the early 1960s, as the real moves from having an external relationship with the symbolic order to being its internal hiccup. Even though the symbolic order creates significance, it also fails to create significance. There are points at which this order breaks down, points of contradiction. Lacan comes to recognize the importance of the failures of the symbolic order, to grasp that the real isn't external or prior to the symbolic order but emerges when this order breaks down. The symbolic order is not perfect; it can't account for everything. The gaps or failures in the symbolic are real, which implies that the relation between the symbolic and real is dialectical.

The move from a dualistic theory of the real and the symbolic to a dialectical one is a move from a Kant-inflected philosophy to a Hegel-inflected one. For Kant, the realm of appearances (the symbolic order) is entirely distinct from the realm of things in themselves (the real). To believe that one can talk about things in themselves is to fall into a philosophical trap that Kant helps us to avoid by conceptualizing the transcendental structure of subjectivity that organizes appearances. This is what Lacan calls the symbolic order.

Hegel sees things otherwise. He contends that we can know about things in themselves through the way that the realm of appearances collapses. Appearances and things in themselves, as Hegel views it, collapse into each other. Contradictions in our appearances point us to the thing in itself. They show that the realm of appearances cannot explain everything. The fact that appearances can fail reveals what appearances cannot directly say. This failure is the source of subjectivity, both for Hegel and for the middle Lacan. Subjectivity arises not in an attempt to solve the symbolic failure but as an expression of it. The divided subject expresses and sustains contradiction. The inability of the symbolic order to symbolize everything without a hitch allows the subject to encounter the real from within its symbolic constraints. The dialectical focus on contradiction reveals the real as accessible in a way that a dualistic view cannot.

In this period of Lacan's philosophy, the real is what constantly makes itself felt despite efforts to symbolize it away. It is the point at which the symbolic structure malfunctions despite everything going according to plan, the point of impossibility within this structure that nonetheless can occur. Whenever a contradiction occurs in the symbolic order, this evinces the disruption of the real. The paradoxes of logic – Zeno's paradoxes, Russell's paradox, the liar's paradox – all indicate that a real fissure inhabits the symbolic.

In the final turn that Lacan's thought takes, the real overcomes the symbolic order. For Lacan, the 1970s is the decade of the real, the phase when the real becomes more determinant than the symbolic. The real goes from being an afterthought in Lacan's early period to being the primary concern of his final philosophy. Thus, it's not surprising that when Lacan devotes a late seminar to the three orders of his system, he leads off with the real rather than the symbolic or imaginary. He calls the seminar *R. S. I.*[26] The order here is significant: By the end of his theorizing, Lacan gives the real pride of place.

When the real emerges as the most important register, its connection to the symbolic that defines the middle period disappears. The real ceases to name the point of impossibility or contradiction within the symbolic. For the late Lacan, the real is what bars access to the symbolic as a mediating force. In this period, Lacan sees subjects as fundamentally isolated from each other, an isolation that he links to the real. It's as if the point of contradiction spills out and gets in the way of all mediation. We no longer partake in a shared relationship to the symbolic order but must instead constitute our own form of organizing the symbolic with the real and the imaginary.

Although Lacan moves considerably from the early period to the late one, these final years in one sense represent a return to the early dualistic conception of the real. The separation between the symbolic and real once again becomes primary. The turn away from impossibility and contradiction is simultaneously a turn away from the dialectical interrelation of the real and the symbolic order. In the late period, dualism trumps dialectics.

Whereas Lacan associates the real with contradiction in the middle period, the late philosophy specifically rejects this line of thought. Rather than emerging at the point where the symbolic order unravels and reveals itself as contradictory, the real makes symbolic connections impossible. In the later work, we cease to be able to know anything except our failure to know. As Lacan puts it in *Seminar XXI: The Non-Duped Err, 1973–1974*, "What is important, what constitutes the real, is that, according to logic, something happens that demonstrates not that *p* and *not-p* are false at the same time, but that neither one nor the other can be logically verified in any way."[27] The real stops us from drawing symbolic conclusions.

At the end, the real names not the internal failure of the symbolic but a separate realm that gets in the way of any shared access to the symbolic. This leads to a loss of confidence in the signifier, even as an agent for conveying its own inadequacy. We become stuck in our own private existence without the symbolic order to give us a public form of interaction. Although psychoanalysis continues to work through the signifier, the role of the signifier diminishes for the late Lacan.

As the real become increasingly primary, Lacan speaks less and less in his seminars. Whereas through the early and middle periods Lacan's lecture would fill the entire time of the session, his sessions during the final years would include long bouts of silence. He would punctuate this silence with occasional oracular proclamations, most often about Borromean knots.[28] The Borromean knot makes its first appearance in Lacan's seminar in 1973, toward the end of his *Seminar XX: Encore, 1972–1973.*

The Borromean knot eventually becomes more important to Lacan than anything he has to say. This type of knot brings together three rings of string in such a way that the integrity of the knot depends on all three rings. If one cuts a single ring, the entire knot breaks apart. Thanks to this structure, the Borromean knot shows the nonrelation of the imaginary, symbolic, and real. The three registers knot together, but there is no relation between any of them, not even a contradictory one. When the Borromean knot has prominence in Lacan's philosophy, each register indicates a separate realm that cannot relate to any other. It is no coincidence that as the Borromean knot gains importance Lacan stops speaking. To resort to the Borromean knot is to admit that we cannot successfully speak to each other, even about the impossibility of speaking successfully. The Borromean knot is a turn away from the possibility of impossibility.[29]

The idea of the real as impossible has nourished political thinkers arising in Lacan's wake. Slavoj Žižek is the most prominent, but the list includes Sheldon George, Anna Kornbluh, Molly Rothenberg, Alenka Zupančič, and many others.[30] Even if they don't explicitly say so, these are thinkers of the middle Lacan, thinkers for whom the symbolic order and the real must be conceived in a dialectical relationship. For these theorists, the real indicates the possibility of an event occurring that the ruling symbolic order has not accounted for. This is what makes the impossible real pregnant with political possibility. It is the necessity of structural impossibility that makes real change thinkable. But the real is visible as a structural impossibility only so long as one theorizes it in a dialectical relationship with the symbolic order. To forsake dialectics for dualism, to view the real as a realm completely distinct from the symbolic order, is to condemn oneself to political silence. The silence that resonates in Lacan's late seminars is a theoretical misstep that portends a political dead end for those who follow him down this path.

Desire

Lacan's emphasis on unconscious desire marks his singular contribution to the theory of subjectivity. Although Freud identifies the unconscious as the determining factor in the subject's activity, he doesn't explicitly formulate the concept of unconscious desire.[31] This falls to Lacan, who (at least until near the end of his life) makes desire the pivot point of his theory. The subject is a being split from itself and incapable of attaining wholeness or oneness, but this lack of wholeness is what leads to desire. Not only can the subject not attain wholeness; it doesn't ever even seek it. Instead, the subject finds satisfaction through its desire and not through attaining the object of desire.

The distinction between the satisfaction that the path of desire generates and the dissatisfaction that occurs with its realization in an object stems from desire's unconscious status. When we consciously consider what we desire, we assume that we will find satisfaction by obtaining the object that we desire – another person, a new car, a piece of cake, or whatever. But unconscious desire satisfies itself through the path that it takes, not through realizing itself in an object. The unconscious status of desire implies that we don't ever desire what we think we want. This warps the subject's relation to its own world.

Desire is the specific distortion that every subject gives to the structure of the social reality that it engages with. Social reality, for Lacan, does not exist apart from the subject's desire.[32] We can never approach reality neutrally but must always relate to it through the distortion of desire. This distortion is not a secondary process that corrupts an original reality. It constitutes social reality for us as subjects.[33]

The most basic distortion that desire creates occurs through what we perceive and what we don't. Certain objects appear more prominently than others because they appeal to our desire while the others don't. If I'm looking at a shelf of books, I might notice Hegel's *Phenomenology of Spirit* while not perceiving the book next to it, Jordan Peterson's *12 Rules for Life*. (Or perhaps if I'm a little misguided, the opposite will occur.) Desire distributes value throughout what we perceive as reality, but it does not distribute value evenly. The distinctions that we make throughout the social reality emerge from how we desire, not from the inherent worth of the objects in this reality.

The structuring role of desire in our comprehension of reality is clearest in the case of potential romantic partners. When one experiences attraction to another person, one notices this person more than everyone else. One might not register the hairstyle or eye color of most people with whom one interacts, but the hair and the eyes of the person one desires stand out and become instantly memorable. Our desire determines what comes to the fore and what recedes out of our social reality.

The distortion of desire doesn't just manifest itself in giving certain objects prominence while obscuring others. It also deforms reality itself. Subjectivity opens up access to the significance of reality, but this access comes with a cost: The subject doesn't treat itself as just another part of the reality but relates to reality through subtracting itself from it. The subject cannot have the status of being a pure object among other objects. Reality is always skewed around the subject's desire. This desire distorts every object that it encounters.

The desiring subject lacks. It lacks the object that would provide it with complete enjoyment. The lack of this object is what drives the subject to continue desiring. But desire doesn't just manifest itself through the subject's lack. It appears also, at the same time, in an excess that distorts the subject's field of perception, an excess that throws the world off balance. Because the world becomes accessible through the lacking subject, there is no way to return it to zero point, no way to escape the distortion that the subject's desire produces.

One cannot imagine a world free from unconscious desire. In such a world, no one would have an incentive to pay attention to anything at all. There is no harmony to which one might return after suffering the contamination of desire. The only path out of the suffering that desire creates is to double down on desire, to find truth through desire's distortion and not outside of it.

Perhaps the best filmic example of how desire distorts social reality is a film often (rightly) credited with being the greatest ever made – Orson Welles's

Citizen Kane (1941). *Citizen Kane* begins with the death of Charles Foster Kane (Orson Welles), who utters one last word, "Rosebud," as he's dying. Since Kane is a politically influential wealthy man, his death causes a sensation. Newspaper reporters want to uncover the enigma attached to his final word by searching into his past and interviewing those who knew him.

The structure of *Citizen Kane* consists in depicting a series of attempts that a reporter makes to find out the truth of Kane's final word and thus to uncover, he hopes, the truth of Kane's subjectivity. The film uses the signifier *Rosebud* to arouse all the activity that it shows and to arouse the spectator's desire. As the reporter moves from person to person in his search, interacting with all those who knew Kane, the spectator views every encounter through the missing object that corresponds to this signifier. This absent object has the effect of deforming the spectator's field of perception while watching the film. One looks at all the objects one sees in Kane's life through the one object that cannot be seen.

By structuring the film in this way, Welles distinguishes between the object that impels our desire and ordinary empirical objects. No matter how valuable these objects might be, they seem valueless relative to the object named by the signifier *Rosebud*. The absent object structures everything that the spectator sees within the visual field. In the film's final scene, the reporter gives up the quest for the object as fruitless, but the film continues on, exposing to the spectator the name *Rosebud* on Kane's childhood sled as it burns in a massive incinerator with all his other worthless objects.

The object appears only to quickly disappear in flames. Although *Citizen Kane* seems to conclude with the presence of the object, the sled doesn't offer the answer that the film's narrative seems to promise. While the sled bears the name *Rosebud*, the truth of Kane's desire – and the spectator's – lies in a series of missed encounters with this object as narrated to the reporter by those who knew Kane. One grasps desire through the way that one misses the absent object, not through making the object present. It is easy to realize how unsatisfying the present object would be if we imagine *Citizen Kane* depicting the reporter quickly discovering the sled as the secret of Kane's desire a few minutes into his search. Such a film would not only be extremely short. It would also be boring. The satisfaction of desire occurs through coming up against the object's absence. This desire suffuses the entire film and forces the spectator to see its distorting influence on the visual field. To watch *Citizen Kane* is to confront the structuring role of unconscious desire in constituting our experience in the way that Lacan formulates.

Lacan adds unconscious desire to the theory of subjectivity formulated by the German Idealists Kant and Hegel. This is his philosophical point of departure. In their philosophy, the structure of subjectivity constitutes what we experience as reality. Kant calls this structure *transcendental* since it doesn't vary according to our experiences but makes our experiences possible. The structure of subjectivity transcends what we experience and gives it a form. As such, it is the condition of possibility for experience. Kant orients this structure around how the subject knows. He examines what it is possible to know through the confines of the form that our subjectivity provides.

Hegel, too, takes subjectivity as his point of departure. In contrast to Kant, however, he sees the contradictions that the subject encounters not just as impasses of knowledge but also as forms of knowledge. Subjectivity finds the truth through its failure to know. For Hegel, a contradiction in thought reveals as much as it conceals. Hegel's subject is a subject of contradiction, but its contradictions occur in conscious thought, not in the unconscious. This is a philosophical limitation that Lacan will eventually rectify.

Lacan turns the focus from knowledge to unconscious desire. As he sees it, what defies the subject's conscious knowledge has the effect of structuring its world and everything that it encounters in this world. Unconscious desire shapes how the subject conceives its world while determining what it cannot know. Theorizing transcendental subjectivity through the distortion of unconscious desire marks Lacan's move beyond both Kant and Hegel. While both make the subject's failure to know it all – a fundamental limitation on knowledge – integral to their understanding of subjectivity, they don't situate this failure in the unconscious. The unconscious, which Freud discovers in the 1890s and theorizes in 1900 in *The Interpretation of Dreams*, is simply not available to them as a concept. This prevents them from taking stock of the subject's proclivity to act against itself and to desire what thwarts its own interests. Lacan adds the self-laceration of unconscious desire to the transcendental subjectivity of Kant and Hegel.

Although desire defines subjectivity, no subject originates its own desire. A subject finds its own specific way of desiring through what Lacan calls the big Other, which is his name for the social authority that the subject confronts. In his very first seminar, Lacan claims, "desire is the desire of the Other."[34] He then repeats this formulation several times during subsequent seminars. It is a formula that he will never renounce, even though he stops repeating it in the later period of his life. This formula describes how the subject discovers its own desire.

The subject confronts a figure of the big Other that issues demands to it. These demands might take the form of "Clean up your room" and "Get a job" or "Talk this way" and "Wear these clothes." Although the authority making the first set of demands is different than the one making the second – the big

Other begins as a parental authority and later becomes a social one – both cases involve a demand made with signifiers. In this sense, Lacan doesn't make a fundamental distinction between the different forms that the social authority assumes – as a parent or a peer group or an influencer. The subject finds itself as the addressee of a demand that obscures a desire it cannot discern.

Every demand occurs with signifiers. It is a symbolic demand that the social authority issues. But every attempt to clarify the desire motivating the demand founders on the problem of the signifier. To articulate the desire straightforwardly would have the effect of putting this desire into signifiers and thereby turning it into another demand that would have to be interpreted. In his essay "Kant with Sade," Lacan claims that "desire . . . cannot be articulated in the signifier even though it is articulated there."[35] The signifier inherently betrays desire by giving it the form of a signifying demand. To articulate one's unconscious desire – or that of the big Other – is already to miss it because demands appear in signifiers and desires correspond to the gap between signifiers. Desire emerges because no statement is ever straightforward. Every demand made on the subject must pass through the structure of signification, a structure that distorts what it expresses. This distortion indicates that an unconscious desire always lurks within every demand.

Demands require conformity on the parts of the subjects receiving them. But at the same time, conforming too enthusiastically or too literally to the demand creates ostracism rather than acceptance. This is because desire is never equivalent to demand. Every demand contains a hidden desire that it cannot directly articulate. Children who perfectly clean their room, vacuuming and dusting throughout, would arouse their parents' suspicion alongside their appreciation. There is always something that the demand can't say, which is the desire.

The subject doesn't just directly assume the desire of the big Other as its own. It confronts this desire as a question that has no ready answer. As a result, the subject's desire emerges through its interpretation of what the big Other desires. In fact, Lacan goes so far as to equate desire and interpretation. In *Seminar XI: The Four Fundamental Concepts of Psychoanalysis, 1963–1964*, he states, "Desire . . . is interpretation."[36] Although the subject's desire is the desire of the Other, the singularity of the subject derives from its way of interpreting this desire.

Because desire always comes in the form of a demand – it is articulated through signifiers – no desire can tell us how to interpret it. This is evident with the big Other that dominates in contemporary capitalist society. This big Other issues imperatives to accumulate, consume, and maximize profit in every possible fashion. All capitalist subjects experience the effects of this capitalist big Other. One subject might respond to the capitalist imperative by doing its best to accumulate all the time, neglecting everything else for the sake of accumulation. Another might respond with feverous consuming that leads to catastrophic debt and bankruptcy. Yet another might respond counterintuitively, by dedicating itself to equality, working for emancipation, and disdaining any accumulation of wealth. Because no one can articulate directly the big Other's desire, no one can say which of these subjects has correctly apprehended this desire. Their singularity consists in their individual responses to it.[37]

Even when we envision conforming our desire to what the big Other demands, we cannot ever fully do so. The subject cannot successfully align its desire with the Other's demand because the Other doesn't exist as a substantial entity that has a specific desire. There is no big Other except through the subject's efforts to conform to it. The big Other that makes demands on us emerges as a social force through our capitulation to it, not through the cunning of the authorities.[38]

Unconscious desire indicates the subject's failure to fit within the social order. Desire is what sticks out. Every interpretation of the Other's desire fails to hit the mark, and it is this failure that gives the subject its singularity relative to the symbolic structure in which it exists. The unconscious dislodges the subject from the path that the social order carves out for it.

The subject is always a subject of desire. Its desire represents an absolutely singular response to the encounter with the symbolic order. When a child is born, it enters a bath of signifiers in which it must locate itself and everyone it knows. This universe of signification exists before the child's birth, and the child will have to orient itself relative to this symbolic order. This orientation is its desire.[39]

A major turn in Lacan's conception of desire occurs during his *Seminar VII: The Ethics of Psychoanalysis, 1959–1960.* In this seminar, Lacan attributes an ethical status to desire that he hadn't earlier and that he would subsequently turn away from. Nonetheless, the claim about the ethics of desire formulated in *Seminar VII* has had as much or more lasting impact than any other part of Lacan's philosophy. The ethics of desire developed in this seminar attracts people as nothing else in his oeuvre does.

Seminar VII marks an important contribution to ethical philosophy because it centers ethics on desire rather than adherence to moral dictates. As he moves ethical philosophy in this direction, Lacan takes another step in the path that Kant lays down. Kant turns morality away from the ideal of the good. In Kantian morality, the subject cannot allow the good to motivate its act. For instance, I must avoid lying to my friend not because telling the truth about his spouse's adultery will improve his life but because my moral duty commands me to tell the truth. The moral law and the duty it implies must be the sole motive. Even though Kant doesn't link desire and ethics, he does dissociate ethics from the good.[40] Likewise, Lacan locates our ethical impulses in desire rather than whatever good we might accomplish with our acts. As Lacan sees it, the good is an ethical temptation that lures us away from our desire.

Although Lacan initially follows Kant's moral turn away from the good, he goes further than Kant when he gives our desire an ethical status. The point of ethics is to heed the dictates of our desire, not to obey the moral law.[41] As Lacan puts it in *Seminar VII*, "the only thing of which one can be guilty is of having given ground relative to one's desire."[42] Rather than abandoning desire for the sake of morality, one must follow one's desire no matter where it leads. To explain this, Lacan turns one of Kant's examples of moral duty on its head. Where Kant argues that one could easily imagine not betraying an innocent person even if the cost of this moral act were being hanged, Lacan imagines a situation in which one has sex with a forbidden person despite the prospect of hanging as the punishment for this act. His claim is that following one's desire even in the face of death is the ethical position. Not giving ground relative to one's desire leads one, Lacan believes, beyond the constraints of the big Other. The subject that doesn't give ground relative to its desire becomes dead symbolically while remaining alive physically, just like Antigone buried alive in her tomb.[43] At the time of *Seminar VII*, Lacan sees this as the only ethical position.

But as soon as Lacan articulates his ethics of psychoanalysis, he quickly turns away from it. Lacan never mentions his ethical maxim about desire after the end of *Seminar VII*, from 1961 to the end of his life. While he incessantly repeats most of his maxims – such as "desire is the desire of the Other" or "the unconscious is structured like a language" – he confines his claim about giving ground relative to one's desire to the end of *Seminar VII*. Given its popularity among Lacan's followers, one would think he would repeat it on at least one other occasion. Lacan's abandonment of the ethics of desire is startling. The seminar of the following year on the transference continues the focus on desire, but desire changes form. The ethical dimension of desire disappears as Lacan theorizes the *objet a* as the object that causes desire, a concept that Lacan had yet to invent when composing the ethics of psychoanalysis. It turns out that the ethics of desire would represent an interval in Lacan's philosophy, a time after his early emphasis on the symbolic order and before the middle period dominated by the *objet a*.

In Lacan's later seminars, desire more and more drops out of his thought as enjoyment replaces it. This abandonment of desire represents philosophical backsliding. The emphasis on desire's emergence through the contradictions of the symbolic order gives way to a consideration of the subject in isolation, a subject unable to connect its own mode of enjoyment with that of others. In Lacan's later theorizing, the subject is no longer what doesn't fit within the symbolic order, as it is for the middle Lacan and for Hegel. At the end of his life, he begins to insist that the impasses of knowledge are just impasses, as they are for Kant. The relative disappearance of desire in Lacan's trajectory marks the reascendence of Kant over Hegel in Lacan's thought.

Jouissance (Enjoyment)

Jouissance rarely stands still in Lacan's philosophy. What Lacan means when he uses this term undergoes a series of transformations from the 1950s to his death in 1981. Even though the definitions of other concepts change along Lacan's intellectual pathway, none goes through as many different iterations as jouissance. Even thinking of jouissance according to three periods seems inadequate when we consider how often Lacan changes what he means by the term. It starts out as the product of an imaginary deception, becomes identified with the phallus in the1950s, moves to an association with transgression in the seminar on ethics around 1960, is linked to the points of failure in the symbolic order in the 1960s, and ends up being divided between masculine and feminine forms in the 1970s.[44]

One controversy surrounding the term *jouissance* is its translation. There are many devotees of Lacan who insist that we not translate this term at all or, at least, that we not translate it with *enjoyment* in English. For instance, Néstor Braunstein leaves no wiggle room in his position. He claims, "It is unthinkable that anyone could translate this notion … into 'enjoyment.' Another problem that the translator faces is the absence of a much needed English equivalent to the verb *jouir*, of which Lacan makes frequent and legitimate use and which, once more, cannot be translated as 'to enjoy.'"[45] Braunstein argues in this way because *jouissance* in French signifies orgasm, which is not necessarily conveyed with the word *enjoyment*. There is also a legal sense of the word absent in the English term that indicates one's right to use something. For these reasons, the common solution among those writing about Lacan is to leave *jouissance* untranslated and attempt to turn it into an English word that readers will understand. This has the unfortunate effect of putting another obstacle in the way of those who want to navigate Lacan's unwieldy prose, which is why we should be wary of it. We should not exacerbate the difficulties created by Lacan's proclivity to speak only to initiates. Thus, contra Braunstein, I will freely interchange the terms *jouissance* and *enjoyment*. My position is that the fetishization of a specialized jargon is far more nefarious than an imprecision of translation.

Since Lacan's idea of what jouissance is changes so much, defining jouissance is necessarily fraught, but he always contrasts it with pleasure.[46] Pleasure is not lesser jouissance but its opposite. Pleasure derives from the release of a build-up of excitation, just like what happens at the conclusion of a sex act. We feel pleasure at the moment of release when our troubles evaporate. Jouissance, in contrast, involves giving oneself trouble, causing problems for oneself that one need not endure. It is not the release of excitation but the amassing of it, the sense of becoming burdened. While the momentariness of pleasure is free from suffering by definition, suffering is integral to jouissance, as an inherently troubling experience.

Jouissance indicates an experience that goes beyond pleasure to the point that it becomes painful. It is an excess of pleasure that the subject suffers. When one enjoys, one attains transcendence relative to the everyday world. And yet, this transcendent experience of jouissance is what makes the everyday world bearable.[47] The excessiveness of jouissance imbues daily life with a significance that it otherwise wouldn't have for the subject, even as it introduces a disturbing imbalance into the subject's existence.

Although jouissance is always excessive in Lacan's theory, how he understands this excess changes. In the early period, according to Lacan's chief disciple Jacques-Alain Miller, Lacan identifies the phallus as the signifier of enjoyment. The phallus doesn't itself enjoy, but it is the signifier of the lost jouissance within the symbolic structure. The process of subjection to the signifier produces the desiring subject, and, in Lacan's early period, desire focuses on the phallus. As Miller puts it, "the signifier annuls *jouissance* restituting it as signified desire."[48] As a result, jouissance becomes associated with the symbolic father who has the phallus. Everyone else is stuck in the position of desiring without access to this jouissance. There is a universal subjectivity that centers on the failure to reach jouissance. The contrast here is not just between pleasure and jouissance but also between desire and jouissance.

In the early seminars, Lacan's great innovation is to distinguish the symbolic phallus – the phallus as a signifier – from the real phallus. The phallus doesn't enjoy but functions as the signifier of the missing enjoyment, which gives it the status of a privileged signifier. The distinction between the real phallus and the phallus as a signifier seemed, at the time, to be an important feminist gesture. The clear implication is that the privilege of the phallus has nothing at all natural about it. Nonetheless, within this early conceptualization, social authority is the site of jouissance. Here, Lacan implicitly accepts the idea that all libido is masculine.

While composing *Seminar VII: The Ethics of Psychoanalysis, 1959–1960*, Lacan moves enjoyment away from the phallus. As a result, it should not be surprising that his example of enjoyment in this seminar is a woman who enjoys. Enjoyment is located not at the site of social authority or the phallus but at the site of social prohibition. One accesses this enjoyment by not giving ground relative to one's desire following the model of Antigone.

Even though enjoyment remains off-limits, it becomes possible to achieve it through an act that defies the figure of phallic authority. Access to the enjoyment occurs through transgression. Jacques-Alain Miller points out that the conception of jouissance articulated in *Seminar VII* portrays "transgression [as] the only way to access it."[49] Lacan even goes so far as to celebrate the jouissance of transgression in this seminar, with the implication that transgression is the only path to jouissance.[50]

This explains the role that Antigone plays in the seminar. Through the defiant transgression of Creon's phallic rule, Antigone attains the zone between symbolic death and real death – the zone between two deaths – that opens up enjoyment. This is what she attains when she goes beyond what the phallic signifier authorizes. It is only through extreme acts of sacrifice that one enters this zone and attains this enjoyment. But the danger of tying enjoyment to transgression is that it remains covertly dependent on the phallic law that it transgresses.

Antigone's dependence on the phallic rule of Creon for her jouissance becomes clear in a joke about their relationship. The joke runs like this: Why is Antigone's apartment in Thebes always hotter than everyone else's in the summer? Because she refuses to put any Creon in her air conditioner. Antigone's heat – her jouissance – depends on the negative relationship to the phallic figure, without whom she would have only her mundane existence bereft of the jouissance she derives from transgression.

The jouissance of transgression that emerges in *Seminar VII* requires the law that it violates. The law opens the space where the subject can transgress. It gives the subject a path to navigate in the direction through which it can discover enjoyment. In this understanding of enjoyment, enjoyment is what defies the phallic authority. And yet, this form of jouissance still remains too tied to the logic of the phallic signifier as what it must transgress. Transgression always relies on what it opposes. Antigone breaks from Creon's rule but nonetheless depends on his prohibition of the burial of Polynices for her act to become possible. The enjoyment of transgression depends on the symbolic authority that it challenges. This is why this conception of jouissance is ultimately a dead end. It remains as invested in the phallus as the way of thinking about enjoyment was in Lacan's early period.

The conception of jouissance in *Seminar VII* has inspired many political thinkers. Antigone serves as a paradigm for the political act in the thought of theorists such as Slavoj Žižek, Joan Copjec, and Alenka Zupančič. But Žižek himself grasps the problem inherent in the appeal to Antigone as a political model. In *The Fragile Absolute*, he turns against his own earlier invocation of her as a revolutionary figure. After lamenting "the overblown celebration of Antigone," he claims, "Antigone is sublime in her sad enumeration of what she is sacrificing – which . . . indicates the transcendent contours of the Thing to which she retains her unconditional fidelity. Is it necessary to add that this Antigone is a masculine fantasy par excellence?"[51] Antigone, as Žižek has it, is more in love with her own sacrifice than with what she hopes to accomplish by the act itself. The image of the self-sacrificing woman devoted to this sacrifice is precisely the problem and precisely what prohibits Antigone from being an authentic revolutionary figure. She remains within the traditional structure of femininity and the confines of the phallic order that she defies.

In the years following *Seminar VII*, Lacan enacts his most important shift in the location of the subject's jouissance. Jouissance ceases to be associated with the phallus or even the act of transgression and becomes identified with what doesn't fit within the symbolic order. It exists where the symbolic authority fails. With Lacan's new twist, jouissance moves from center to margin. This move represents a fundamental challenge to the conception of the libido as inherently masculine and puts to rest any residual privileging of the masculine position that inhered in the celebration of Antigone.

To be fair, from its inception, psychoanalysis challenges the structure of phallic authority. Beginning with Freud himself, it recognizes phallic authority as inherently fraudulent, that it has its basis in imposture. It is akin to the bully who wilts when someone finally stands up to him – or, as an ironically phallic expression from the American southwest has it, the phallus is "all hat and no cattle." And yet, as long as Freud and (following him) Lacan identify jouissance with the phallus, they limit the radicality of the psychoanalytic project. They successfully deflate the phallus, but they don't yet dissociate it from jouissance. A blurring between social recognition and jouissance remains.

What's most important about Lacan's turn to locating jouissance with what doesn't fit in the symbolic order is that it reveals that jouissance is opposed to symbolic recognition. As long as the phallus appears to function as the signifier of jouissance, symbolic recognition seems to confer enjoyment on those who receive it. Those occupying the position of phallic authority are more proximate to jouissance than those who don't belong to the symbolic structure. Nonbelonging is the index of distance from jouissance. Although this changes in *Seminar VII* with the figure of Antigone, Lacan's conception of jouissance there remains too indebted to the phallic order that it contests. Jouissance still operates from center to margin, even if the margin involves a dramatic transgression of the center.

This completely changes in the middle period of the 1960s, which begins after *Seminar VII*. In this period, the phallic signifier becomes not the location of jouissance but the signifier of its absence. Libido is no longer masculine. Rather than embodying the libido, the phallus now comes to represent the flight from it. The phallus marks the betrayal of jouissance for the sake of recognition.

The political valence of Lacan's thought changes dramatically with this new theorization of jouissance. The political charge ceases to be limited to exposing phallic authority as a fraud and becomes a reorientation of how we should map the social terrain. Once Lacan conceptualizes jouissance as occurring in the gaps of signifying structure, he associates it with those who lack the social recognition that comes from a symbolic identity. With this move, jouissance itself becomes radicalized, even though Lacan himself doesn't pursue this line of thought.[52] His gives the tools for others that he himself doesn't use.

According to the conception of jouissance in the middle period, social belonging corresponds to missing out on jouissance, since it occurs only in the gaps of the symbolic structure. Subjectivity enjoys insofar as it is alienated from the social order out of which it emerges. The subject can enjoy because it doesn't simply exist in the identity that has been laid out for it. The failure to fit is the basis for success at enjoying. This is what Alenka Zupančič is getting at in *What IS Sex?* She writes, "enjoyment appears at the place of the nonexistent ('originally missing') signifier, which – with its very nonexistence – dictates the logic of the signifying chain, 'declines it' in a certain way."[53] This positioning of jouissance in the holes of the symbolic order gives it a radicality in this period of Lacan's thought that it lacked earlier when it was linked to the phallus. Enjoyment doesn't come through defiance of the phallic law but through the possibilities opened up by its inherent failure. The phallic signifier becomes the signifier of the failure to enjoy. Enjoyment becomes located at the site of an absence that defies the realm of signification altogether. The signifier remains important, but it is important only for the gaps within the signifying structure that it cannot account for.

This jouissance associated with what doesn't fit in the symbolic order becomes apparent in jokes that show jouissance occurring where the figure of phallic authority cannot see or experience for himself. These jokes, in contrast to sexist jokes, find comedy in what doesn't fit within the phallic order. One such joke goes as follows: A wealthy old man, his young wife, and a handsome stranger are shipwrecked on a desert island. Seeing the situation, the young wife loses interest in the wealthy husband and starts to flirt with the handsome stranger. As this flirtation goes on, the three build a lookout tower to watch for passing ships that could rescue them from the island. The stranger offers to take the first watch. As the husband and wife gather driftwood on the sand, the stranger yells, "Hey! No sex on the beach! Get back to work!" The husband yells back, "We're not having sex! There's nothing going on here!" Later, the stranger yells out to them the same thing again. And again, the husband, annoyed, yells back and corrects him. Finally, the husband takes his shift in the tower. While he's in the watchtower, his wife and the good-looking stranger make passionate love on the beach. The wealthy husband on watch exclaims, "Wow, it really does look like sex from up here!" In this joke, the husband has the phallus: He has wealth that allows him to attract an appealing female romantic partner. But his possession of the phallus is what excludes him from jouissance. The young lover is able to dupe him by acting as if he sees the husband enjoying when he knows full well that he isn't.

The joke plays on the symbolic father's inability to see enjoyment while believing himself to have a monopoly on it. As Lacan situates jouissance with what doesn't fit symbolically, he takes the side of those who can enjoy where the symbolic father looks but cannot see. The phallus cannot see where it fails, which is what blinds it to jouissance, just as in the desert island joke.

The radicality of jouissance becomes even clearer with Lacan's critique of Marx in *Seminar XVI: From an Other to the other, 1968–1969*. The association of jouissance with the absence of social recognition leads Lacan to reformulate Marx's notion of surplus value as what the capitalist takes from the working class. As Lacan comes to see it, the capitalist doesn't expropriate surplus value but surplus enjoyment.[54] Capitalists are constantly trying to capture a complete jouissance that always escapes their grasp, which is what drives their continued exploitation of the worker.

By changing how we understand capitalist exploitation, Lacan makes clear not just how capitalism works (which is what Marx does) but why it works, why the capitalist is so motivated to exploit the worker in such a ruthless fashion. The capitalist is not driven by self-interest but by the prospect of an enjoyment that the worker seems to produce. But the capitalist project ultimately fails to attain the enjoyment that it seeks. It slips through the capitalist's hands just as the wealthy man in the watchtower fails to see the couple having sex beneath him.

Unfortunately, Lacan never works out a socioeconomic theory focused on surplus enjoyment. He never goes beyond the limited critique of Marx because he quickly moves on in the next seminar, *Seminar XVII: The Other Side of Psychoanalysis, 1969–1970*. This seminar begins with Lacan's philosophical turn to no longer considering the symbolic order as a shared terrain. It is the beginning of the late period. As the weight of the symbolic order recedes, the power of jouissance increases, but it ceases to be identified with what doesn't fit within the symbolic order because nothing fits anymore. Jouissance now bespeaks the disconnection of everyone from everyone else. In the late theory, everyone is stuck in their private form of jouissance. All that one can do is embrace one's private jouissance, which holds one together as a subject.

The full-throated embrace of jouissance in Lacan's late period represents the loss of its value as a political concept. Although Lacan himself never explored this political value, others did. It's not surprising that Lacan's politically oriented followers focus much more on the middle period than the late one. Several of those indebted to him – such as Jennifer Friedlander, Sheldon George, and Slavoj Žižek – have taken up jouissance as a political category for emancipatory politics. If jouissance derives from the failure of the phallic order, it must function as a site for emancipation. Lacan helps us to see that politics names the struggle for the relationship to jouissance that the society will have.

Drive

The drive doesn't go through as many transformations as jouissance does in the unfolding of Lacan's thought, but it's close. These changes, like those that the concept of jouissance undergoes in Lacan's thought, cannot be reconciled with each other. Lacan genuinely changes his mind and comes to positions that are incompatible with ones that he previously held. But what stays the same in Lacan's thinking about the drive is the fundamental status that it has for the subject.

The drive is what impels subjects to act and produces satisfaction in their actions. Lacan insists on the difference between the drive and instincts, a difference obfuscated in the English translation of Freud's works, which Lacan, even though he's working in French, criticizes. English translator

James Strachey uses the word *instinct* as a translation for Freud's term *Trieb*, which has the effect of causing the drive to seem natural. For Lacan, the distinction between drive and instinct, between *Trieb* and *Instinkt* in German, is of paramount importance.[55] While drives have only an impossible object and exert a constant force, instincts have clear objects that allow them to be temporarily satisfied through the act of obtaining the object, such as when a lion eats a gazelle or a zebra has sex with another zebra.

The object is strictly secondary in relation to the path that the drive follows. There is satisfaction in pursuing the drive that isn't tied to obtaining an object. The cliché, "It's not where you're going but how you get there," captures where the satisfaction of the drive lies. By stressing how drives replace instincts in speaking subjects, Lacan emphasizes the inherent hostility of psychoanalysis to any heteronormativity or association of human sexuality with reproduction. Unlike instincts, our drives are not natural. They do not drive us to reproduce ourselves as biological entities, which means that heterosexual or reproductive sex has no priority for the subject. One might even say that it's the most misleading form of sexuality because it has the illusion of being natural. The drive is not heterosexual or homosexual because it is indifferent toward the object. The drive satisfies itself through its own movement, not through any specific object choice. Its impulse is divorced from any instinct for reproduction.[56] The repetition of the drive provides satisfaction for the subject.

Lacan inherits the concept of the drive, like many of the concepts in his theory, from Freud, but his thinking departs from Freud's in important ways. Freud always maintains a dualistic perspective.[57] Initially, he separates the drives into the sexual and the ego drives. Whereas the sexual drive is the source of desire for objects, the ego drive seeks self-preservation. This opposition later undergoes a dramatic transformation as the idea of a distinct ego drive disappears from Freud's thinking. The sexual drive or Eros comes to encompass self-preservation because it can take the ego as its object. Beginning in 1920 with the publication of *Beyond the Pleasure Principle*, the drive opposed to Eros is the death drive. Even while Freud's conception of the drives undergoes a considerable shift, the dualistic structure remains the same. Lacan would break completely with this dualism.

Freud's initial revolution in the 1890s concerns the libido. He recognizes the priority that the sexual drive has over our conscious control. When Freud speaks about the power of the unconscious, at least in his work before 1920, he emphasizes its libidinous form. The sexual drive is what disturbs the functioning of the subject in society and demands repression, which is itself the indication of sexuality's predominance as a psychic force. The disruptiveness of our sexuality renders it unconscious, at least in the way that Freud theorizes it in early works like *The Interpretation of Dreams* (1900).

In contrast to the sexual drive or libido, the death drive names our self-destructiveness in Freud's later theory. *Beyond the Pleasure Principle* identifies the death drive as the force that leads us to undermine ourselves and sabotage our prospects for flourishing. Freud envisions this self-destructiveness ultimately driving us to return to an inorganic state. That is, under the impulse of the death drive, the subject seeks to destroy itself to the point of death. It wants to die, as Freud puts it, in its own way.

Lacan departs from Freud's dualism of the drives and from his emphasis on the primacy of sexuality. While Freud makes his original splash by seeing sexuality where others do not, Lacan's first contribution concerns the analysis of violence. Lacan's doctoral thesis on paranoid violence contrasts with Freud's development of psychoanalysis through the treatment of hysterics. From this starting point, the role of the death drive in the psyche would play a central role in Lacan's theorizing. While he never excludes considerations of the libido, he always considers the libido within the scope of the death drive. Sexual desire, for Lacan, becomes activated in the death drive, which marks a break from Freud that Lacan himself doesn't fully acknowledge.

In the process of giving primacy to the death drive, Lacan asserts it as the only drive. While Freud insists that Eros and the death drive battle it out in civilization, Lacan comes to see the libido or Eros as a manifestation of the death drive.[58] The death drive provides the structure for our libidinal desire. Our desire is unconscious because of its link to the death drive, not because it is libidinal and a taboo within society. There is a clear link between sexual satisfaction and the self-destructiveness of the death drive in Lacan's thinking. Sex always relies on an act of creating an excessive stimulation, an act of seeking out disruption rather than just directly seeking pleasure. The drive is responsible for the build-up of sexual tension, not for the final release that brings pleasure.[59] As a result of Lacan's theoretical insight, we don't need to distinguish between Eros and the death drive. The drive itself becomes singular.[60] The death drive is the drive as such.

But the death drive undergoes significant revision during Lacan's life. The evolution in his understanding of the drive is not the same as Freud's, but it is just as dramatic. In the early 1950s when Lacan begins giving his seminars, the death drive operates through the symbolic order. For this early Lacan, the pleasure principle dominates the imaginary order. But the realm beyond the pleasure principle – the death drive – is that of the signifier. The signifier insists regardless of the subject's pleasure. A death drive animates the symbolic order as it carves out a repetitive path for the subject. The repetition that characterizes signification is the repetition of the death drive, according to the early Lacan.[61]

This changes dramatically in the middle period of the 1960s. At this point, Lacan begins to associate the drive with the real instead of the symbolic order. As one of the fundamental concepts that Lacan outlines in *Seminar XI: The Four Fundamental Concepts of Psychoanalysis, 1963–1964*, the drive involves an encounter with the real at the point where signification breaks down. Lacan stops identifying the drive with the logic of the signifying order. It becomes what interrupts signification. In the late period, the drive ceases to be a central theoretical concept for Lacan. It almost drops out of his thinking entirely, which is one of the reasons why the late period holds less philosophical interest.

During the middle period, Lacan conceives the drives as a result of the subject's subjection to the signifier and the relation that it takes up to signification. Rather than conceiving the death drive as a drive to die, Lacan sees it as a repetition that continues not because it succeeds but because it incessantly fails. The death drive is the repetition of failure. By translating Freud's theorizing into the terms of signification, he breaks from Freud's flirtation with a biological idea of the death drive – the idea that all living things are driven to return to an inorganic state.

Seeing the drive as a failed repetition rather than as self-annihilation raises the question of the relationship between the drive and desire. While it initially seems as if these two forms are irrevocably at odds with each other, desire and drive have the same structure and trace the same path. The difference between them consists solely in their relationship to the object. Unlike desire, the drive operates with the unconscious knowledge that it has no object that it pursues.

Desire follows a metonymic movement from object to object. It seeks out an object that will realize it, finds the object, and then moves on to the next object after attaining the first. A constant movement forward characterizes desire, as it fails to discover the satisfaction that it anticipates in the object it gets. Whereas desire always seeks something more, drive finds satisfaction with what it doesn't have. Desire's object is always disappearing out in front of it, receding the closer that the subject comes to it. The drive's object is absent from the start, as the repetition encircles a fundamental void. Desire's movement from object to object obscures the basic repetition of the drive, which grasps the nothingness of its object – or takes nothing as its object.

But the distinction between drive and desire ultimately breaks down because the apparent forward movement of desire from one object to the next masks the repetition of the drive. While desire appears to move, it actually repeats. The object that it chases may change, but what animates it is the same absence that animates the drive.[62] Recognizing that desire and drive share the same missing object and follow the same path offers a shortcut for conceiving the psychoanalytic cure in Lacan's terms.

This is what Lacan articulates at the end of *Seminar XI*. He theorizes the end of analysis as a move from desire to drive. Embracing one's drive comes at the expense of abandoning the illusion of desire's future object. One must give up the image that desire has something it might possibly obtain. The object is absent, and it provides the satisfaction of the drive only through its absence. As long as one remains in the position of desire, this is not evident. In the position of the drive, the emptiness of the future becomes clear. The turn from desire to drive is emancipation from the seductions of commodities that promise a future of unlimited enjoyment and oppressive regimes that tempt us with the lure of true belonging.

Big Other

Authority is not confined to its political guises. We are used to thinking of political leaders – presidents, prime ministers, judges, mayors, and the police – as the only genuine sources of authority. State rulers and cultural elites seem like the ones responsible for determining the course of our lives. But Lacan conceives of a diffuse social authority, an authority not confined to discrete powerful people, as primary. Whereas political leaders tell people how to act, social authority infects subjects on the level of their unconscious desire. Lacan's name for social authority is the big Other.[63] In contrast to most of his other concepts, the big Other stays basically the same throughout the development of Lacan's thought. It is important for the analysis of society because it enables us to see that social authority, while it appears in external guises, is not just external in the way that political authority is. It has the power that it does through the way that subjects invest themselves in it.

Lacan contrasts the big Other with little others. The big Other is the force of social authority, while the little others are the people with whom I interact. We don't interact directly with these little others but do so through the mediation of the big Other. The big Other gives us the terms that we use and indicates how we should use them. This is why Lacan claims, in *Seminar VI: Desire and Its Interpretation, 1958–1959*, "Every discourse is the Other's discourse, even when it is the subject who speaks it."[64] When we speak to the little other, we do so through the big Other. Its authority rests in the background of every social interaction.

The distinction between the big Other and the little other enables Lacan to indicate the difference between general social forces and the distinct entities affected by these forces. Lacan doesn't lament the emergence of the big Other as an obstacle in the way of the subject's relationship to the little other. The detour through the big Other – the mediating effect of social authority – enables the little other to emerge as a relatable entity. It gives the subject a way to position the little other and make sense of what it says. As Lacan sees it, there is no such thing as a one-on-one relationship between the subject and the little other. There would be no path for making sense of anything that the other did.

The big Other represents a necessary force of indirection that comes first. This is why Lacan titles his sixteenth seminar *From an Other to the other* and not *From an other to the Other*. It is only through the path that the big Other lays down that the subject has the possibility to encounter the little other. There is no way that subjects can relate directly to other subjects. For Lacan, there is no intersubjectivity. Every interaction occurs through the big Other, the social authority that emerges out of the symbolic order.[65]

Although Lacan discusses intersubjective relations in his early seminars, just before the middle period (in the late 1950s) he turns against the possibility of subjects relating to other subjects. The error in theorizing intersubjective relations is that such theorizing imagines that the subject can bypass entirely the reign of the big Other. By the time of *Seminar VII: The Ethics of Psychoanalysis, 1959–1960*, the term *intersubjectivity* acquires a critical thrust. It comes to signify a false manner of thinking about how a subject engages with others. After 1959, Lacan ceases to believe in the possibility of intersubjectivity. The big Other is in the way of such relations. Rather than being a social tendency to combat, the primacy of the big Other provides the necessary terrain for subjects to interact with others. Without any social authority, there would be no terrain at all for this interaction.

The mistake that subjects make about this social authority is that they believe it to have a substantial status that it lacks. They appeal to the big Other as a reliable authority that can guide their lives by telling them how to act. But it is not reliable. Even as he comes up with the concept of the big Other, Lacan insists that the big Other does not exist, or, as he puts it in *Seminar XIV: The Logic of Fantasy, 1966–1967*, "there is no Other."[66] The big Other plays a social role but cannot function as an existential security blanket for the subject. Its status depends on everyone investing themselves in it. The big Other is nothing on its own.

While this line of thinking seems contradictory – the big Other constitutes the social field and yet doesn't exist – it nonetheless captures Lacan's thinking.

To imagine that we just relate directly to others without the big Other mediating these encounters is to fall for one form of ideological deception. But to believe that the big Other has a substantial status and can orient our actions is to fall for another. One must recognize the impact of the big Other while not investing in it as a substantial entity. That is the basic challenge for the subject.

Lacan's critique of our investment in the big Other is a critique of conformity. Subjects sell themselves to the big Other without realizing that it cannot offer the support for their identity that they demand from it. The claim of psychoanalytic theory, as Lacan sees it, is that the subject must give up its reliance on the big Other as a social authority and take responsibility for its desire. Rather than investing itself in the big Other, the subject must come to recognize its own singularity in its unconscious desire.[67]

The demands that the social order makes on us come from the big Other. The big Other issues demands for us to obey, and we approach the big Other with a corresponding demand for its recognition. We conform to the dictates of the big Other in an effort to gain the big Other's recognition. But no matter how strenuously we sacrifice ourselves for the sake of conforming, we can never go far enough for the big Other. The more we capitulate to it, the more it asks of us. Successful conformity is not possible because we are trying to conform to a force that has a purely symbolic status. There is no substantial big Other to grant us the recognition that we seek. But rather than lead us to quickly turn away from conforming to the big Other's demands, its nonexistence has the effect of luring us toward capitulation.

This becomes evident with our ways of dressing. We purchase clothing to appeal to the big Other, in an effort to accommodate ourselves to the big Other's demands. The practical concerns that clothing addresses are secondary thanks to the influence of the big Other. Under its spell, one person wears a shirt with *Nike* blazoned across the front, while another wears a pair of jeans that announce themselves as *Levi's*. A third person buys an expensive suit, and a fourth purchases designer boots. Such decisions about apparel derive from an investment in the big Other rather than a concern for what any particular others might think. We don't typically dress for others but for the abstractness of the Other. But it is exactly this abstractness that misleads us. We don't see the big Other issuing orders, and this deceives us into thinking that it's not demanding anything.

The problem with the big Other is that it is not a purely external authority for the subject. This is what makes it so much more psychically dangerous than the typical political authority. The subject's demand for recognition plays a crucial part in the erecting of the big Other's authority. When the subject strives for social recognition, it doesn't seek this recognition from one or two little others but from the big Other.

When we capitulate, the big Other rewards us by giving us the semblance of a secure symbolic identity. But this identity is never secure, due to the insubstantial status of the big Other. For the subject invested in the power of the big Other, this symbolic identity appears as a solution to the problem of subjectivity. Rather than confront the unanswerable question of who I am, I receive a message from the big Other that I am identical to my position in the symbolic order. I am a professor and a father and a tennis player. Whatever symbolic identity I have the big Other gives to me. This is what makes it completely insecure and ultimately worthless, due to the big Other's nonexistence.

One of the advantages of coming-of-age films is that they show the big Other manifesting itself in a few characters who dominate the psychic space of the high school. These films, such as *The Breakfast Club* (John Hughes, 1985), *Heathers* (Michael Lehmann, 1989), and *Mean Girls* (Mark Waters, 2004), typically depict a small clique as a social authority that demands conformity from everyone – and ostracizes those who don't capitulate. This type of film reveals the big Other at the moment of its emergence as a force in the life of teenagers. The big Other is not more powerful at the time when one comes of age, but it is more apparent than later in life. During the teenage years, the social authority's demand must conquer the subject so that it will remain psychically pliant throughout its adulthood. Capitulation when one comes of age prepares one psychically for a lifetime of it.

The power of the big Other over the teen manifests itself in *Heathers*, where social authority resides in a clique known as the Heathers. The leader of this clique, Heather Chandler (Kim Walker), has no institutional authority at Westerburg High School, but she rules it socially. As the leader of the Heathers, approval or denunciation from her can make or break the high school career of another student. At one point early in the film, she merely looks with disdain on one of the unpopular kids during lunch. When he sees her look at him, the guy spits up the milk he's drinking and expresses delight, telling his friends, "Did you see that? Heather #1 just looked right at me." As an embodiment of the big Other, Heather's recognition, even when it takes a negative form, means more to the people in the school than that of anyone else. She is aware that she rules the school and does so with an unrelenting severity.[68]

Other coming-of-age films show the big Other taking on a less oppressive form. Its representatives in *The Breakfast Club*, Claire (Molly Ringwald) and Andy (Emilio Estevez), evince more sympathy for those beneath them than

Heather Chandler does. But what characterizes these films as a genre is their determination to concretize the big Other in a few figures, which makes it easier to get a handle on the concept. The time in life that they focus on lends itself to an exploration of the big Other and how it operates.

The term *coming of age* itself indicates a shift in the subject's big Other. To come of age is to shift from a parental form of the big Other to a social one. For the child, the parent functions as its big Other, the ultimate authority for how the child should direct its desire. As the child becomes an adult, it transitions from a parental to a social big Other and becomes concerned with pleasing this new authority rather than its parents. The coming-of-age film shows the power of new authority as it is in the process of displacing the old one.

For instance, a teen might violate the curfew that the parent establishes to drink with friends. From the parent's perspective, this act looks like a transgression, not obedience. When we take the changed big Other into account, its valence changes. While disobeying the parent, the teen obeys the new figure of the big Other. Underage drinking while driving around town violates the law and the parent's demand, but it heeds the teen big Other, which demands stricter obedience than most parents do. This big Other pushes the subject coming of age to all sorts of disobedience, but in each case, the disobedience masks an extreme capitulation. Although teens in this situation experience themselves transgressing, they are instead moving from one form of conformity to another.[69]

The big Other doesn't change only when one moves from a parent's authority to that of the larger society. It also varies from group to group within the social order. While a larger big Other is operative in the society, groups have their own that can often act as an alternative to that of the society. Adhering to an alternative form of the big Other doesn't spare one from the problem of conformity. It can often worsen conformity by creating a sense of transgression relative to the societal form of the big Other. If one transgresses through an investment in another big Other, one is not really transgressing at all. Conformity takes the big Other as a substantial authority, no matter what form this big Other assumes.

The subject's obedience to the big Other becomes increasingly complicated when we introduce the law into the equation. The relationship between the big Other and the law is not what one might expect. The big Other does not simply demand that subjects obey the law. Its demands can dictate how they should behave when the law is silent. Or they can even compel subjects to disobey the law, which is how public transgression can manifest private capitulation.

The noncoincidence of the big Other and the law reveals itself when the big Other demands that we break the law in some way. This is what occurs in a joke about a woman who arrives in Rome on vacation and takes a taxi from the airport to her hotel. As they head to the hotel, the cab driver speeds through a red light. Frightened, the woman says to him, "Hey, you missed the red light back there." The cabbie responds, "Oh, it's all right. The great Italian philosopher Giorgio Agamben does it all the time. He believes we shouldn't view the law as a rigid thing but should play with its restrictions." The woman feels somewhat calmed by this explanation, until the man drives even faster through a second red light, this time narrowly missing an oncoming car. She exclaims, "You're going to get us killed with this driving." He says, "No, no, it's OK. This is exactly how Giorgio Agamben drives, and he's the most important contemporary philosopher." The woman is not much comforted, but she sits back in the seat. Just then, the cab driver slams on the brakes at a green light. The woman asks, "Now what are you doing?" The driver explains, "You never know. Agamben might be coming the other way."

The taxi driver in this joke views himself as someone simply transgressing the law in the way that Giorgio Agamben advises. As a follower of Agamben, he believes that the law is inherently oppressive and that one must refuse to capitulate to it. One must play with the law rather than obeying it. But he brakes at the green light because he obeys his own form of the big Other that appears in the form of Agamben. This appearance of transgression hides the comfort of obedience, an obedience that props up the big Other it follows. Even if one's big Other is an anarchist like Agamben, the point is to break from this figure's power, not to find a more palatable authority to which one might conform. The taxi driver breaks the law but remains an obedient subject. Lacan's insistence on the difference between the big Other and the symbolic law helps us to grasp how far obedience extends.

The distance that separates the dictates of the law and the demands of the big Other explains organized criminal activity. It's tempting to say that those involved in organized crime adopt a different big Other than ordinary people in society. They adhere to omertà and refuse to cooperate with the police. They receive social recognition for killing, for stealing, and for verbal aggression, activities that damage their status with the big Other outside of organized crime.

But the code that governs organized crime is entirely conscious. It replaces the public law to some extent but doesn't serve as a new big Other. While these criminals disobey the law, they most often obey the society's big Other. In fact, criminality usually involves more capitulation to the big Other than obeying the law.[70] Criminals turn to crime so that they can gain a social status that would otherwise escape them. They can purchase a spacious house, wear expensive jewelry, and drive a luxury car – all of which will garner them recognition with the big Other. Even the criminal's violence and sexual conquests lead to increased recognition from those inside the criminal organization and outside alike. The life of crime pays in the sense that it provides a quicker and easier path to the big Other's approbation than the law-abiding life. Criminality has its basis in a fundamental obedience. The criminal breaks the law in order to conform to the dictates of the big Other. This is why, from the perspective of psychoanalysis, criminality represents a psychic dead end. Its devotion to the big Other bars it from the path to freedom.

Lacan theorizes psychoanalysis as a response to the power of the big Other. It is an attempt to help the subject respond with its own singularity as an alternative to this power. Lacan aims at offering the subject a path out of capitulation to this authority that doesn't end up erecting a new authority in its stead. The subject must confront the nonexistence of every form that the big Other might take, including that of the psychoanalyst or even Lacan himself. To embrace the Other's nonexistence is to see Lacan's status as a divided subject, to refuse to treat him as a substantial authority.

Name-of-the-Father (Paternal Metaphor/Master Signifier/S_1)

Signifiers acquire their signification through their relationship to other signifiers. No realm of signification external to the whole symbolic order provides a reference point for signifiers. The signifier doesn't point directly to real objects or to images that aren't themselves part of the symbolic order. Instead, signifiers explain signifiers. This is evident when one looks up a word in a dictionary. The dictionary doesn't use a mathematical formula or a picture to define the word but relies instead on other words.[71] The result of this is that there is a degree of tautology in every definition: We define a signifier with another signifier, but then we define the second signifier through the first. When we look up the term *Earth*, for example, we find that it refers to the planet that orbits around the Sun. But if we subsequently search out the definition of *Sun*, we learn that it is a star that Earth orbits. Most definitions aren't this circular but have a more elliptical relationship to each other. Nonetheless, all definitions rely on words that they must define with recourse to other words. At some point, the definition collapses into itself, sometimes sooner for one than for others. We end up defining a word with a version of itself.[72]

This slippage from signifier to signifier when attempting to discover signification is what Lacan calls – following the structural linguist Roman Jakobson – the *metonymy* of the symbolic order. Metonymy involves the replacement of one word for another close to it. The symbolic order is replete with metonymy, especially when it comes to definitions. In their metonymic relations with each other, the signification of signifiers undergoes continual slippage. One word bleeds into another, as its signification affects the signification of the other word. Defining *love* requires knowing what *affection* means, but defining *affection* in turn necessitates being able to understand the word *fondness*. The cycle goes on and on. We need this metonymy to have at least some signification, and yet it threatens to render the symbolic order senseless. If the symbolic order were only tautological, it would be unable to signify. Lacan wagers that there must be another force that trumps the metonymy of the signifier.

To explain why the symbolic order doesn't devolve into endless slippage of one signifier into another in a mass of tautology, Lacan insists on the priority of metaphor relative to metonymy. The foundation of the symbolic order occurs through a metaphorical substitution, not of one signifier for another but of one signifier for nothing. Metaphor reaches outside the symbolic to refer to nothing at all, not to unsymbolized real things. The signifier that structures the symbolic order has no signified, which allows it to act as an anchor for signification. It is the one signifier not defined through its metonymic relations with other signifiers. But this is because it has no definition at all. It is a nonsensical signifier.

Lacan's name for the metaphor that structures the realm of signification, the symbolic order, is the *Name-of-the-Father*. He indicates its metaphorical status by also referring to it as the *paternal metaphor*. In the middle and late periods, he will refer to it as the *master signifier* or S_1 (which stands for the first signifier). Although Lacan sees the former two terms as slightly broader than the latter two, we can use them interchangeably. The Name-of-the-Father or master signifier is what it is. It is the signifier without a signified. To seek to define it is to miss how it operates relative to the symbolic order.

The absence of any signified for the Name-of-the-Father augments its authority. It doesn't have to refer to other signifiers to justify or explain itself. Its assertion of self-identity helps immunize it to critique, as we can see with the ideological justifications proffered by one of the most successful coaches in the history of American football. Bill Belichick, longtime coach of the New England Patriots, was fond of telling players, reporters, and fans, "It is what it is." Belichick often used this line in response to questions about his team or challenges to his decision-making. Doing so allowed him to implicitly invoke the authority of the one signifier that appears self-identical, the Name-of-the-Father, the only signifier that is what it is. This self-identity invests the Name-of-the-Father with a potential authority beyond what any other signifiers could have, the authority that Belichick tries to invoke when he responds to questions not with answers but with a claim to self-identity.

The signification of every signifier has its basis in the master signifier, which anchors the symbolic order by referring to nothing external to it. One can see this in the Soviet Union, where Marx's name functioned as the master signifier. Every decision that the government made, every turn of major events that occurred, and every setback that the people endured acquired its ultimate significance in reference to Marx's doctrine. The justification for everything that one does is that Marx says one should do it, but there is nothing behind Marx, no justification for this ultimate source of justification. *Marx* had a metaphorical primacy that elevated it above all other signifiers and provided a ground for them, regardless of what Marx himself might have thought about the situation.[73]

Every paternal metaphor that grounds a symbolic order acts like Baron Munchausen, who pulls himself out of the water by his own hair to avoid drowning. Obviously, no one can do this, any more than someone could lift up a chair while sitting on it. This impossible gesture of acting on itself is what characterizes the Name-of-the-Father. It starts the signifying order off by referring to nothing but itself. This gives every other signifier something apparently solid to refer to.

By linking the metaphorical basis for the symbolic order with the symbolic father, Lacan identifies this first metaphor as a figure of prohibition. The basis of signification is always also a symbolic law that issues a fundamental prohibition for the subjects within the structure. This prohibition restricts the metonymic sliding of the signifier in order to make signification possible. Within the symbolic order, one cannot just do anything at all. One cannot simply use signifiers such as *Earth* and *Sun* interchangeably but must keep each confined to its role. Signification depends on such restrictiveness.

This function of the Name-of-the-Father certainly seems oppressive. It keeps signifiers in their symbolic place and abridges their free movement. But at the same time, the sliding of one signifier into another – using *Earth* to refer to *Sun* and vice versa – would devolve into nonsense. The Name-of-the-Father is a nonsensical signifier that prevents the symbolic order from collapsing into nonsense. It is the signifier that tells everyone that they cannot just do as they please with the signifier.

There is no justification for the Name-of-the-Father's prohibition. While all other symbolic prohibitions have some symbolic justification, this foundational one doesn't. It is akin to the final word of parents who tire of explaining themselves to their children. The prohibition that the Name-of-the-Father lays down proclaims, "No, because I said so." This experience of an ungrounded law authorized only by its own performance is what brings home the stubbornness of symbolic castration to the subject. The Name-of-the-Father can only appear as an arbitrary command of the law because it lacks metonymic connections with other signifiers. It is a pure injunction to obey, which is why it makes symbolic castration evident to the subject.

For Lacan, the Name-of-the-Father announces the prohibition of incest. Whereas Freud believes that actual fathers play the decisive role in the Oedipus Complex by prohibiting the bond with the mother, Lacan sees prohibition in symbolic terms. The figure of prohibition is a symbolic father, a signifier, not an actual father. As a result, even though the term evokes male authority, the Name-of-the-Father doesn't specifically refer to men. It points to a symbolic position that has a structural necessity.

To underline the dissociation between the Name-of-the-Father and masculine subjectivity, Lacan will gradually replace the term *Name-of-the-Father* with that of *master signifier*.[74] The transition to the latter term allows Lacan to break completely with the baggage of the Oedipus Complex and its focus on the primacy of the family that he inherits from Freud.[75] It furthers his socialization of psychoanalytic theory.

Breaking the link between actual fathers and the Name-of-the-Father highlights the fact that the signifier is a social necessity that doesn't rely on the actions of any individual parent. The symbolic law is social, not familial. Social existence occurs through the mutual acceptance of the signifier of prohibition. The signifier, not some person, is the agent of this prohibition. To be a subject within the symbolic order means that one agrees to abide by the fundamental prohibition. One must accept the limit that the master signifier, the signifier of prohibition, introduces.

In Lacan's early period, he is relatively sanguine about the role that the Name-of-the-Father plays in harnessing our tendency toward aggressiveness, an aggressiveness that stems from our investment in an imaginary perspective on our relationships. To accede to the symbolic law and its fundamental prohibition is to discover life in common, to break the hold that the imaginary has on the subject. Although the Name-of-the-Father is a signifier without a signified, a nonsensical signifier, it does have beneficial effects, as Lacan sees it at this time.

Things change dramatically by the time of the late period. In one sense, the transition from the Name-of-the-Father to the master signifier in the last decade of Lacan's life was not felicitous. While it rightly separated symbolic authority from any necessary relation to the father – which is why we should freely substitute *master signifier* for *Name-of-the-Father* – it had the deleterious effect of leading Lacan to lose his belief in the social link. In his last years, he became convinced that each subject can forge its own version of the master signifier that has no relationship to others. Even in its inability to connect to others, the subject can get along on its own through recourse to a self-made master signifier, one with no ties to the social link. Its theoretical invention corresponds with a turn away from dialectical relations between the subject and the social order to isolation in a private form of jouissance. Or, to put it in the terms laid out so far in this book, it involves a regression from Hegel back to Kant. Hegel's philosophy focuses on the dialectical relationship between the subject and the social order, whereas Kant theorizes by taking the individual subject as the starting point. This is where Lacan ends up in the late period.

The middle period, however, represents the time where Lacan insists on the nonsensical status of the Name-of-the-Father.[76] The idea that the symbolic law is meaningful, that the Name-of-the-Father is anchored in something rather than nothing, seduces people. They come to believe that the paternal metaphor has real authority. They fall for the idea that the leader is a real man, that the paternal metaphor refers to a substantial thing. Psychoanalysis helps to disabuse them of this belief as it reveals again and again the nonsensical status of the Name-of-the-Father. It is a signifier that subjects invest themselves in to avoid confronting the fact of symbolic castration.

Every subject must wrestle with its symbolic castration, which is the result of its insertion into the signifying structure of language. Every subject is lacking because its desire always goes beyond itself, blocking any attainment of self-identity. One gains awareness of symbolic castration when one experiences the structural determinations of one's subjectivity and the limits that one cannot transgress. These limits are embodied in the master signifier. The master signifier symbolizes the limitation that confronts the lacking subject. But at the same time, this signifier suggests that there is one subject – the authority itself – that avoids castration. Investment in the master signifier reconciles the subject with its own castration by referring to one subject beyond lack.

The Name-of-the-Father is the signifier not of specific laws that limit what we can do but of law as such. It has to have an exceptional status in relation to all other signifiers in order to authorize the law. As Lacan states in *Seminar V: Formations of the Unconscious, 1957–1958*, "there is something that authorizes the text of the law. Effectively, it is sufficient that what authorizes the text of the law is at the level of signifiers. This is what I call the Name-of-the-Father."[77] The authorization of the law must come from outside the social field if it is to cover the symbolic field. The Name-of-the-Father is the signifier that totalizes the symbolic order through its exceptional status relative to this order. The exceptional signifier creates a whole of all the other signifiers. As an exception, it is what closes the set of all signifiers. While every other signifier has its meaning in relation to other signifiers, the Name-of-the-Father doesn't rely on relationality, which allows it to orient everything around itself.

The prohibition that the Name-of-the-Father authorizes hides the impossibility lurking within all desire. The limit that the subject encounters in its desire is not the result of the prohibition that the Name-of-the-Father decrees. There is an inherent impossibility in all desire. Failure is written into the structure of desire because what drives the subject's desire is not the object of desire toward which it strives but what blocks its path. But prohibition plays a precise role for the desiring subject. The prohibition allows the subject to believe in the possibility of attaining its object but for the existence of the law.

The Name-of-the-Father takes the responsibility for castration away from the subject and places it within the law. This has the effect of creating an illusory conception of desire. Prohibition is the primary external hindrance designed to obscure the impossibility of desire.[78] But at the same time, simply bypassing the Name-of-the-Father is not the path to emancipation. It symbolizes a structural impossibility that no subject can escape.

To accept symbolic castration, one must allow oneself to be duped by the fundamental social lie that the Name-of-the-Father embodies. To refuse the structuring symbolic fiction is to find oneself not in the truth but rather completely misled. As Lacan puts it in *Seminar XXI: The Non-Duped Err, 1973–1974*, "the non-dupes are two times duped."[79] Thinking that one can pass straight to the truth without going through the detour of the controlling symbolic fiction – thinking that one can avoid the Name-of-the-Father or master signifier – leaves one in complete disarray.

The unavoidability of the master signifier stems from its status as first. Lacan calls it S_1, the first signifier that structures the symbolic order. According to Lacan's theory of the signifier, there must be an S_1, but there is no binary signifier or S_2. Other signifiers exist, but none of them completes S_1 and gives it a decisive signification. There is no complementary signifier that would allow the process of signification to conclude. When one is in the structure of signification, one never arrives at an end point. One signifier (S_1) starts the process, but there is none (no S_2) to end it. This means that the structure of signification is inherently incomplete and has no possibility for reaching completion. Every ending point is always provisional.

Instead of a binary signifier or S_2, there is knowledge. Knowledge replaces the missing binary signifier. The subject accumulates knowledge in the hopes of bringing signification to an end point, but knowledge is inherently endless. No matter how much knowledge one accumulates, there is always more out there. A fundamental impasse characterizes the signifying order.

What is crucial is that we register the absence of any possible complementarity or harmony within the symbolic order. The idea that relations might work if everyone sticks to traditional gender roles or, from the opposite perspective, if everyone gives up traditional gender roles, fails to internalize the structural impasse of the signifying structure. This structure is fundamentally out of balance. The master signifier, whatever it might be, can have no complementary binary signifier. Moving on from the Name-of-the-Father to some other master signifier does not ameliorate the imbalance that structures the symbolic order. The imbalance, the disharmony, is here to stay as long as we have a symbolic order.

The political point of psychoanalysis is not to change our master signifier. Believing in a salutary master signifier always leads one astray. There is no such thing as a just or egalitarian master signifier, no master signifier that allows things to work out, such as *Marx* or *communism*. Every master signifier operates just like the Name-of-the-Father and is equally oppressive. We need not change the master signifier but must instead insist on its stupidity, on its inability to have a signification.

On the other hand, advocating the abandonment of all master signifiers courts political disaster. This seems like the egalitarian play, but it actually feeds the oppressive desire for a meaningful master signifier. The rejection of the master signifier as such operates from within the field of signification underwritten by a master signifier. It is a project that saws off the branch on which it sits. If successful, it takes itself down alongside the master signifier it combats. The more we eliminate the master signifier, the more people clamor for a real master.

We need a master signifier, but we must insist on its nonsensical status. Reactionary movements come to power with the promise that they will give us a meaningful master signifier, a Name-of-the-Father rooted in a real man or the nation's blood and soil. This promise always fails because there is nothing significant outside the symbolic order on which any version of the master signifier might rely. The promise of psychoanalysis goes in the other direction. It reveals the nonsensical status of every master signifier. Every father, as psychoanalysis makes clear, is a fool. There is nothing outside the symbolic order, and this nothing is the basis of every version of the master signifier. As a result, no master signifier can save us.

Phallus

The phallus is an important category in Lacan's socialization of psychoanalytic thought. Lacan refers to the phallus where Freud refers to the penis to draw attention to its status as a signifier rather than as a bodily organ. This distinction has widespread ramifications for the theoretical ambit of psychoanalysis. With this transition from penis to phallus, all of a sudden the significance of psychoanalysis for feminism becomes much clearer because the phallus is a signifier and not a bodily organ. At the same time, the interventions of the analyst gain a new direction.

The symbolic status of the phallus receives its first articulation and most thorough theorization in "The Signification of the Phallus" from 1958.[80] This essay appears toward the end of the early period. By insisting on the phallus as a signifier, Lacan offers an original interpretation of Freud's theory of sexual difference, a theory that appears to give significance to biological difference between the sexes. Through his approach to what is actually at stake in Freud's way of thinking, seeing how straightforward biology is not at issue, Lacan shows that what Freud calls the penis takes on its value not as a bodily organ but as a signifier. That is, we should understand the penis in Freud's works as a phallus, which is what Lacan's contribution makes evident. The phallus has the importance that it has in the psychic economy of both sexes because of its status as a privileged signifier, not because of any natural privilege that the penis as a sexual organ enjoys or even because of any cultural investment in the penis. Recognizing the phallus as a signifier implies going beyond the divide between nature and culture.

As a signifier, the phallus is not just any other signifier. It plays the central role among all signifiers as the signifier of signification as such, the signifier that stands for every signified.[81] All meanings must refer to this phallic signifier. Nothing authorizes the phallus to be in this position, and yet one signifier must perform this operation. If we recognize that the phallus is not the penis and thus has no natural privilege, we can relate to its privilege as structural rather than ontological.

More importantly, Lacan insists that the seeming privilege of the phallus is illusory. If the phallus is merely a signifier with no substantial status, this implies that its status is that of an impostor. The symbolic father figure who wields the privilege of the phallus can only do so through recourse to imposture, not because this figure really has authority. When the phallus shows itself, as happens within psychoanalysis, its imposture becomes visible to everyone. If the veil is lifted, phallic impotence becomes evident, and the phallus ceases to function. This is what psychoanalysis attempts to accomplish.

The imposture of the phallic signifier renders all phallic power precarious. Since it has its basis in semblance rather than actual power, it is constantly on the verge of collapse. In *The Feminine Look*, Jennifer Friedlander draws attention to the difficulties inherent in the phallic position of imposture. She writes, "imposture carries the burden of accomplishing an identity based on the illusion of knowledge."[82] Phallic imposture is always on the verge of having its impotence exposed, which is why Friedlander compares it to the act of wearing a toupee. At any moment, a gust of wind could reveal that the symbolic father is impotent – or worse, bald. Phallic imposture hides phallic impotence.

One can easily imagine a little joke about Lacan himself that would illustrate phallic imposture. As he is explaining his philosophy to his wife, he comes to the concept of the phallus, where she stops him because she can't fully grasp it. Lacan tells her, "I can't explain but have to show you." At this point, he pulls down his pants. His wife responds, "Oh, I get it now. It's like the penis, only smaller."[83] The phallus promises omnipotence but delivers impotence. Its imposture hides that there is nothing to hide.

Imposture results from the special relationship that the phallic signifier has to the signified. Whereas every other signifier has a signification through its relationship to other signifiers, the phallic signifier signifies significance as such. In consequence, it has no one signification of its own. Whereas the master signifier has no signified, the phallic signifier has every signified. The master signifier signifies nothing, while the phallus as a signifier signifies everything. It is the difference between not enough and too much. The phallus is the signifier too full of meaning. The privilege of the phallic signifier allows it to function as the signifier of all signification, but this is at the same time the source of its impotence.

The problem is that we don't recognize this impotence when we fail to understand the phallus as a signifier and instead view its centrality as a result of nature or culture. We believe that phallic privilege derives from its status in human reproduction, or we assume that masculine dominance within society has given it its privileged status. The great feminist insight of psychoanalytic theory is that the privilege of the phallus lies in its status as neither natural nor cultural.[84]

The recognition that the phallus is a signifier leads us beyond two basic errors that predominate in the contemporary theoretical universe. The first is naturalism, a position that treats the subject as a biological entity not fundamentally altered by its subjection to the signifier. What this position misses is that the event of subjection to the signifier produces a radical disruption in an entity's needs, so that the subject of the signifier cannot obtain direct satisfaction in an object. Need becomes desire, leading to the existence of subjects who disdain their needs and pursue desires that are at odds with what they need. The discovery of the role of the phallic signifier allows Lacan to understand the distortion that the signifier introduces to subjectivity, the way that it tilts the symbolic field through one signifier that sticks out from all the others.

The opposed error is culturalism, which, like naturalism, fails to account for the distorting effects of the signifier. The culturalist sees subjectivity as simply an effect of the imprint of power. According to this theory, we are what the ruling structure makes us into. For someone such as Michel Foucault, desire emerges in response to the compulsion effectuated on the individual. In this view, power creates the symbolic field and determines what happens within it. But what the culturalist doesn't see is that the phallic signifier causes a distortion within the symbolic field, so that the symbolic demand doesn't produce a direct effect in the subject that receives it.

Lacan's engagement with the question of the phallus enables him to make a major contribution to the debate between naturalism and culturalism. Rather than identifying psychoanalysis with either side in this debate, the existence of the phallic signifier provides evidence for a third position beyond nature and culture, a position that results from the collision between the natural entity and the cultural formation. This discovery is Freud's legacy, but, as Lacan recognizes, he fails to place enough emphasis on the primacy of the signifier and symbolic castration. One reason that he misses the primacy of symbolic castration is his preoccupation with the Oedipus complex.

Freud openly gives priority to the Oedipus complex relative to the castration complex. For him, the Oedipal bond to the mother comes first, followed by the father's threat of castration that interrupts this initial bond. The Oedipus complex triggers the castration complex. Its structural priority gives its discovery pride of place within the claims of psychoanalysis. Freud writes, "I venture to say that if psycho-analysis could boast of no other achievement than the discovery of the repressed Oedipus complex, that alone would give it a claim to be included among the precious new acquisitions of mankind."[85] Freud's pride in the Oedipus complex is not something that Lacan would share. He does discuss the Oedipus complex, especially in the early period, but he would not count it among the great insights of psychoanalysis.

Lacan inverts the priority of the Oedipus complex and castration complex that Freud establishes. Castration takes on the central position in the subject's destiny. It becomes central for Lacan because he theorizes it differently than Freud does. Castration becomes symbolic castration. Rather than being the fear of losing an organ, it is the lack that defines subjectivity as such and that results from entrance into the realm of signification.

One might expect that the phallus is the cause of castration, but instead Lacan sees it as the signifier of castration. The phallus signifies what the subject has given up in order to be a subject. This is precisely what makes the phallus a fraud: The subject lacks as a subject, but it lacks nothing that it ever had. What the subject gives up is what exists only insofar as it has been given up. One has sacrificed nothing but an imaginary object – an imaginary phallus – and nothing real.[86] The imaginary phallus is the image of complete jouissance, jouissance unencumbered by any lack. The phallic signifier then substitutes itself for this missing object by signifying it. The phallus signifies a plenitude that doesn't exist and that never existed – what the subject believes that it lost when it entered the symbolic order.

Seeing the phallus as a signifier is Lacan's method for attenuating the aura of mystery that surrounds it and that gives it its power. It is insofar as people don't speak about the phallus that they allow it to remain a mysterious entity. The phallus acquires the aura of mystery because of its special status within the structure of signification. As the signifier of all signfieds, it is not just a random signifier. The phallus signifies the distortion of animal needs into subjective desires that occurs through the introduction of the signifier. When we can recognize and theorize its signifying function, it ceases to have the substantial authority that it gains as long as it remains undiscussed and veiled. Drawing attention to the privilege of the phallic signifier is thus part of a battle that Lacan wages against the power of the phallus.

But the place that the phallus has in Lacan's thought doesn't stay the same. It reaches a high point in the late 1950s and then recedes during the middle period. As the signifier of desire, the phallus structures how Lacan theorizes desire during the 1950s. This undergoes a thorough transformation that begins just after *Seminar VI: Desire and Its Interpretation, 1958–1959.* In this seminar, the phallus still plays a determinative role in the subject's desire.

When Lacan formulates his ethics of desire in *Seminar VII: The Ethics of Psychoanalysis, 1959–1960*, he doesn't refer to the phallus at all. When he lays out the four fundamental concepts of psychoanalysis in *Seminar XI: The Four Fundamental Concepts of Psychoanalysis, 1963–1964*, not only is the phallus missing as one of these concepts, but he barely mentions it at all in the seminar. This near omission evinces the waning importance of the phallus in Lacan's middle period, even though he never fully abandons the notion of the phallic signifier.

Just as the Name-of-the-Father gradually becomes subsumed within the master signifier, so does the phallic signifier. The Name-of-the-Father and the phallus come together as Lacan's thought advances, and they merge under the rubric of the master signifier, which is the signifier that begins the signifying process.[87] Although the phallus recedes in importance in Lacan's own thought, his conception of it had lasting importance for feminist theory.

It is not surprising that when Juliet Mitchell and Jacqueline Rose opt to collect Lacan's work on feminine sexuality for translation into English they choose to include "The Signification of the Phallus."[88] They recognize that distinguishing the phallus from the penis is a major feminist insight. Mitchell and Rose entitle the volume *Female Sexuality: Jacques Lacan and the école freudienne* (1982), which places Lacan's theory alongside feminist theory.

Alenka Zupančič claims that Lacan emphasizes the phallus to such an extent not because of his investment in phallic authority but precisely in order to undermine that authority, to draw attention to its contingent status. Historically, people have wrongly viewed phallic authority as structurally necessary and ontologically sanctioned. Psychoanalysis remedies this error. In *The Odd One In*, Zupančič says, "By spelling out the link between the traditional almighty phallus (which, by the way, functioned symbolically, and as a symbolic power, long before Lacan came along) to an anatomical particularity, he (and psychoanalysis) made a crucial contribution to the removal of the phallus from the mode of necessity to that of contingency."[89] When we articulate the centrality of the phallic signifier in the way that Lacan does, we demystify its operation and undermine its ability to confer privilege to masculine subjectivity.

The point is not to eliminate the privileged signifier as such, whether the phallus or some other signifier that takes its place. In the middle and late periods, Lacan sees the function of the master signifier and the phallus coming together in a single privileged signifier that both signifies itself and signifies the field of the signified as such. But even when we theorize the two functions as united in one signifier as Lacan begins to do after the early period, there must a privileged signifier. There will always be one signifier that serves to signify the entire field of signification. The key political struggle lies in recognizing that privilege of this signifier also entails its impotence. Any subject presenting itself as the bearer of this signifier does so as a fraud, always on the verge of having the imposture exposed. Although Lacan himself failed to articulate this as a feminist insight or to insist on the feminist inflection of psychoanalysis, grasping the fraudulence of the phallus marks one of Lacan's contributions to feminism.

Quilting Point

Employing a quilting point is an act of punctuation that ends the openness of every statement. Every sentence reveals what's at stake with the quilting point because every sentence begins with an open signification. I can say, "I want you to come here . . .," and signify an infinite number of things. It isn't clear until the point at which I place a period at the end of the sentence. I might conclude with ". . . so I can congratulate you" or ". . . so I can rob you." The signification of the opening becomes evident when I add the final punctuation, but not until then. The quilting point doesn't just conclude a sentence. It punctuates an entire signifying instance, such as what occurs in a psychoanalytic session or a political struggle.

The quilting point has structural necessity for the functioning of the symbolic order. Statements that don't at some point refer to a quilting point don't make any sense. Without the quilting point, nothing ends the act of signification. The result is that undecidability infiltrates every aspect of the statement. Even though the quilting point is never fixed once and for all, it nonetheless is what allows the subject to be understood. It gives signification a stopping point.

The quilting point has a much too brief career in Lacan's philosophy. Toward the end of his third seminar in 1956, Lacan develops this concept as a key to understanding psychosis. After this introduction, it receives a passing mention in a seminar two years later and in the essays "The Instance of the Letter in the Unconscious or Reason Since Freud" (1957) and "The Subversion of the Subject and the Dialectic of Desire" (1960). Then it disappears. The quilting point does not become a constant reference point for Lacan's thinking, as the real or jouissance would, even if what Lacan understands by these terms evolves. Lacan's abandonment of the quilting point seems to suggest its unimportance within his theory. But despite being barely a blip on Lacan's theoretical trajectory, it merits close attention not just for its role in making sense of psychosis but for the central role that it plays in all signification and in Lacan's practice of the short session, his technique of ending the analytic session at the point when an opening to the unconscious appears rather than after the standard fifty minutes.

The quilting point is an English translation of the French *point de capiton*, which is a term of art used to indicate the button sewn on a quilt to prevent the stuffing inside from sliding around during use. The translator of *Seminar III: The Psychoses, 1955–1956*, Russell Grigg, chose the term *quilting point* to mirror the French term that quilters (and Lacan) employ. When Bruce Fink later translated the *Écrits* (2006), he changed this translation to *button tie*, which undoubtedly makes more sense to non-quilters but loses the technical resonance of the original, which Lacan himself was certainly aware of.[90]

The starting point for understanding the symbolic order is grasping that nothing intrinsically relates signifiers to particular signifieds. There is, instead, a generalized sliding of the signifier that constantly takes place. This sliding leaves signification up in the air, as becomes clearest in the case of puns. Puns can be humorous because they capture the contradictions of language, but they also indicate the openness of signification, the fact that it is always up for grabs. In the title of an essay deconstructing Lacan's interpretation of the short story "The Purloined Letter," Jacques Derrida employs a pun that works through its undecidability. "*Le Facteur de la vérité*" means both "The Factor of Truth" and "The Postman of Truth." Derrida wants readers to keep the signification of the title open without ever closing it down. The quilting point is what provides the closure that Derrida here leaves in abeyance.[91]

Nowhere is the influence of structuralist semiotician Ferdinand de Saussure more evident than in Lacan's theorization of the quilting point. Saussure himself never invokes the term *quilting point*, but he should have. Saussure envisions a flow of signifiers just below a flow of signifieds – words below their meanings. In his semiotic theory, signifiers and signified simply line up with each other. There is no risk of the sliding of the signifier making a sentence unintelligible because every signifier is anchored to its signified. This anchoring occurs even though the relationship between signifiers is what determines what signifiers mean or what the signified is in Saussure's theory.[92]

While Lacan owes an immense debt to Saussure and his understanding of structural linguistics, he is much less sanguine about the relationship between the signifier and the signified than his theoretical forerunner. The word and its meaning are not bonded together. They are constantly on the verge of becoming dissociated from each other. Or, as Lacan puts it in *Seminar III: The Psychoses, 1955–1956* where he develops the idea of the quilting point, "The relationship between the signified and the signifier always appears fluid, always ready to come undone."[93] Far from seeing an intrinsic link between signifier and signified, Lacan identifies a troubled and evanescent linkage. This is where the quilting point enters the scene. It solidifies the connection, at least as long as it is operative for the subject.[94] The symbolic order is meaningless without the quilting point. It has the effect of creating a total transformation of the subject's relationship to the signifying structure.

Although Lacan doesn't mention the term when introducing the quilting point in *Seminar III*, the quilting point effectuates a process that Freud refers to as *Nachträglichkeit* or retroactivity. The articulation of a quilting point works backward to the past to determine the signification of what comes before it chronologically. One can add a quilting point intentionally or not, consciously or unconsciously. Everything that follows after the introduction of the quilting point bears its imprint. But even more importantly, this signifier retroactively changes the signification of the words that come before it. This is the effect of *Nachträglichkeit* or retroactivity. The introduction of a new quilting point provides a fundamental reorientation of the world.

This is what occurs when, for instance, the term *climate change* became part of the everyday lexicon of the world. It is not just another signifier for many people but a quilting point. All other fears – fear of criticism, fear of hatred, fear of violence – disappear relative to this signifier for those employing it. Movements such as Fridays For Future take *climate change* as their quilting point and organize around it. In doing so, they attempt to persuade others and hopefully the whole world to see it as the signifier that marked an end point for the contemporary world. Grasping this end point changes how one looks at something like an airplane flight. The significance of the flight undergoes a complete reversal with the introduction of this new quilting point, *climate change*. Rather than a fast mode of travel allowing one to get from Berlin to Hong Kong, it becomes a way of contributing to making the planet uninhabitable. It goes from being a great opportunity for those with enough money for it to being a horrible mode of travel. Not to see this, according to Fridays For Future, is to turn away from our shared reality. The group's political struggle consists in convincing others to acknowledge the quilting point that they embrace. To see *climate change* as just another signifier – one to be dealt with as other signifiers – is to miss the point altogether. One grasps the impact of climate change only when one takes it up as a quilting point, in the view of Fridays For Future.

The primary practical intervention that Lacan in the working of analysis makes derives from his theorization of the quilting point. It is the introduction of the short session. According to the theory of the short session, having a psychoanalytic session go a standard length – fifty minutes – has a deleterious effect on the treatment. The short session enables the analyst to quilt the session when the analysand says something psychically significant, even if this is unbeknownst to the analysand. The act of quilting the session gives the analysand something to ponder between sessions.[95] This is the primary way that the quilting point survives in the middle and late periods.

In "The Field and Function of Speech and Language in Psychoanalysis," Lacan describes the benefit of the short session for the analysand (and for the analyst as well). He discusses a particular analysand who has a habit of prolix discussions during his analytic sessions that, despite being very erudite, work to block the movement of the analysis. It is the short session that frees Lacan and the analysand from these soliloquies. Lacan writes, "in experimenting with what have been called my 'short sessions,' . . . I was able to bring to light in a certain male subject fantasies of anal pregnancy . . . in a time frame in which I would normally still have been listening to his speculations on Dostoyevsky's artistry."[96] This insight comes out thanks to the use of the short session, which cuts short the analysand's psychically insignificant babble.

Lacan never refers to the quilting point when discussing the short session, but the latter clearly occurs within the theoretical ambit of the former. Although it disappears from Lacan's theory after 1960, it has a posthumous career in the form of the short session. In the short session, the analyst forces the emergence of signification by punctuating the psychoanalytic session at a crucial point. By stopping at a specific moment, the analyst arrests the flow of signifiers and causes a specific signified to emerge for the analysand. If done right, the analysand must confront a significance that the flow of signifiers – about Dostoyevsky, say – aims to avoid.

By quilting in a timely fashion, an unconscious significance can come to the fore. This is why the quilting point doesn't just survive in the form of the short session but also in the theorizing of politics and society among thinkers indebted to Lacan. One can envision theoretical engagement in politics manifesting itself through the contribution of a timely quilting point. By quilting social relations with a term like *class struggle*, a barrier to equality becomes visible in a way that it wasn't prior to the act of quilting. Although this is far afield from what Lacan himself would embrace under the banner of the quilting point, it represents one of the most significant parts of his legacy.

Slavoj Žižek makes the quilting point central in his influential form of ideology critique. Ideological fantasies work, according to Žižek, by quilting a social situation in a tendentious way. One of his examples for this is Hitler in interwar Germany. As Žižek puts it in *For They Know Not What They Do*, "the simple evocation of the 'Jewish plot' *explains everything*: All of a sudden 'things become clear,' perplexity is replaced by a firm sense of orientation, all the diversity of earthly miseries is conceived as the manifestation of the 'Jewish plot.' In other words, the Jew is Hitler's *point de capiton*."[97] The quilting point enables a fantasy to anchor significance around a central signifier that mobilizes an ideological position, as Hitler's use of the quilting point does here. One way to fight against this political use of the quilting point is with the concept itself. By theorizing it in operation, one has a weapon to use against its political deployment, a weapon that those fighting against Hitler lacked.

What neither Lacan nor Žižek says is that we might benefit theoretically from distinguishing between the master signifier and the quilting point. According to Lacan in *Seminar III*, the master signifier (what he calls the Name-of-the-Father at the time) is one version of the quilting point among others. But my contention is that the master signifier and the quilting point function differently. The master signifier or Name-of-the-Father, as the exceptional signifier that signifies itself, provides the basis for signification. It is the initial point of reference for all other signifiers, while the quilting point punctuates the signifying order, providing it with a stopping point. Simply put, the master signifier is the nonsensical beginning point, and the quilting point is the ending that creates a sense. To reduce them to a single concept, as both Lacan and Žižek do, is to mingle together the nonsense of the signifying structure and the moments of sense that arise out of this nonsense.

We can see this distinction at work in Žižek's own example of Nazism. He's certainly correct that the Jew operates as the Nazi quilting point, as the signifier that completes Nazi symbolic identity. So far, so good. But it doesn't serve as a master signifier for Nazis to rally around and to define themselves through. Here we can see how the master signifier and the quilting point function differently. The signifier *Jew* has a clear sense for Nazis, which precludes it from being a master signifier. The Nazi master signifier must be something akin to *Aryan* or *Deutschland*. These terms provide the foundation for what it means to be a Nazi, the foundation for the Nazi's symbolic identity. One cannot ask what this signifier means for the Nazi because it is the basis for all meaning, the ultimate justification for everything a Nazi does or thinks. As a quilting point, the signifier *Jew*, in contrast, explains why the symbolic identity based on this master signifier isn't completely satisfying. The quilting point rescues the Nazi from the failure of the master signifier, which is why Nazism could not give up the idea of a Jewish conspiracy, no matter how many Jews the Nazis killed. As Nazism shows, the master signifier and the quilting point work in tandem, but they occur at opposite ends of the process of signification.

Although it might be obvious, it's important to note that the quilting point doesn't function in the same way for the psychoanalyst as it does for the Nazi. The psychoanalyst brings the analytic session to a close by quilting at a moment that undermines rather than secures the symbolic identity of the analysand. If one quilts at a point where the unconscious manifests itself, the self-division that the subject's symbolic identity obscures comes to the fore. The Nazi recourse to the Jew as a quilting point renders the nonsensical status of the master signifier invisible. Using the Jew as a quilting point hides the unconscious because it helps to secure the status of the master signifier. It is a quilting signifier that supports the fabrication that the Nazi's symbolic identity requires. Nazism would become unthinkable for one who confronted the subject's self-division in the act of quilting. By promoting a quilting that insists on the unconscious, psychoanalysis shows us how we might envision a political challenge to Nazism and its still vibrant descendants.

For Lacanian practitioners, the short session is indisputably the most important residue of Lacan's brief flirtation with the quilting point in *Seminar III*. But for those concerned with politics, it must be instead the role that the quilting point plays in the critique of ideological fantasies. Although Lacan never envisioned this destiny for his concept, this use bespeaks its enduring value. The quilting point lets people know how to read explanations that are designed to put one over on them.

Das Ding

The first mention of *das Ding* (translated as "the Thing") in Lacan's work occurs in *Seminar VII: The Ethics of Psychoanalysis, 1959–1960*. It emerges as a concept between the early and middle periods but disappears almost entirely soon after its invention. Although Lacan devotes precious little attention to it in his seminars and almost none in his writing, this concept has played an outsized role in Lacan's reception. Many theorists following in Lacan's wake have found the idea of *das Ding* a fecund avenue for thinking about the subject and its desire. Lacan's followers like *das Ding* much more than he does.

As Lacan conceives it, *das Ding* is an inaccessible and unknowable void that attracts the subject's desire. It provides a structuring absence in the world of objects that orients the subject toward this world. Each subject has its own *Ding*, and it pursues others to the extent that they seem to harbor this *Ding* within them. But *das Ding* has its status thanks to its inaccessibility for the subject. No one can possess *das Ding* because it is an emptiness that recedes the closer one comes to it. To grasp it would be simultaneously to lose it. *Das Ding* is a central absence that structures desire through its position beyond the field of all other accessible objects. Our inability to encounter *das Ding* directly gives it its appeal.

Das Ding is different from other things not simply because we fail to integrate it smoothly into our conceptual apparatus. It doesn't fit within this apparatus because it doesn't have any materiality at all. *Das Ding* is a hollowed-out emptiness within the material world, a blank space that we confront within the world of other things.

Lacan primarily uses the German term to indicate the difference between *das Ding* and everything else. German allows Lacan to distinguish between an ordinary thing and the Thing through the terms *die Sache* and *das Ding*. French (like English) has only one term, *la chose*, for the thing. Although we can translate both German words with "thing," the distinction between them has significance. It is a distinction that Martin Heidegger stresses in his essay "*Das Ding*," an essay, along with Sigmund Freud's *Project for a Scientific Psychology*, that serves as an inspiration for Lacan's concept.[98] While Lacan will sometimes refer to the French "*la Chose*" when discussing *das Ding*, most often he refers to the German term to underline its extraordinary status.

Lacan's examples of *das Ding* all refer to the creation of an emptiness through the erection of a barrier. The vase, the jug, and the matchbox all exemplify *das Ding*. Lacan even makes a passing reference to macaroni in *Seminar VII* as having this form. But the privileged instance of it involves a form of romantic love. Lacan devotes an entire session of *Seminar VII* to one example of *das Ding* – courtly love. In the situation of courtly love, the (male) lover treats the Lady he courts as *das Ding*. The courtship emphasizes the inaccessibility of the Lady for the lover: the point is not to have sex with the Lady. The courtly lover avoids actual sex because not obtaining the beloved as an object sustains her as the absent *Ding*. In courtly love, the lover ensures that the Lady remains inaccessible. If she's locked up in a tower, all the better. The poetry that the lover dedicates to the Lady underlines her distance from all ordinary objects. The psychic barrier surrounding the figure of the Lady produces her status as a transcendent value.[99]

The turn to *das Ding* enables Lacan to articulate his own distinct theory of sublimation, a theory that departs from Freud's, even though Lacan never mentions the disagreement between them on this issue. Freud conceives of sublimation as a vicissitude of the subject's sexual drive, a modification that allows the drive to function in an indirect way. When the subject sublimates, it finds sexual satisfaction in a nonsexual object. The most conspicuous form of sublimation occurs when we work. The satisfaction that work produces is, according to Freud, a sublimated form of sexual desire. For Freud, it is possible to have direct sexual satisfaction through accessing an overtly sexual object, but sublimation allows us to find this satisfaction elsewhere. For Lacan, however, sublimation plays a much more fundamental role in our desire. Without sublimation, we wouldn't desire at all.

In the theory that Lacan develops in *Seminar VII*, sublimation creates a *Ding* for the subject. Rather than representing a nonsexual detour of the drive, it makes an object desirable in the first place.[100] For Lacan, our drive has no natural object. Sexuality doesn't inhere in certain privileged objects but must be forged through the act of sublimation, an act that turns the ordinary into the transcendent. As he puts it in this seminar, sublimation "raises an object ... to the dignity of the Thing."[101] Through sublimation, the subject gives itself a path for its sexual desire. In order to have any satisfaction at all, the subject must sublimate.

There is an utter singularity to *das Ding*. The subject's act of sublimation that gives it its transcendent value doesn't give it this value for everyone. This value exists for the subject that creates it but not for others. From the perspective of others, the sublimating subject overinvests itself in one object while neglecting the obvious importance of everything else. But this commonsensical perspective fails to recognize how overinvesting in *das Ding* is essential for the subject to desire at all. Without this overinvestment, there would be no subject of desire.

Das Ding is not just external. The subject takes up a position relative to its internal opacity through the act of sublimation that marks out this *Ding* in the world of objects. The subject's relationship to the *Ding* that it creates is a way of relating to the *Ding* of the subject itself. In this sense, *das Ding* has what Lacan calls extimacy, a neologism that brings together the external and the intimate: *das Ding* is part of the external world but also intimate to the subject itself.[102] This implies that the act of sublimation through which the subject constitutes its *Ding* is at once the way that the subject discovers itself. One finds oneself in the inaccessible Thing that structures one's desire.

When Lacan theorizes *das Ding*, he doubles down on Immanuel Kant. In his early theorizing, Lacan works out a psychoanalytic Kantianism, a transcendental theory of subjectivity that takes the unconscious into account. The conception of *das Ding* brings Kant's thought to the fore as this early period comes to an end in 1959–1960. Lacan's conception of *das Ding* suggests Kant's thing in itself or *Ding-an-sich*.

Kant's philosophy depends on a contrast between knowable appearances and the unknowable thing in itself. For Kant, the thing in itself doesn't lie beyond the realm of appearances but rather constitutes the limit of that realm. We can know appearances with certainty because we can't know things in themselves. This barrier within our apparatus of knowledge is a productive one that makes our limited knowledge possible. Were we to try to know things in themselves, we would have no means of ordering them in a coherent way.

Das Ding is a version of the Kantian thing in itself translated from knowledge (where Kant has it) to desire. It isn't what we can't know but what our desire can't reach. *Das Ding* is a Kantian concept through and through. At the same time, *das Ding* leads Lacan to a dead end in his early Kantian approach, which is why he moves on from it so quickly. Its position beyond the world of objects, beyond the field of representation, highlights a contradiction that Kant sidestepped. If *das Ding* really has a transcendent status, one should not be able to theorize it in the way that Lacan does in *Seminar VII*. Even our ability to talk about *das Ding* suggests it isn't really a *Ding* but exists on the same plane as other objects. This is a genuine problem. When Lacan runs into this contradiction, he turns away from theorizing *das Ding*.

When Lacan moves from an emphasis on *das Ding* in *Seminar VII* to a focus on the *objet a* two years later, the object continues to play a structuring role for the subject's desire. The crucial difference is that the *objet a*, unlike *das Ding*, has an immanent status for the subject, not a transcendent one. The *objet a* does not reside in the beyond but disturbs the field of representation from within. It disrupts the symbolic space from inside this symbolic space.

One of the central divides in the reception of Lacan's thought concerns which object one privileges – *das Ding* or the *objet a*.[103] As Lacan orients his thought around the *objet a*, the term *das Ding* more or less drops out of his thinking. His references to it are seldom and always brief. He identifies proximity to *das Ding* as the source of anxiety in *Seminar X: Anxiety, 1962–1963*, but the focus of this seminar is the *objet a*. Years later, in *Seminar XVI: From an Other to the other, 1968–1969*, Lacan makes his only statement relating *das Ding* to the *objet a*. He says, "The *objet a* . . . is what tickles *das Ding* from the inside. That is what comprises the essential merit of everything known as a work of art."[104] While this statement continues the association of *das Ding* with the sublimation at work in artistic creation, it nonetheless reflects the priority of the *objet a* in Lacan's later thinking. Not only is the mention of *das Ding* confined to a couple of sentences, its importance is confined to how it relates to the *objet a*. This is what leads most theorists following Lacan to privilege the *objet a* relative to *das Ding*. But not all.

The two most important theorists of *das Ding* are Richard Boothby and Mari Ruti. For both, the discovery of *das Ding* represents Lacan at his most far-reaching. In their thinking, *das Ding* is a more significant theoretical discovery than the *objet a*. Everything that occurs before this point is preparatory for it, and everything that comes after is a retreat from this great breakthrough. Boothby sees *das Ding* as the impetus for the development of all religion, while Ruti theorizes it as the paradigm for artistic creation.

In Boothby's view, our religious belief is a response to the inescapable absence that structures the world of our experience. The origin of faith is not simply a power play on the part of priests but a nod to what cannot be known. The reference to God indicates a gap in what we know, a failure of the subject's mastery. Boothby sees *das Ding* as Lacan's effort to grant a place within his system to what necessarily exceeds that system.[105]

Ruti insists on the contrast between the desire oriented around *das Ding* and all other desires. *Das Ding* gives our desire an ethical bearing because it forces us to insist on what really matters and sideline the banality of everyday life. The desire centered on *das Ding* offers an alternative to the capitalist universe of limitless consumption. It gives the subject a way to limit itself and defy the imperative to always seek more. Ethics, for Ruti, must have its basis in the distinction between *das Ding* and all other things.[106]

Even if we accept – contra thinkers such as Boothby and Ruti – Lacan's own decision to deemphasize *das Ding*, we must nonetheless recognize the role that it plays in the theoretical path to the *objet a*. *Seminar VII* is a hapax. It doesn't belong to Lacan's early theory or to his middle period. But it has the virtue of pushing his early Kantian thinking to the point at which it tips over into a Hegelian approach. In this Hegelian approach, the subject's limit ceases to be external to its system and becomes an internal disturbance. The discovery of *das Ding* marks the end of the early Lacan.

objet a (*objet petit a/object a*)

The *objet a* is Lacan's most important concept. His importance as a theorist ultimately stands or falls with our verdict on the *objet a* (or what he also calls the *objet petit a*). Lacan himself is aware of the magnitude of its importance for his philosophy, which is why he says, in *Seminar XXI: The Non-Duped Err, 1973–1974*, "the *objet petit a* is perhaps what I had invented."[107] If there is one concept that Lacan himself wants to be known for, it is the *objet a*. Lacan insists that this term not be translated – an insistence that he reserves for this concept alone, despite what certain people claim for *jouissance* – because it indicates a point of singularity that functions as the engine for desire. To translate it would betray its singularity. This audacious assertion is justified because Lacan is the first to focus a theory of desire around not what the subject wants – its object of desire – but what blocks what it wants, what Lacan calls the *objet a*.

Lacan uses the term *objet a* in order to distinguish the *objet a* from the real-life, tangible object of desire. Rather than being what the subject desires, the *objet a* triggers the subject to desire the object of desire.[108] It is the object-cause of desire. While the object of desire might be any ordinary object, the *objet a* gives that ordinary object an extraordinary quality that makes it desirable. Without the *objet a* – which infuses the real-life object with an intimation of exceptionality, even of sublimity – the latter would remain just one among a heap of indifferent objects.

The *objet a* sparks the subject's desire for a mundane object by hindering the subject's direct and full access to it. For instance, the wrapping paper that covers a gift functions as an *objet a* for the gift. Without the wrapping paper, the gift, however nice it might be, is just an ordinary object, an object that one might exchange for some other (as one often does after unwrapping it). But the wrapping paper adds something special to the object's ordinariness, making it a site that draws the subject's desire. If one laid out unwrapped presents under a Christmas tree, they would not attract the desire of children in the way that the wrapped ones do.[109] In one sense, the wrapping, like the *objet a*, is unnecessary. It doesn't change the materiality of the gift in any way. But it does nonetheless fundamentally transform the gift. This transformation occurs as the *objet a* spurs desire by erecting a barrier between the subject and the object of desire, a barrier that makes the object desirable in the first place. A wrapped object is no longer like every other object but has the promise within it of something much more.

At times, the *objet a* is able to render an object of desire desirable even without augmenting it with any enigmatic intimations of exceptionality, without spicing it up with any added desirable qualities. In such instances, the opposite approach of marring or obfuscating the object in some way functions equally well. For example, a defect that a person has can generate desire for that person in a way that physical perfection does not. A mole that slightly impairs the attractiveness of someone's face is also what, for Lacan, makes the face appealing. The mole is the *objet a*, while the perfectly attractive face itself might be the object of desire. The mole prevents the subject from experiencing the face in its perfection, but it is also what produces the possibility of a perfect face. The defect is the condition of possibility for the desired object that exists just outside of our reach. Because the perfect face does not exist (or does not exist as a desired object) the defect is necessary to make the face desirable. Direct access to an object is always stultifying, which is why Lacan sees the barrier – whether this barrier consists of a tinge of sublimity or of imperfection – constituted by the *objet a* as the sine qua non of desire itself. Without this obstacle, one would have no impetus to desire the object.

By barring direct access to the object of desire, the *objet a* distorts the subject's perceptual field. It generates a curvature in the subject's space of perception, rendering it impossible for the subject to look neutrally at what it sees. For instance, the *objet a* might cause someone to look at a face through the mole that seems to detract from the face's attractiveness or to regard a scene through a detail that does not seem to fit in it. Paradoxically, as an obstacle to complete perception of the object, it provides the perspective through which the subject perceives. The distortion that the *objet a* creates is constitutive of what it discloses. We perceive through the distortion, which is its condition of possibility. Without this distortion, Lacan contends, one would not be able to perceive anything at all. The *objet a* stains the field of perception with the distortion that the subject's desire introduces into this field.

The *objet a* marks the subject's inability to perceive without the distortion of its own desire. In the visual field, the *objet a* represents the way that the subject's desire distorts what appears as visible. In other words, every perceptual field is organized around a desire that renders a neutral perspective on that field impossible. Yet the *objet a* does not just distort the perceptual field; it also makes the perceptual field accessible in the act of distorting it. This field results from the subject's desiring perspective that leaves it unable to perceive the field neutrally. In this sense, what opens up the perceptual field is also what makes it impossible to perceive this field without the distortion of desire. This distortion manifests itself within the field as the *objet a*.[110]

Although Lacan's examples of this distortion tend to derive either from painting or from his own experiences, cinema offers some of the most compelling illustrations of how the *objet a* as a cause of desire distorts the field of the spectator's perception. Because desire is unconscious, we typically avoid confronting the *objet a* in our daily experience. We do not see the importance of what distorts our vision but merely the positive objects within our visual field: We consciously try to look at the attractiveness of the face rather than the mole that distorts it. We think about the gift beneath the wrapping paper rather than the wrapping paper itself. Consciousness is a barrier to a confrontation with the *objet a* and its distorting power because it directs our perception to what seems pleasing rather than to what disrupts our pleasure. But cinema can foster just such an encounter with the distorting power of the *objet a*, given that the spectator is not calling the shots and directing the structure of the perceptual field in the cinematic experience.

Let us look at the ending of Jonathan Demme's *The Silence of the Lambs* (1991). The film recounts the assistance that the serial killer Hannibal Lecter (Anthony Hopkins) provides for the fledgling FBI agent Clarice Starling (Jodie Foster) in apprehending another serial killer, nicknamed "Buffalo Bill." Through the offer to help the FBI in its investigation, Lecter manages to escape from police custody and flee the country. At the end of the film, he is free somewhere in the Caribbean. At this point, he calls Starling.

As Lecter talks with Starling, the film shows his former jailer, the head of the psychiatric prison where he had been held, arriving on the island. Dr. Chilton (Anthony Heald) had not only acted sadistically toward Lecter but also sexually harassed Starling when she came to the prison. The film also highlights his unctuous manner in all his dealings with other characters. This background sets up the final scene when Chilton's arrival coincides with Lecter's call to Starling. In his last line of the film, Lecter tells her, "I'm having an old friend for dinner." At this moment, the film cuts to an image of Chilton, which signals that he is the "old friend" whom Lecter plans to eat.

Rather than setting up the spectator to be repulsed by Lecter's continued cannibalism (a practice that certainly violates the spectator's conscious moral convictions), the film pushes the spectator to enjoy the prospect of Lecter eating Chilton. One watches the final scene convinced that Chilton will get his just deserts, despite one's attitude toward cannibalism. In this way, the film forces spectators to confront the *objet a*, the manifestation of an unconscious desire as it is structured through the narrative form. Lecter eating Chilton is not in itself a desirable object, but it is an *objet a* that triggers the spectator's unconscious desire.

The *objet a* is the device through which unconscious desire is written into what is perceived. It is a detail in the structure of the perceptual field that does not fit, that throws the field off and subjectivizes it by permeating it with the subject's desire. The distinction between the subject's conscious will and its unconscious desire – and how this unconscious desire shapes what is seen – becomes discernible. Under normal circumstances, the subject cannot gain direct consciousness of this distortion in order to correct for it, but it can encounter it through moments like the end of *The Silence of the Lambs*. At such times, the effect of one's unconscious desire becomes evident as a subjective distortion in what one perceives. Lacan's theorizing of the *objet a* enables us to pay attention to such encounters and to recognize their significance for grasping subjectivity.

Alexandre Kojève's seminars on Hegel during the 1930s occupy a critical position in Lacan's development of the *objet a*, even though Kojève employs no related concept himself. When Kojève interprets Hegel's *Phenomenology of Spirit*, the desire for recognition in this work occupies a central position within Kojève's philosophy, so much so that Kojève interprets the entire history of the world through the desire for recognition and its various failures. Historical development occurs through the unfolding of the struggle for recognition. This development comes to an end, he postulates, when this desire for recognition concludes in a state of mutual recognition, which occurs with the ultimate victory of the slave.

Although Lacan does not inherit Kojève's propensity for philosophizing about the end of history, he does take up, with a significant modification, Kojève's understanding of desire. But what Kojève sees as the desire for recognition, Lacan reconceptualizes as a desire for what escapes the realm of recognition.[111] Lacan sees that Kojève's philosophy of recognition has a crucial blind spot: It fails to account for the unconscious status of our desire. This is Lacan's most original innovation and the point at which he brings together Kojève and Freud in a way that goes beyond both. If we just desire the Other's recognition, there is no role for the unconscious. Lacan gives desire an unconscious dimension that turns its focus beyond recognition. By introducing the *objet a* as what is irreducible to recognition, Lacan accomplishes a great theoretical leap. The introduction of the unconscious into the struggle for recognition results in Lacan coming up with the *objet a*.

What Kojève theorizes as the desire for recognition Lacan rechristens as the demand for recognition. According to Lacan, the subject's conscious demand for recognition houses an unconscious desire driven by the *objet a*. This unconscious desire motivated by the *objet a* yearns not for the Other's recognition but for its desire: the subject doesn't desire the Other to recognize it but desires the desire of the Other – to capture the Other's desire (to become the object of this desire) *and* to access what the Other desires. Obviously, these two senses of "the desire of the Other" are at odds. To desire to become what the Other desires is not the same as to desire what the Other desires. Lacan nevertheless understands "the desire of the Other" in both of these senses, which contributes to the impossible status of the Other's desire for the subject. It is impossible to figure out the desire of the Other, so the subject must interpret it according to the subject's own fashion. The desire of the Other that the subject interprets is the *objet a*.

Lacan starts to develop the *objet a* in the seminar immediately following *Seminar VII: The Ethics of Psychoanalysis, 1959–1960*, in which he first theorizes *das Ding*. The seminar of the following year on the transference contains elements that point toward the *objet a*. In this seminar, Lacan does not yet name the *objet a* or *objet petit a* but, in a lengthy discussion of Plato's *Symposium*, refers to an enigmatic object called the *ágalma* that causes desire to erupt in precisely the way that the *objet a* will in the seminar of the following year. The *Symposium* recounts a series of orations on love that take place at a dinner party. Alcibiades barges in and interrupts the proceedings to express his unreciprocated desire for Socrates. According to Lacan, Alcibiades desires Socrates because he believes that Socrates possesses an especially powerful version of the *ágalma*, a secret treasure that he hopes to access through a sexual relationship with Socrates. The *ágalma* marks the way that the desire of

Alcibiades distorts what he sees. The *ágalma* is a direct forerunner of the *objet a* insofar as it drives the desire of Alcibiades and yet remains irreducible to any positive object of desire – in this case, Socrates – or to any characteristic that Socrates possesses. It is, as Lacan will later describe the *objet a*, what is in Socrates more than Socrates. The *ágalma* triggers the desire of Alcibiades, but he would never be able to find this *objet a* within Socrates even if he managed to convince Socrates to have sex with him (which he does not in the *Symposium*).

The first mention of the *objet a* occurs in *Seminar IX: Identification, 1961–1962*. In this seminar, the *ágalma* from the previous year now becomes the *objet a*. Lacan characterizes the *objet a* as what is nonspecular in an image, what cannot be seen directly as just another object within the visual field. The subject's unconscious desire distorts what it sees, and the *objet a* indicates the distortion from within the perceptual field. The *objet a* emerges in the gaps of the signifying order, but it does not belong to the imaginary either. Because signification always fails to say it all, the *objet a* appears not as a positive object but as what is missing. That is, the *objet a* is the missing element of the symbolic order, which links it to the real.

The seminar that fleshes out the concept of the *objet a* in the clearest fashion is *Seminar XI: The Four Fundamental Concepts of Psychoanalysis, 1963–1964*.[112] Interestingly, despite the attention that Lacan gives to the *objet a* in this seminar, it does not have the status of one of the four fundamental concepts of psychoanalysis, which are the unconscious, repetition, transference, and the drive. Yet the *objet a* plays a central part in the operation of each of these concepts. The *objet a* exists only insofar as it remains unconscious. The subject repeats its failed encounter with the *objet a*, its inability to possess this object. The *objet a* leads to a transferential relationship wherein the subject believes that the Other has an *objet a* that attracts its desire; rather than grasping the *objet a* as a structural phenomenon, the subject attributes it to the Other and seeks it within the Other. And finally, the drive perpetually circulates around the *objet a* without being able to ever reach it. The *objet a* is not one of the fundamental concepts of psychoanalysis because it is the fundamental object of psychoanalysis – an object without which the fundamental concepts would not possess the centrality that they do.

For Lacan, the *objet a* reveals how the subject's unconscious desire distorts what the subject perceives. It indicates that there is no neutral perception of the world. My unconscious desire manifests itself in what doesn't fit within the world, which is what Lacan calls the *objet a*. How desire misshapes the world is itself irreducible to the subject's perceptual field.[113] It shapes what the subject perceives but is not part of what the subject perceives. The *objet a* is how one perceives, not what.

We can only encounter the *objet a* at moments when it takes us by surprise. There is no way to look directly on how desire distorts what we perceive. We must experience it through disruptions within our everyday perception, through jolts that reveal how our unconscious desire distorts what we perceive. When these jolts occur, the *objet a* shows us that we are inextricably involved in the world that seems to be at a distance from us.

Lacan focuses his discussion of the *objet a* on two forms that it can take – the gaze and the voice. Gaze and voice are objects, but they are not empirical objects. The gaze is the *objet a* in the visual field. The subject's desire focuses on what is missing in the visual field, which, as we have noted, is the point where this very desire distorts the visual field. The gaze is where the subject's own desire manifests itself as a stain in what it sees. The subject cannot see the gaze since the gaze is nothing but the way that its desire affects what and how it sees. Through the gaze, the subject inhabits the visual field in the form of an impossible object, the *objet a*.

The voice is even more enigmatic than the gaze. It is what the subject hears in the aural field that goes beyond signification. It is how others speak rather than what they say.[114] In this voice that doesn't have any signification in itself – in which the affect conveyed by its tone takes precedence – the subject confronts the desire of the Other imposing itself on the subject.

The *objet a* is not a positive object that one perceives but the distortion that the subject's unconscious desire produces in the very structure of perception. Every time one looks, one sees in a way that is structured around the distorting gaze. And every time one listens, one hears through the distorting voice. Even though the *objet a* is specific to each subject, it provides an opening to the Other for every subject, no matter what form it takes, thereby ensuring that the subject does not lose its ability to relate to the outside world. We relate to the world through the singular distortion of the *objet a*. It is how the subject disturbs the world, but it is through this disturbance that the subject relates to the Other because it provides an orientation for the subject that it otherwise would not have. For Lacan, the *objet a* names the orientation of the subject's desire that allows it to relate to the Other, even as it indicates the subject's failure to fit in the world. The *objet a* reveals how we are a part of the world through our distorted relation to it.

Gaze

None of Lacan's concepts have been as thoroughly misunderstood as the gaze. Thanks to developments in the field of film theory, the gaze became widely conceived as a look of mastery that subjugates what is seen. According to this view, the gaze is synonymous with power and demands strategies of resistance.[115] This way of conceiving it understands the gaze as necessarily on the side of the subject looking, not as a part of what is seen. While such a gaze might exist and might be something to lament, it has nothing to do with Lacan's concept of the gaze, despite the fact that critics theorized it in his name. One might say that film theory confused the subject's look for the gaze as *objet a*. For Lacan, the gaze is an object in the field of the visible, not the act of a subject looking at objects. To understand what Lacan is getting at with the gaze, one must separate it from the look. Our look sees the visual field and doesn't see the gaze within it.[116]

According to Lacan, the gaze is the form of the *objet a* that emerges in the visual field. As a form of the *objet a*, the gaze acts as an object causing the subject to desire. It is an engine for desire rather than for mastery. When theorizing the *objet a* in relation to the drive, Lacan adds two objects and two partial drives to those found in Freud. Freud contends that there is an oral drive with the breast as its object and an anal drive with the feces as its object. Lacan adds to this list an aural drive and a visual drive. These take the voice and gaze as the two forms of the *objet a* that correspond to them. Of these different forms that the *objet a* takes, the gaze receives the most detailed discussion both from Lacan himself and from those following in his wake.

The gaze is the point at which the subject's desire warps the image. It is the point that we cannot directly see in the image that draws our desire to it, the point at which the subject looking appears as a curvature in what it sees. The subject's desire distorts what it sees, and, according to Lacan, this distortion manifests itself at a specific point within the visual field, which is the gaze.

The existence of the gaze indicates the impossibility of a neutral or objective look. The distortion that the gaze as an impossible object creates in the visual field is the manifestation of the desiring subject looking on this field. This desire distorts what it sees, and the distortion takes the form of the gaze. No one can see the gaze because it is only how the subjectivity of the one looking distorts what is seen. But this is also why no one can see without the gaze. It haunts every look as the mark of the impossibility of the look being neutral.

Due to the influence of Michel Foucault and his theory of the panopticon, it is typical to think of the gaze in terms of mastery and domination.[117] Foucault's gaze is one of surveillance. The gaze in the Lacanian sense has nothing to do with mastery and domination, nor does it occur on the side of the subject looking. Ordinary objects populate the visual field, but the Lacanian gaze stands out among them. The subject can have mastery over ordinary empirical objects. When it comes to the gaze, the subject loses its sense of mastery. It is the point at which the subject's look stumbles and encounters an obstacle that cannot be integrated into the world of meaning. The gaze is the unconscious manifested in the visual field.

The encounter with the gaze, this nonsensical point, forces subjects to become aware of their investment on the level of desire in the images on the screen. The gaze is the point at which the visual field reaches out and grabs hold of the subject, the point at which the subject confronts its own unconscious desire in the objectivity of the visual field. We can see how this happens in Steven Spielberg's first (and greatest) film, *Duel* (1970), where an unknown truck driver pursues and tries to kill David Mann (Dennis Weaver) as he drives up the coast of California. Throughout the entire film, the spectator never learns the identity of the truck driver, nor the reason for his murderousness, nor why he targets Mann. Spielberg shows the truck driver only with images of his windshield under the glare of the sun. Rather than see the truck driver's face, the spectator sees the glass reflecting the sun. This image – and the lack of knowledge it embodies – is one of the paradigmatic cinematic depictions of the gaze.

Spectators can see here the way that desire shapes experience, which is the gaze. The truck driver remains unseen even in death, and we never learn what motivates this murderous rampage against the protagonist, even when the truck driver dies. And yet, the truck driver's motivation is the focus of the spectator's desire throughout the film. This is why the view of the blank windshield in *Duel* is an encounter with the gaze for the spectator. The blank windshield indicates what we cannot consciously know about desire, what remains constitutively unknown, and yet what shapes everything that transpires in the film. The gaze is an obstacle to our knowledge that manifests our unconscious desire. It objectifies the blank space of the unconscious within what we can consciously perceive in the image.

The gaze is the way the subject's way of looking manifests itself as an object within the visual field. As a subject looking, one is always part of what one sees, although this involvement is itself not visible except as a distortion in the image. As Lacan puts it in a key passage from *Seminar XI: The Four Fundamental Concepts of Psychoanalysis, 1963–1964*, "I am not simply … located at the geometral point from which the perspective is grasped. No doubt, in the depths of my eye, the picture is painted. The picture, certainly, is in my eye. But I am in the picture."[118] That is to say, the gaze marks the point in the visual field where this field takes the subject's look into account, the point at which the subject's desire deforms the structure of this field.

The translation of the above passage into English manages to convey the exact opposite meaning of what Lacan says in French, which may account for some of the difficulties in understanding the concept of the gaze in the English-speaking world. The last line of the paragraph in French reads, "Mais moi je suis dans le tableau." Lacan clearly indicates that the subject is in the picture being seen in the form of what doesn't fit. English translator Alan Sheridan translates this as: "But I am not in the picture." The *not* emerges from nowhere to reverse what is being said and make it incomprehensible.[119]

If the subject is not in the picture (as the English translation would have it), then there is no gaze. Because the gaze marks the point at which the subject's desire manifests itself visually, it has the ability to disrupt the subject's look and make clear that the subject is part of the world that it assumes to be purely external. But the subject is not just part of what it sees in the form of the rest of the objects seen. It is a point that sticks out in the visual field, an excess that distorts this field

Lacan begins his discussion of the gaze in *Seminar XI* and picks it up again in *Seminar XIII: The Object of Psychoanalysis, 1965–1966.* He gives two concrete examples of the gaze in his seminar on the *Seminar XI.* The first occurs in the painting entitled *The Ambassadors* (1533). In this painting, Hans Holbein depicts two wealthy world travelers surrounded by many objects that they have acquired. Lacan pays attention to the stain or smear across the front bottom of the image. This stain is actually a skull, which signifies the death that awaits the two men, despite all that they have acquired. This was known in the Renaissance as a memento mori, a reminder of death.

What is important about the skull is that it is a reminder of the death that awaits not just the two wealthy men in the painting but also the viewer. Staring directly at the painting from the front, the skull simply appears as an unidentifiable blot. One can see the skull only while looking awry, looking at it from the upper right. In order for the skull to look like a skull and not just a blot stretching across the painting's foreground at the feet of the two men, one must look at the painting from the upper right at a sharp angle. This indicates that the image itself takes the position and subjectivity of the viewer into account.

The painting doesn't simply exist on its own, but it is painted to be seen. It includes the viewer within the image, not directly but as a stain or failure within the image. This stain is the gaze as *objet a*. The problem is that most of the time we fail to see how the image takes us into account as viewers. We believe that the image has an objective reality that we simply are catching sight of. This is the fundamental deception of looking that the anamorphic quality of *The Ambassadors* attempts to correct.[120]

Lacan's other example of the gaze occurs in an autobiographical story that he relates from his youth. As a young bourgeois university student, he spent a summer in a village in the south of France, where he was on a fishing boat with a young fisherman named Petit-Jean. Once they saw a sardine can floating in the water, and Petit-Jean pointed out to Lacan that, while he might see the can, the can didn't see him. By saying this, Petit-Jean attempted to convey to Lacan that he was, regardless of his class privilege, unimportant and insignificant in the world of the fishing village. He didn't belong in this locale.

But in his recounting of the story, Lacan notes that despite this, the can does see him, in the sense that the sardine can takes Lacan into account, just as the painting *The Ambassadors* takes its viewer into account. Even though the can is just floating aimlessly in the ocean, it marks a point where the ocean is no longer just a vast and meaningless expanse. It disrupts the vision of the whole as an object of human production that has been discarded so that it no longer fits in the world but instead exists as a remainder or piece of excess. The gaze is what doesn't fit and thereby draws attention to the fact that our world or our field of vision is not whole. It is fractured, and our desire is drawn to the point of the fracture. This sardine can doesn't fit in the picture just as Lacan himself doesn't fit in the fishing village. The disturbance that it creates in the picture is Lacan's own disturbance – the way that the picture is skewed around his own desire.

Lacan discusses a third instance of the gaze two years later in *Seminar XIII*. It involves the painting by Diego Velázquez entitled *Las Meninas* (1656). This painting depicts a painter who appears to be painting a royal couple, although the couple is visible only in a mirror on the back wall while various other figures populate the foreground. The most obtrusive object, however, is the back of the large canvass that the painter works on in the image, which dominates the left side of the painting. This is where Lacan locates the gaze in his interpretation of the painting, an interpretation that contrasts with the one that Michel Foucault gives in the first chapter of *The Order of Things*.

According to Foucault, the painting reveals the epistemological structure of what he calls the Classical era. In the Classical era, representation becomes a field apart from what it represents and no longer resembles it. The key for Foucault is that everything in the field of representation has a correlate in the field of what is represented. He sees clear answers in the painting, not blank spaces.

The central question of *Las Meninas* is what the painter within the painting is painting. As a result of this gap in the visual field, our question as spectators concerns the desire of the painter. It seems like it must be the royal couple who are being painted – Foucault believes that this goes without saying – but

Lacan insists that the canvass is too large for the king and queen alone to be the object of the painting. In this way, Lacan undermines Foucault's interpretation without ever mentioning that he's doing so.[121]

Whereas Foucault views *Las Meninas* as indicative of the emerging world of representation, where everything can be represented from the world, Lacan focuses on what fails to be represented or what resists representation. The system of representation that emerges in the seventeenth century is not perfect at representing the world. It has limitations, and these are what interest Lacan. The limitations are the points at which the gaze becomes evident as an absence disrupting the field of representation.

Within representation, the gaze appears as a stain in our perspective – and in perspective painting. Unlike other critics of perspective who see it as a form of mastery over the visible world, Lacan recognizes the gaze within this form of painting. The vanishing point in perspective painting is the gaze. All perspective painting is based on the vanishing point and thus on the gaze. The gaze sustains the subject's relation with the visible world, but it is art that renders the gaze sensible.

In the interior of a perspective painting, the painter positions the spectator who will look at the painting. As a result, the spectator's relation to the painting is structural, not simply the result of the spectator's choice of how to look. The distance between the spectator and the painting is inscribed internally within the painting. This shows that the distinction between internal and external actually breaks down, as the internal dynamics of the painting form the external act of looking at it.

The problem with a realist approach to the world is that it conceives of the subject and the world as two opposed and closed off spheres. Lacan wants to theorize how the internal and the external are engaged with each other. Our subjectivity isn't internal because the gaze as *objet a*, the kernel of our subjectivity, is outside us. It is our intimate desire that manifests itself externally as a distortion of the visual field. Our unconscious is not located deep inside us but outside in what we fail to see.

Our encounter with the gaze is definitely first and foremost unconscious. It is an encounter, like every genuine encounter, that takes us by surprise. In this sense, the encounter with the gaze functions like the Freudian slip: We recognize ourselves unconsciously in what initially appears absolutely foreign to us. The gaze shocks us into grasping ourselves as part of what we are seeing, grasping that we are in the film we watch in the form of a distortion of the visual field. This happens unconsciously, but then the encounter almost forces an awareness on us. The encounter with the gaze, in other words, is where the unconscious action leads to conscious awareness.

The encounter with the gaze is traumatic because it eliminates our distance from what we see. It is always safer to remain at a distance and to believe that one is uninvolved in what one sees. But the fundamental wager of Lacan's theory is that we are never really at a distance from what we see. We are always externalized in the world that we see in the form of the gaze that distorts this world. Once we see the gaze, the possibility of a retreat into oneself from what one sees becomes impossible. The trauma of the encounter with the gaze is the trauma of the absence of any safe distance from the world. Once one recognizes the gaze, one cannot retreat anymore.

Lacan's theorization of the gaze in *Seminar XI* and *Seminar XIII* is the high point of his philosophical trajectory. Coming in the middle of the middle period, the gaze shows us how we are unconsciously implicated in what we view as foreign. It impels us to confront that we are never at a safe distance from what we perceive. With the concept of the gaze, Lacan pushes his theory to its most dialectical point – where we can see our subjectivity manifested in the field of objects. He sees how the subject is always unconsciously other to itself.

Fantasy

Lacan often deals with important concepts in a way that is suggestive rather than exhaustive. He seems to be leaving the terrain open for further development by others following in his wake by not fully working out a concept that he mentions. Certain concepts, such as the quilting point and *das Ding*, make an appearance and then disappear almost completely. Others appear sporadically but never receive a full development or sustained elaboration. This is the case with fantasy. Even the year-long seminar that Lacan devotes to the logic of fantasy spends precious little time addressing its purported subject matter. One can safely say that Slavoj Žižek has explained Lacan's theory of fantasy in much more detail than Lacan himself has done.

Fantasy is an imaginary scenario that provides a path for the subject's desire. It enables the subject to envision a way out of the deadlock of desire – the impossibility of attaining its object – by creating a narrative that makes the object possible. The fantasy narrative possibilizes the impossible. The impossibility of desire becomes accessible through its translation into the imaginary scenario of the fantasy. Through this process, the imaginary scenario offers a form for the subject's enjoyment. Fantasy is the way that we organize our enjoyment.

Often, the narrative structure of the fantasy is conscious for the subject. What is unconscious is the point of the real that the fantasizing subject enjoys.

In *Freud as Philosopher*, Richard Boothby claims that this point of the real beyond the image is how the fantasy attracts the subject's desire. He writes, "phantasy is always a picturing, an imaginal figuration, yet also aims toward something unimagable. What is most deeply sought by desire in the phantasy cannot be given in the register of the image."[122] By presenting the subject with a scenario that aims at the impossible real, fantasy offers it a way to enjoy what would otherwise remain inaccessible and off-limits. Fantasy brings us closer to the real than real life does. This is the radical edge of fantasy for Lacan. It inherently takes us beyond the conditions that govern our everyday lives by providing a scenario that aims at what cannot be represented according to the rules that govern the ruling order.

With many of Lacan's other concepts, such as jouissance or the drive, it is evident that the concept undergoes a transformation as Lacan's thought moves forward. Jouissance in the 1950s is not, for Lacan, the same concept as it is in the middle of the 1960s, for instance. The same pattern holds for fantasy, except that Lacan uses the same formula for fantasy throughout his life, even as the meaning of the terms within this formula change. This makes understanding Lacan's conception of fantasy challenging.

Lacan's most extensive discussion of fantasy occurs in *Seminar VI: Desire and Its Interpretation, 1958–1959*. In this seminar (which is the last of the early seminars), Lacan lays a formula for fantasy that will largely stay the same until his death, although a decisive change occurs in it due to the transformation in one of its terms. What will remain consistent is Lacan's insistence that fantasy provides the matrix through which the subject relates to its world. Rather than situating itself in relation to a series of positive objects in the world, the subject orients itself through the structure of fantasy. Fantasy provides the coordinates for the subject's perception and gives a direction to its desire. Without fantasy, the subject would not know where to look or what to value in the field of perception. This is an idea that Lacan never gives up on.

Understood in this way, fantasy functions for psychoanalytic thought in the same way that the schematism functions in Kant's critical philosophy. Kant believes that we know the world through various categories that allow it to make sense of things, but we cannot just directly apply these categories to our experiences. We need a guideline that would relate abstract categories to the rough-and-tumble world of objects that don't simply correspond to our categories. This is where the schematism comes into play. The schematism shows us how to apply the categories to objects. It is the connective tissue that holds together our categories and the object world of our experience.

This is exactly the role that Lacan gives to fantasy in his theory. Although Lacan never makes reference to Kant when discussing fantasy, it is clear that this is how he envisions fantasy operating. In *The Parallax View*, Slavoj Žižek picks up on this connection. He writes, "fantasy mediates between the formal symbolic structure and the positivity of the objects we encounter in reality; it provides a 'scheme' according to which certain positive objects in reality can function as objects of desire, filling in the empty places opened up by the formal symbolic structure."[123] In this sense, fantasy is structurally necessary for the subject. It provides a way for the subject to map its desire onto the world that it perceives. There is no such thing as a free-floating desire not rooted in fantasy. Fantasy's guidelines permit desire to map onto the world that it encounters.

At the same time that he theorizes fantasy as a mode of access to the world, Lacan defines it as the relationship between the subject and the imaginary other. In *Seminar VI: Desire and Its Interpretation, 1958–1959*, he states, "Whenever you come up against something that is a fantasy, strictly speaking, you will see that it can be articulated in these primary terms, qua relationship between the speaking subject and the imaginary other. This is what defines fantasy."[124] At this point in time, Lacan sees fantasy as an affair of two of his three registers – the symbolic and the imaginary. The real has no place in fantasy, in large part because at this moment the real coincides with the subject's psychic reality, which is what fantasy flees from.[125]

What is confusing is that in the early seminars Lacan refers to the imaginary other with the shorthand *a*, which later, beginning in *Seminar IX: Identification, 1961–1962*, becomes the term that designates the impossible real that acts as a cause for the subject's desire – the *objet a*.[126] In this later period, Lacan will retain the formula for fantasy that he develops in the early *Seminar VI*, which is the barred subject relating to the *a* (or $ <> *a*), but when he uses this formula again in the essay "The Subversion of the Subject and the Dialectic of Desire" or *Seminar XI: The Four Fundamental Concepts of Psychoanalysis, 1963–1964*, the denotation of the term *a* has undergone a complete transformation. When the *a* becomes the *objet a*, it indicates the real of the subject's desire, the point around which the fantasy scenario is organized.

This organization both provides access to enjoyment and protects the subject from its own enjoyment. The source of the enjoyment that the fantasy produces does not lie in its imaginary scenario. The imaginary and symbolic structure of the fantasy form the basis of its narrative, but this narrative itself is not enjoyable for the subject. The imaginary scenario narrates a path around the impossible *objet a*, which is what energizes the fantasy with enjoyment.[127] The point of the real is decisive in the fantasy. The imaginary narrative is constructed in an attempt to explain this real, but it can do so only through dissembling about its status.

Fantasy protects the subject by subtracting subjectivity from the scenario that it depicts. It is always the other enjoying, not the subject itself. One can encounter the impossible real in the fantasy in a way that one cannot in the social reality because there is never a subject of the fantasy. The fantasy scenario keeps the enjoyment at a distance so that it doesn't overwhelm the subject. The excessiveness of enjoyment renders it traumatic. When the subject enjoys itself, it must encounter a trauma. But the fantasy scenario domesticates this trauma and delivers it in a palatable form of the enjoying other. Fantasies provide access to enjoyment while minimizing the disruptiveness of this encounter.

The basic scenario of fantasy narrativizes our failure to enjoy by showing an other blocking our path to enjoyment or enjoying in our stead. This is clear in the antisemitic fantasy of the figure of the Jew or the banal fantasy about the popular clique or even one about a celebrity influencer. In each case, some other is both inhibiting the subject's enjoyment and enjoying where the subject hopes to enjoy itself. The Jew is swindling the subject, while the popular clique is having wild sex and the celebrity is enjoying all the best commodities. Even though each of these scenarios depicts someone depriving the fantasizing subject of enjoyment, this is actually the way that they allow the subject to access enjoyment. In a fantasy, one enjoys through the other who is enjoying in one's stead. This is what makes fantasy so conducive to political exploitation. One can proffer a fantasy of Jews enjoying in the stead of Aryans and thereby get a mass of people on board with a pogrom that they wouldn't desire without the fantasy.

Lacan never refers to fantasy in societal terms but confines his discussion to individual subjects. But there is nothing in Lacan's philosophy that precludes a move toward thinking about collective fantasies that operate just like those of the subject. The collective fantasy appeals to people because it fills the same role in the psyche that the private fantasy does. It maps out a terrain of enjoyment for the subject amid the prohibitions of the symbolic law and demands of the big Other.

Collective antisemitic fantasies and private fantasies have the same structure. I might, for instance, fantasize about driving a new sports car. In such a fantasy, it doesn't seem as if there is anyone enjoying in my stead or blocking my own access to enjoyment. But a closer look reveals this dynamic at work even here. I opt to fantasize about the sports car because it is an object that I don't have and that others do. I see them appearing to enjoy this object, and this triggers my fantasy about it. If there were no association between the sports car and the other enjoying it, it would not come up as a possible fantasy object, nor would my fantasy narrate the act of driving the car.

Without fantasy, the subject has no way to navigate the terrain of the big Other's desire, which is the central problem confronting someone in any social relation. The question of one's own desire is always the question of the big Other's desire. This is one of Lacan's most important insights with ramifications for how he theorizes fantasy. Every fantasy is an interpretation of the big Other's desire, an attempt to translate that desire into a narrative structure that gives it a sense. The big Other's desire is never directly articulated, only spoken between the lines of its explicit demands, and finally indecipherable for the subject. Confronted with the enigma of the big Other's desire, the subject resorts to fantasy to concoct a solution to this unanswerable question. Through fantasy, desire ceases to be fundamentally unanswerable and becomes a problem that one can solve. The solution to the big Other's desire is the little other's enjoyment. Fantasy charts the relationship between the big Other and the little other in terms of a movement from desire to enjoyment.

Fantasy misleads the subject because it is premised on the actual existence of a concrete desire in the big Other. When the subject fantasizes a solution to the big Other's desire, one imagines that the big Other has a consistent and substantial existence. In this way, fantasy buttresses the dominance of social authority by granting this authority a substantiality that it doesn't actually have. The big Other doesn't actually know its own desire but relies on the subject's response to find out. It is an inconsistent entity internally at odds with itself, but fantasy creates the impression of a knowable desire of the big Other that it has uncovered, even if that desire is nothing more than driving a sports car.

The big Other establishes a paradigm for the social order and directs its desire, but it cannot control its own desire. The moment that I fantasize a solution to the Other's desire, I accept that the social authority knows what it's doing and therefore submit to the justification for its rule, even if I don't accede to the authority's demands. Fantasy works hand-in-hand with the big Other to lead subjects to capitulate. If we return to the problem of how popularity in high school works, this function of fantasy becomes quite clear.

The popular clique represents one figure of the big Other in contemporary society. Though the popular kids technically don't rule the school, they do have a social authority that the school's titular authorities do not have. No one uses the commodities that principals and teachers do or adopts their ways of talking, but they do respond to the popular students in these ways. Everyone in the school would choose having the popular group recognize them over the school principal doing so. The subject who enters the high school confronts the desire of the Other in the form of the secret of popularity. Fantasy provides this subject a roadmap toward popularity and gaining the acceptance of the popular crowd. This roadmap tells one to wear particular clothes, speak with certain words, appreciate the proper music, like specific people, and so on. If the subject adheres to this roadmap through fantasy, popularity seems assured. But the path is not so easy. The solution that fantasy provides to the desire of the big Other is only an imaginary solution, and it assumes that the big Other has a consistency that it doesn't have.

Let's look at a joke about popularity to see how fantasy leads us astray. The most popular guy in his high school is able to do everything. He has perfect grades, is the captain of the football team, writes publishable short stories, teaches himself computer programing, and even helps at the food kitchen during his free time. To expand his interests, in his senior year he decides to take up the plastic arts. But every sculpture that he tries ends up being a bust. The key to the popular guy's failing is the pun on the word *bust*. The role that the pun plays in undermining the status of the popular guy is essential for understanding why fantasy is inherently misleading. In this joke, the popular guy stands in for the big Other. His failing in sculpture indicates how the big Other is necessarily inconsistent, even if it appears to know what it wants.

No one can know what they desire because desire must be articulated in language, at which point it becomes alien to whoever is desiring. One can never just tell someone what one desires because this straightforward articulation of desire would manifest itself as a demand that hides another desire beneath it. Fantasy tries to circumvent this problem but always relies on the subject's own interpretation of the big Other's desire.

Fantasy directs us to misrecognize the site of our enjoyment. We align it with an object of desire that the enjoying other takes from us and blocks us from having. Due to the fantasy scenario, we fail to see that the *objet a*, the object that causes us to desire, is not actually the object of desire but the obstacle to that object. Confusion between the object of desire and the *objet a* unleashes hatred on those preventing us from accessing the object of desire. This is the problem. The subject turns its political energy against this agent that deprives the subject of its object, when in fact it is the obstacle to the object of desire that itself generates desire.

Those insisting on the absolute danger that immigrants pose to a social order indulge in a national fantasy. This fantasy posits the immigrant as the source of the loss that undermines the nation, and the elimination of immigrants becomes a pathway to restoring what the nation has lost, even though the nation has no former greatness to recover. Fantasy stages loss in order to convince subjects that they once had what they never had. In this way it provides a narrative for explaining the absence that exists within every signifying structure.

But this is not the last word on fantasy. How we relate to fantasy is tied to both our situation as subjects and to our political destiny. It is possible to shift our relationship to the *objet a* within the fantasy, to recognize the *objet a*, not the object of desire, as the site for our enjoyment. This transformation is at the heart of the psychoanalytic politics that many have taken up in Lacan's wake and that Lacan himself points toward.

One of the most suggestive remarks that Lacan makes about fantasy occurs in *Seminar XI: The Four Fundamental Concepts of Psychoanalysis, 1963–1964*. Many commentators and other theorists have picked up on this remark, even though Lacan himself never repeats it beyond this one instance, which is strange given how often one hears it mentioned. In the final session of this seminar, he asks, "How can a subject who has traversed the radical phantasy experience the drive?"[128] With this question, Lacan links the act of traversing the fantasy with the breakthrough that psychoanalysis aims to achieve. For many theorists, traversing the fantasy serves as the paradigm for the psychoanalytic cure.

The standard interpretation of traversing the fantasy is moving beyond it, ceasing to have one's desire constrained by the fantasy scenario. Where fantasy offers the subject the possibility of realizing desire, one recognizes that the object is constitutively impossible, that desire cannot be realized. According to this interpretation, accomplishing the traversal of the fantasy frees one from the lure of attaining the impossible through which fantasy seduces the subject.

Richard Boothby offers a different way of looking at this process. For Boothby, traversing the fantasy doesn't entail getting beyond the fantasy. It doesn't allow the subject to free itself from fantasy's power. Instead, when one traverses the fantasy, one finds oneself completely given over to the impossible real within the fantasy. Boothby claims, "To traverse the phantasy in the Lacanian sense is to be more profoundly claimed by the phantasy than ever, in the sense of being brought into an ever more intimate relation with that real core of the phantasy that transcends imaging."[129] As long as we remain preoccupied with the imaginary scenario that leads to the desired object, we fall for the basic deception of fantasy. But Boothby points out another possibility implicit in the fantasy structure. Fantasy brings us closer to the impossible real, closer to the point at which the symbolic order breaks down. This point is what makes the fantasy enjoyable, but it is also the point that we usually ignore. When we traverse the fantasy, we devote ourselves to this real disruption.

After the traversal of the fantasy, the subject doesn't escape the fantasy but instead comes to take responsibility for the enjoyment that it derives from the fantasy. It recognizes this enjoyment as its own rather than believing that it belongs to the little other. Coming to this position involves an act of rereading the structure of the fantasy. In the fantasy, the enjoyment appears to belong to the other who leaves the subject deprived of it. But the fantasy scenario allows the subject to enjoy through this figure of the other. The subject's own enjoyment manifests itself through the other. The problem with fantasy is how it prompts us to see our own enjoyment as completely foreign to us.

That's why traversing the fantasy is so important. When one traverses the fantasy, one accepts the foreign enjoyment within the fantasy as one's own. One ceases to envy the enjoying other and recognizes oneself in this other. To traverse the fantasy, nationalists would have to recognize themselves in immigrants. In this way, the subject would go beyond its ideological situation. This act reveals the political possibility hidden within fantasy's political dangers.[130]

Fantasy always has a double edge. While it ensures the subject's subjection to the order of the signifier in its most constraining dimension, it also creates an avenue for moving beyond the symbolic regime. This is why fantasy is vital to any psychoanalytic conception of politics. Fantasy both explains why we are tied to oppressive regimes and opens up the path to challenging such regimes.

Four Discourses

The late period in Lacan's thought begins with the development of the four discourses in *Seminar XVII: The Other Side of Psychoanalysis, 1969–1970.* This seminar occasions one of the fundamental breaks in Lacan's thought. It is the beginning of what I am calling the late period. Prior to this theoretical move at the end of the 1960s, Lacan had a singular conception of the symbolic order: It always had the same form, even though it had an infinite number of possible manifestations. All of a sudden in *Seminar XVII*, there are four different forms that the symbolic order can take on, forms that Lacan labels the discourses.

According to his thinking before this seminar, the symbolic order has a master signifier that orients the structure of signification. But the universe of signification that the master signifier authorizes always contains a point of failure, a site where contradiction becomes evident. Because every symbolic order runs into a contradiction, no symbolic order is ever complete. This failure indicates that the symbolic order is necessarily at odds with itself. The symbolic order, no matter what its content, always has this same contradictory formal structure.

In *Seminar XVII: The Other Side of Psychoanalysis*, Lacan identifies the discourse of the master, the university, the hysteric, and the analyst as the four possible discursive structures that the symbolic order might have. The identification of four distinct discourses enables Lacan to indicate how the symbolic order might function differently depending on the social and historical situation in which this order is set. For instance, the symbolic order operates in one way when people base their lives on their faith in God but in another way when their ultimate point of reference is science. Likewise, hysterical revolt doesn't have the same discursive structure as that which operates during psychoanalysis. Lacan envisions four different discourses that correspond to four ways that significance can be grounded.

Each of the four discourses has the same four positions – the agent in the top left of the diagram, the Other in the top right, the product in the bottom right, and the truth in the bottom left. Each discourse also has the same four elements – the master signifier (S_1), knowledge (S_2), surplus enjoyment (*a*), and the barred subject ($). What differentiates the discourses from one another is the positioning of the elements within the formal positions. Each of the four discourses involves these terms located in different positions, but their ordering remains the same. Lacan locates these positions on a diagram that he uses to illustrate the discourses and contrast them with one another.

In the first position on the top left of the diagram, there is the agent that drives the discourse and from whom the discourse acquires its name. The agent in the discourse of the master is, as one would expect, the master signifier. In the master's discourse, the master signifier (S_1) animates the activity that occurs within the symbolic structure. The master signifier provides the basis for all signification within this discourse. All significance ultimately refers back to this signifier.

The second position in a discourse is the Other, the one to whom the discourse addresses itself. This position is located in the upper right of Lacan's diagram. The Other in the discourse of the master is knowledge (S_2). This knowledge explains the master signifier by fleshing out its significance and building on its foundation. The problem with the accumulation of knowledge is that the master signifier, although it acts as the ground for signification, can never itself acquire a sense. Let's look at the master signifier *God.* We study the world as God's creation and recognize everything that we encounter as the result of a divine plan. But no matter how much knowledge about the world we acquire, we will never gain any insight into the purpose of God's plan itself. The signifier *God* makes possible a form of knowledge, but this knowledge will never encompass the master signifier that generates this field of inquiry. It is not that we gain so much knowledge that we recognize the inadequacy of the master signifier but that no amount of knowledge can grasp the nonsensical excess of the master signifier. No matter how complete the world of knowledge is, it will always fail to grasp the master signifier that lies beyond this world.

The failed relationship between mastery and knowledge produces an excess that is its product. The product is the third position in the diagram, found at the bottom right. The discourse of the master produces surplus enjoyment (*a*) in the form of an excess that emerges in the space that opens up through the master signifier's relationship to the field of knowledge. This surplus enjoyment both sustains the structure and challenges it. It is the enjoyment of obedience to the master's nonsensical imperative to obey, but it is also the enjoyment found at the limit of the master's authority. The existence of this surplus leads to the emergence of the subject.

The fourth and final position in the bottom left of the diagram, below the agent, is the truth of the discourse. The truth escapes conscious awareness within the discourse and yet reveals what motivates the discourse all along. The repressed truth of the master's discourse is the barred or lacking subject ($). Even though it stems from the master's discourse, the lacking subject represents a challenge to the master's authority. This challenge is the truth of the master's unconscious desire, a desire that flies in the face of what the discourse itself commands. As Lacan sees it, the truth of every discourse defies the conscious demand that animates it: The truth of mastery is the desiring subject; the unconscious truth of the university is mastery; the truth of analytic discourse is knowledge; and the truth of hysteria is a surplus enjoyment that derives from the hysterical questioning itself. The formal structure of the discourses points to a truth that the agent in the discourse cannot recognize. No master believes that it desires the subject's challenge to its rule, just as no hysteric grasps that it enjoys its own dissatisfaction. In this sense, Lacan's discovery of the four discourses doubles down on his commitment to emphasize the role that the unconscious plays in the social order.

One can see an example of the master's discourse in the philosophical text that Gottfried Leibniz wrote in 1710 and the response to this text. Leibniz wrote the *Theodicy* to justify the ways of God to humanity, making it a paradigmatic expression of the master's discourse. In this treatise, Leibniz provides knowledge (S_2) to support *God* as a master signifier (S_1). According to the *Theodicy*, God created the best of all possible worlds. Any apparent failings in this world result from our misperception rather than God's lack of omnipotence or omniscience. The problem is that in Leibniz's system the signifier *God* can justify the greatest horrors. These horrors have the status of a surplus (*a*) that Leibniz cannot explain away. The disconnection between the rational system of his theodicy and the horrors that we must attribute to God's plan generate Voltaire's satirical response in his novel *Candide*. Here, the figure of Pangloss, the champion of Leibniz's philosophy, loses his fingers and nose, suffers from syphilis, and is hanged for heresy. In the master's discourse that Leibniz enacts, Voltaire occupies the position of the desiring subject ($). He responds to the excess that the discourse presents but cannot contain on its own terms. *Candide* reveals the ultimate failure of the master's discourse to attain the mastery that it proposes. We should view Voltaire's novel as the truth of the master's unconscious desire.

In the university discourse, Lacan turns the diagram of the master's discourse a quarter turn to the left. Knowledge becomes the agent, while surplus enjoyment functions as the Other, the lacking subject as the product, and the master signifier as the truth. Through his conception of this discursive form, Lacan criticizes the knowledge enterprise in operation at the university. The discourse that emanates from the university has a pretense to neutrality. It appears to challenge the masters of the social order. The university claims to speak truth to power. But university discourse has the effect of offering a hidden support for mastery, which is why the master signifier is in the position of the truth of this discourse, at the bottom left of the diagram.

We can see this in the way that a university researcher might examine what factors lead people to become stuck in poverty. Through its focus on factors internal to the capitalist system such as education level or marital status, the exploration of this question enhances the acceptance of this system among those who perform and read the research. The support for the master signifier doesn't derive so much from the tendentiousness of the results of the study but from the decision to study this phenomenon in the first place. The research undertaken in university discourse finds its truth in the master signifier even when those involved in it believe that they are fighting against the master.

The Other of university discourse is surplus enjoyment. Lacan rejects the idea of a neutral quest for knowledge. Not only does this quest provide support for a master, but it also finds its motivation in enjoyment rather than in truth. The researcher seeks what doesn't fit within the symbolic universe – what no one has yet discovered or explored – and yet university discourse never arrives at this point. Its product is thus the barred subject, the researcher who always has something new to look for, no matter how apparently satisfying the results of the previous experiment. The product of university discourse is the endless seeking of the lacking subject. University discourse never reaches an end point but keeps searching again and again for more results. The point of this discourse is the ceaseless production of knowledge.

Both university discourse and the hysteric's discourse appear to mount a challenge to mastery while actually supporting it. The hysteric's discourse places the lacking subject as the agent. In this position, the lacking subject represents the figure of the hysteric. The agent of this discourse, the lacking subject, confronts the master as its Other. But it does so only to demand an adequate master. All hysterical questioning is performed in service of mastery. As the agent of the discourse, the hysteric cannot do without the master that it questions. Hysterical challenges to mastery reflect the desire for a nonlacking master, not existence without one. The hysteric's questioning of the master generates knowledge as its product through its incessant call for a more adequate master. The truth of the hysteric's discourse is the surplus enjoyment located at the bottom left of the diagram. The hysteric enjoys the process of challenging the master, not the change demanded, which is why hysteria cannot be a radical position.

One can identify hysterical discourse by its investment in the master that it criticizes. No matter how much the person in the position of the master accedes to the hysterical demands, the demands continue unabated. If the master cedes on one point, the hysterical subject will quickly raise another objection. There is no end point to the questioning that occurs in the hysteric's discourse because the enjoyment of the questioning is the aim.[131] The challenges that this discourse poses to mastery are sham challenges. The only discourse that highlights the master's lack is that of the analyst.

The agent of the analyst's discourse is surplus enjoyment. As Lacan understands it at this time, psychoanalysis involves the analyst adopting the position of surplus enjoyment (the *objet a*).[132] Lacan believes that this enables the analyst to avoid the problem of mastery that besets all other discursive formations. He compels the psychoanalyst to refrain from acting like a master by giving advice or instructions to the analysand. Instead, Lacan theorizes the position of the analyst as an enigmatic one. Rather than telling an analysand what to do, the analyst refuses to offer a clearly definable position for the analysand to rely on. The Lacanian analyst must embody the idea that the big Other does not exist, that there is no secure external basis for meaning on which the subject in analysis can rely. Or, to put it in Lacan's terms, the analyst takes up the position of what falls out of signification, not what grounds it.

The Other of the analyst's discourse is the barred subject. The analyst engages the desire of the barred subject during the psychoanalytic session in order to produce a new master signifier. But this new master signifier is radically different than the usual ones. The analyst's discourse generates a new form of master signifier, one that points toward its own incompleteness. As Lacan puts it in *Seminar XVII*, "perhaps it's from the analyst's discourse that there can emerge another style of master signifier."[133] This discourse allows the subject to ground subjectivity on its own desire rather than on an investment in a master. The analyst avoids the problem of mastery that besets the other discourses because the analyst leads to a new master signifier established on a radically different basis – that of surplus enjoyment.

Analysis produces a lacking subject. But this lacking subject is not the same as the agent in the hysteric's discourse or the truth of the master's. This subject no longer attempts to hysterically flee its lack. Through the analyst's discourse, a lacking subject emerges that embraces its lack as the source of its surplus enjoyment. This discourse has the same reference points as the others, but their significance undergoes an important change, a change also evident in the truth of the analyst's discourse.

The truth of the discourse of the analyst is knowledge. This knowledge is dissimilar from the knowledge of the other discourses because it is a knowledge based on the failure of the master and the nonexistence of the Other. Knowledge in the analyst's discourse grasps the absence of any ultimate ground. It is a knowledge of the master's failure, not its success.[134] In the discourse of the analyst, Lacan envisions a path for the subject to overcome its investment in mastery and to recognize how enjoyment derives from disinvesting in the master.

When one surveys Lacan's conception of the four discourses, it becomes evident that one discourse bypasses the problem that besets the other three. The discourse of the analyst receives a distinct privilege in Lacan's theory because it avoids becoming caught up in the illusions of mastery. In contrast, each of the other discourses succumbs to the problem of mastery, even if this occurs in a disguised form, as is the case with university discourse and hysterical discourse. As Lacan sees it, the analyst doesn't impose on the analysand as a master but instead prompts the subject to desire. This is a theoretical problem because it represents a failure on Lacan's part to recognize how mastery operates.

Lacan believes that the analyst remaining an enigma to the analysand will thwart the analyst's mastery. Nothing could be further from the truth. When someone confronts us with an enigmatic stance, this doesn't prompt us to recognize this person's lack of mastery. It does the opposite: It multiplies the person's mastery. Comporting oneself as an enigma doesn't dismantle authority but gives one heightened authority. The more Lacan acts as an obscure figure impossible to decipher, the more analysands invest themselves in his word.

The error in this line of thinking becomes clear when we consider Lacan's style as a speaker and writer. Quite intentionally, Lacan speaks and writes in a completely obscure fashion. He believes that Freud opens himself up to misunderstanding because he wrote too simply and directly. As Lacan sees it, Freud doesn't force readers to think for themselves but gives them an easy path to submit to him as a master. Lacan thinks that he has a solution to this Freudian misstep. In stark contrast with Freud, Lacan develops a style that no one could unpack without multiple rereading and careful study. It has the effect of turning Lacan himself into a master.

But Lacan's mastery is not the end of the theoretical difficulties that the development of the four discourses occasions. This development suffers from the curse of multiplicity. When theorizing a multiplicity, one must navigate the arbitrariness of the structure's end point. As we examine the theory of the four discourses, an obvious question arises: Why not five or six or any number? Once one journeys down the path of multiplicity away from a single contradictory structure, there is no necessary stopping point. The turn to multiplicity leads to the continuing demand for more and more particular options. Lacan himself responds to this demand in the years following his development of the four discourses. During a talk at the University of Milan in 1972, he theorizes a fifth discourse, the discourse of the capitalist.[135]

Lacan arrives at the controversial fifth discourse by changing up the order of the terms in a way not permitted when he first introduces them. In the first four discourses, the terms remain in the same sequence even when they shift positions. In the capitalist discourse, the lacking subject is the agent (as in the hysteric's discourse), and its Other is knowledge (as in the master's discourse). The product is surplus enjoyment, while the truth is the master signifier. This reshuffling of the order of the terms represents a major shift in Lacan's thinking about the discourses. Once Lacan makes this move, the floodgates are open. It is a fifth discourse that opens the door to multiple others, without Lacan himself having a theoretical reason to limit this expansion.[136] This is undoubtedly why Lacan was reluctant to integrate this fifth discourse fully into his thinking. It received a few mentions here and there outside the talk at Milan, but it remained marginal in Lacan's own thought. The reception to the invention of the capitalist discourse has been divided. Certain theorists have taken up this fifth discourse enthusiastically, while others have confined their discussion to the canonical four.[137]

When Lacan introduces the four discourses, he never acknowledges that they mark a radical change in his thinking. Perhaps as a result, Lacan's interpreters have not theorized them as such. Instead, they have assumed the existence of a continuity between the theory of the signifier in Lacan's early seminars and the theory of the four discourses in *Seminar XVII*. This assumption of a continuity misses the dramatic change that occurs as Lacan develops the four discourses. The introduction of the four discourses occasions a considerable change in Lacan's conception of the master signifier.

In the early and middle periods, Lacan's relationship to the master signifier was unambiguous. The point was to grasp this signifier, no matter what its content, as nonsensical. There was a political gain in asserting the stupidity of the master signifier. After the development of the four discourses, Lacan's view of the possibilities for the master signifier becomes more sanguine. Out of the analyst's discourse, one can create new forms of the master signifier through which the subject can assert the lack in the big Other. This more positive conception of the master signifier reflects Lacan's own belief in the analyst as one who could guide the subject while avoiding the pitfalls of mastery. Prior to the articulation of the four discourses, mastery was always a fraud. Once Lacan formulates the discourses, he sees a path to a viable form of mastery, to a master signifier that would take on a liberatory form. This represents a profound misstep.

The problem with this move in Lacan's trajectory is that it fails to recognize how mastery remains fraudulent no matter what approach we take to it. Within the realm of signification, there is no way to avoid a fraudulent master signifier for structural reasons. There must be one signifier that acts as the basis for the signification of all others. When it is in this position, it cannot itself have a signified. Its nonsensical status is requisite. Any attempt to avoid confronting the nonsense of this master signifier paves the way for despotism. The despotic master finds support in the illusion of a meaningful master signifier, while emancipation occurs through exposing the fraudulence of this same signifier. To grant any significance to the master signifier, as Lacan does when he formulates the four discourses, is to turn from emancipation to conformity. The late Lacan promulgates conformism in the guise of multiplicity.

Sexuation

The mantra defining Lacan's late period is that "*there is no such thing as sexual relation*."[138] By this he means that there is a fundamental impasse between the masculine and feminine forms of subjectivity that renders any stable relationship between the sexes impossible. This idea begins to come to the fore in his philosophy beginning in 1970, and it never recedes in importance until his death in 1981.[139] Lacan comes to believe that the sexual nonrelation is the central motivating idea of psychoanalysis – what brings people into analysis and what animates the analysis itself. The late emphasis on the sexual nonrelation occasions a sea change in his understanding of the structure of signification. Lacan divests himself from the notion that we can grasp how the signifying chain works. The sexual nonrelation trumps the relations that occur in the chain of signifiers and leaves each subject isolated. The dialectical relationship of the subject and the social order disappears as the sexual nonrelation takes the stage in Lacan's philosophy. Although the formulas of sexuation contain moments of incredible insight, the turn away from dialectics in Lacan's late period is something to be lamented.

The sexual nonrelation manifests itself through formulas of sexuation that articulate the structural logic that constitutes each sex. Lacan envisions the nonrelation as a logical impasse that he can articulate through logical formulas that correspond to each sex. This logical formalization has the benefit of divorcing sexuation from both biological organs and from gender identities.

While the formulas seem to map physiological differences onto the structure of the psyche, Lacan insists that sexuation does not correspond to physiology.[140] One could have the physical characteristics of a human male while existing in the woman's position, and vice versa. Sex, for Lacan, defines the specific way that the subject fails to achieve self-identity, the specific way of failing to relate to the signifier. There are two ways to fail, which is why there are two sexual positions.

Just as sex is irreducible to biological difference, it is also distinct from gender identity. For Lacan, sex is between biology and culture, an impasse that both biology and culture seem to elude. While gender can be multiple, it also presents the deception of self-identity. Gender creates the illusion that one can take it up fully without being divided from oneself. Sex, in contrast, is the way that one assumes one's self-division as a subject.[141]

The formulas of sexuation have the benefit of laying out a logical structure of sex that makes evident the impasse it indicates. Sexuation revolves around what Lacan calls the phallic function or symbolic castration. Each structure of sexuation has two interrelated ways of relating to castration, through which male or female subjectivity forms. The formulas provide a way of showing the two distinct logical impasses that occur for a subject within language.

Male sexuation is the simpler form for Lacan. It revolves around an exception. One accedes to male subjectivity through the figure of the exception who does not submit to prohibition, who escapes symbolic castration. This is the ideal man who doesn't lack. All of the other men who are subjected to castration form a whole through the exclusion of the one who isn't. In the case of men, the exception makes the rule. The one not subjected to castration enables all those subjected to castration to define their subjectivity relative to this ideal that is constitutively excluded as a possibility. To be a man means to orient oneself relative to an ideal that one can never attain.

One might imagine the masculine exception in the figure of someone like John Wayne. Wayne appears completely independent, strong, and invulnerable. He doesn't suffer from the same potential pitfalls that undermine every other man. No matter what Wayne does, his status as a lacking subject never becomes evident. He is an ideal of noncastration.

Like women, men are subjected to symbolic castration, but in contrast to women, they live in relation to an ideal of noncastration. The ideal of the man who really has the phallus and doesn't lack haunts everyone who struggles with this form of subjectivity. This ideal stands before the male subject, but there is an absolute prohibition against reaching the ideal. Men must strive to be like John Wayne, but they are not permitted to be John Wayne. Not even John Wayne himself can reach this ideal. The male subject takes its bearings relative to prohibition. Those situated on the masculine side are reduced to trying to transgress the barrier and become the ideal man. But this project always fails, and it fails because the structure of male subjectivity is deceptive in a way that the structure of female subjectivity is not.

There is no corresponding ideal on the feminine side, which is why there is also no corresponding group of all women. This side is much more complex than the masculine side, and, at the same time, the feminine side is much more politically suggestive. The formulas of the feminine side begin with the negative relationship to castration: there is no one not subjected to castration. But then Lacan adds the twist. Rather than indicating that all women are thus subjected to castration, the second formula on the feminine side claims that not-all women are subjected to castration. This not-all (*pas tout* in French) states that the feminine side does not form a whole because it lacks the exception that the male side has, the exception which permits the clear definition of the outside.

Lacan's claim that not-all women are subjected to castration has led to a misreading that posits feminine subjectivity existing outside the dynamic of symbolic castration. According to this conception, part of feminine subjectivity – or certain women, Lacan isn't clear in the structure of the not-all – escapes from the symbolic order. This is a misreading because it romanticizes feminine subjectivity as being outside of language. In *Seminar XX: Encore*, Lacan clarifies the feminine position. He states, "It's not because she is not-wholly in the phallic function that she is not there at all. She is *not* not at all there. She is there in full. But there is something more."[142] Women avoid the preoccupation with the outside that men have. While men have the exceptional ideal that escapes castration defining their subjectivity, women have no investment in the outside. There is no prohibition against escaping the symbolic order and reaching the ideal because there is no ideal at all.[143]

The discovery of the not-all as a way of theorizing the subject's relationship to the group represents Lacan's great insight of the late period. Many subsequent thinkers have translated the not-all into a schema for emancipatory politics. One can think of universal emancipation in terms of the not-all rather than as a fully constituted whole that requires an exception to be excluded. The emergence of the not-all is the theoretical justification for the last ten years of Lacan's life.

The not-all is the way that the feminine side offers a corrective to the masculine side. The absence of a feminine exception eliminates the need for a prohibition against transgressing and reaching it. The feminine side thus makes clear the impossibility of going beyond the symbolic order. This impossibility is the truth of the masculine side's prohibition. Masculine sexuation involves the prohibition of an impossibility that causes the impossibility to appear as possible. Feminine sexuation directly confronts the impossibility.[144] The formulas of sexuation demonstrate two structurally opposed ways of the subject failing to achieve a full self-identity – the prohibition against doing so and the impossibility of doing so.

Lacan develops the formulas of sexuation in the last decade of his life as a way of reformulating his earlier conception of sexual difference. For most of his intellectual trajectory, Lacan differentiates masculine and feminine subjectivity through the contrast between having and being the phallus. The man has the phallus, while the woman is it. He has the status that derives from the phallus, while she is the desired object. Of course, the phallus is only symbolic for Lacan. It is the phallic signifier. But this way of theorizing sex associates all sex with the phallus and doesn't envision enjoyment rooted in the feminine position, which is what changes in Lacan's later thought.

When Lacan develops the formulas of sexuation in *Seminar XVIII*, the idea of a subject having the phallus drops out of his theory.[145] It is only the masculine exception, a position that no actual man can attain, who has the phallus and avoids castration. In this sense, the formulas of sexuation represent an advance on the allotment of sex on the basis of having or being the phallus. With the formulas, having becomes a clear deception.

Sexuation is a division into two. The first question that this division raises is why the division must stop with two and not proceed to a multiplicity. Those who oppose Lacan's idea of sexuation most often promote a multiplicity of positions in opposition to the two. The problem with the turn to multiplicity is that it blunts the contradiction that exists between the two positions. The failure of the relation becomes blurred with the introduction of multiplicity, which is why Lacan is suspicious of this seemingly progressive gesture. With multiplicity, one has a series of differences rather than contradiction. Because difference avoids contradiction, it opens up the possibility of a stable relation, which is what the formulas of sexuation rule out.

While Lacan does divide the terrain of sex into two, he tends to avoid talking about sexual difference because the term *difference* suggests a relation between the two sides. The most important claim in the articulation of the formulas of sexuation is that they describe a nonrelation. The two sides of sexuation do not line up with each other. He will later add that not only is there no relation, there is a nonrelation.

The two sides of the formulas of sexuation do not exist in a complementary relationship to each other. Instead, the formulas describe a nonrelation. This is what Guy Le Gaufey is getting at when he explains, "the absence of phallic trait has no *complementary* value as compared to its presence, opening up by this very fact another space, liable to other rules."[146] The formulas of sexuation capture the existence of a split between the two antagonistic logics and a split within each position. The implications of this antagonistic split go beyond what Lacan himself attempts to explain. This has become one of the most fecund parts of Lacan's theory in spite of the controversy surrounding it.

No one has done more to unlock the theoretical significance of the formulas of sexuation than Joan Copjec. In the final chapter of her book *Read My Desire: Lacan Against the Historicists*, Copjec demonstrates how the formulas of sexuation align exactly with Immanuel Kant's antinomies of pure reason. While it might seem as if recognizing a parallel between two disparate lines of thought is interesting but unremarkable, the force of Copjec's interpretation introduces a shift in the understanding of both thinkers. All of a sudden, thanks to Copjec's discovery, the limitations of reason become inherently sexualized, and the ontological bearing of sex becomes evident.

Copjec also reveals the late Lacan's return to Kant away from Hegel. It is not by chance that Copjec is able to map the formulas of sexuation onto the antinomies of pure reason. They are Kantian formulas that formulate what we can't think, not what we can. Whereas the Lacan of the middle period thinks that we can know the social order through the contradictory point – the *objet a* – that it cannot integrate into its functioning, the late Lacan moves from contradiction to nonrelation. As he insists on the sexual nonrelation, Lacan gives up any prospect of thinking through the whole signifying structure and grasping the contradiction that inheres in this whole. But subsequent theorists, taking Copjec's reading as their starting point, have marshalled the formulas of sexuation to political ends by focusing on the feminine not-all as a rallying point.

The politics of the formulas begin with the critique of constructivism. According to Copjec, the development of the formulas of sexuation reveals psychoanalysis as an anti-constructivist position, one that undermines constructivism by showing sex as the point where construction fails. One cannot just construct masculine or feminine subjectivity without running into a logical impasse. The theory of construction makes sense up to a point – the point at which identity forms. But when one looks below identity to the structure of sex, construction loses its explanatory power.

Sex emerges through the inability of the symbolic order to complete itself. Sex is the point at which the social construction of identities fails. As Copjec puts it, "sex is produced by the internal limit, the failure of signification. It is only there where discursive practices falter – and not at all where they succeed in producing meaning – that sex comes to be."[147] Lacan comes up with the formulas of sexuation as a way to express how sex intrudes into subjectivity and prevents it from fully constituting itself.

One might imagine that the development of queer theory or the trans movement would target Lacan's theory of sexuation as hopelessly heteronormative since it takes as its point of departure two sexes (rather than none or three or more). To some extent, this has been the case. It is the basic tenor of Judith Butler's critique directed at Lacan's theory of sexuation, a theory that she always refers to in terms of sexual difference. Butler translates sexuation into sexual difference in order to create a target that is easier to hit.

Butler contends that Lacan erects sexual difference as a transcendental binary that subsequently prescribes all social relations. The discussion focuses on the relationship between sexual difference as a transcendental structure and the actual sexual practices in society. Butler writes, "as a transcendental claim, sexual difference should be rigorously opposed by anyone who wants to guard against a theory that would prescribe in advance what kinds of sexual arrangements will and will not be permitted in intelligible culture. The inevitable vacillation between the transcendental and the social functioning of the term makes its prescriptive function inevitable."[148] For Butler, there are transcendental structures and social practices with nothing in between. But as Copjec's analysis shows, sex stands directly between these two. It is neither transcendental nor social but corresponds to how both the transcendental and the social fail to constitute themselves. Sex is how neither the transcendental nor the social works out.

In response to Butler's critique of the transcendental binarism of sexuation, Patricia Gherovici argues for the appropriateness of sexuation for thinking about trans. In *Transgender Psychoanalysis*, she writes, "The sexuation formulae offer a way of thinking about trans because they are free from the shackles of anatomical constraints. The model of sexual difference still recognizes that there is only one logical operator, which is the phallus, but acknowledges that some individuals are placed in a position in which the phallus is not operative."[149] Lacan's formulas of sexuation provide a way to think about trans not as an aberration but as the paradigm for all subjectivity. No one simply is their sex because sex is the failure of self-identity. Conceiving sex in this way reveals that everyone is a trans subject, although most people fail to confront this fact and believe themselves to be fully men or women. To believe oneself cisgendered is to fall for a fundamental deception. Instead of putting Lacan's theory of sexuation to rest once and for all, the development of trans theory has actually breathed new life into it, as Gherovici and others show.

The formulas of sexuation can provide a basis for theorizing gender dysphoria that the ruling constructivist theory cannot. The constructivist thesis is that all gender – and ultimately sex itself – is a social construction and thus malleable. If one takes this theory seriously, it rules out the possibility of gender dysphoria from the get-go. One's gender could not misalign with one's sex if both are just constructions. According to this theory, there is no real sex relative to which one's gender might be misaligned.

Although he doesn't theorize sex as a biological category, Lacan's anti-constructivist conception of sex offers a way out of this theoretical dilemma. One's sex emerges as a result of how the subject enters into signification. It derives from the collision between biology and the signifying order. Sex does not involve a conscious choice, nor is it the product of cultural determinations. It is not symbolic but real.

Gender, in contrast, is a purely symbolic category. Social forces determine one's gender before one has the opportunity to choose it for oneself. There is no guarantee, in Lacan's thinking, that gender will align with sex. One can enter the symbolic order in the feminine way while being gendered as a man. Lacan doesn't ever discuss the possibility, but his theory provides a compelling background for the concept of gender dysphoria. He can think through this concept in a way that constructivism cannot.

The formulas of sexuation have received considerable attention since their introduction at the beginning of the 1970s. Much energy has been spent deciphering their form and translating them into everyday language. An equal amount of energy has been directed at making sense of the feminine not-all. Although the masculine formulas are straightforward, the feminine ones are anything but. The primary task that the formulas of sexuation leave is uncovering their political bearing. Lacan is notoriously quiet about the political implications of his theorizing, despite hinting about a link between feminine jouissance and politics in *Seminar XX*.[150]

There is a political charge to insisting on the sexual nonrelation.[151] Believing the sexes to be complementary always places one sex in a subordinate position. Complementarity sounds nice, but when one lists the complementary relationships, its positive sheen vanishes. The relationships of master and slave, husband and wife, boss and worker, or predator and prey all have a complementary structure, and none works out so great for the second term. The overthrow of the idea of complementarity is the political dimension of Lacan's formulas of sexuation that he himself doesn't develop. That task falls to Joan Copjec, Jennifer Friedlander, Hilary Neroni, and other feminist thinkers, including Alenka Zupančič.

Zupančič's *What IS Sex?* tackles the ontological question of sex. In this work, she tries to integrate the antagonism of sex into ontological speculation. In the process, the political significance of sexuation comes to the fore. She claims that insistence on the sexual nonrelation is not just a political act but the political act. Zupančič states, "The most oppressive societies have always been those which axiomatically proclaimed (enforced) the existence of the sexual relation: a 'harmonious' relation presupposes an exact definition of essences (involved in this relation) and of roles pertaining to them."[152] Oppressive regimes love complementarity and – implicitly at least – hate Lacan's theory of sexuation. According to Zupančič, the sexual nonrelation has a political import.

This political bearing is different than the one Lacan develops in the middle period. When he develops the concept of the *objet a* in the 1960s, Lacan contends that subjectivity emerges through a point of contradiction in the social order. His thought from this time enables us to consider social relations from where they break down. But in the 1970s, the turn to the sexual nonrelation marks an explicit refusal to consider the social order as such. It ceases to be constituted through failure because nonrelation so thoroughly trumps all relationality. One can no longer talk about the social order as a whole at all. This limits those following Lacan on prioritizing the sexual nonrelation to an isolated form of politics that can resist oppressive relations without proposing an alternative form of contradictory relationality. There is theoretical richness in the formulas of sexuation, but the turn away from a universal theory has an unfortunate downside.

Sinthome

The symptom always has a double valence for psychoanalysis. It indicates the existence of a repressed desire – if there were no repression, the symptom wouldn't have developed – but at the same time, it expresses that desire in a symptomatic form. The symptom satisfies the subject. This satisfaction is what prevents the subject from just giving up the symptom. Symptoms bring excess suffering for the subject, but the subject is attached to them for the satisfaction that they provide. This is what leads subjects into psychoanalytic treatment.

Psychoanalysis interprets symptoms by linking them to an underlying neurotic disorder. A patient comes to an analyst with a persistent cough that has no physiological cause. The analysis treats this cough as a symptom of the patient's neurosis, the form of expression that the patient's drive adopts due to the pressure of the disorder. Through the work of psychoanalysis, the patient becomes capable of interpreting this symptom rather than just suffering from it. This process doesn't necessarily eliminate the symptom but allows the subject to recognize the satisfaction that it receives from the symptom. One can see one's desire manifesting where one formerly saw just unnecessary suffering.

Late in his career, Lacan adopts a new position relative to the symptom. In *Seminar XXIII: The Sinthome, 1975–1976*, he creates his final new concept – the *sinthome*. The *sinthome* is the privileged symptom within the subject's psyche. Lacan uses the old spelling of the word *symptom* in order to distinguish this privileged symptom from ordinary ones. The *sinthome* has a privileged status because of what it accomplishes for the subject. It holds subjectivity together by operating in the stead of a missing master signifier. A subject lacking access to a master signifier can replace its function through the turn to a *sinthome*. The final concept from Lacan marks his last theoretical misstep, a misstep that cements his turn away from the dialectical relationship between the subject and the symbolic order. It is impossible to integrate the concept of the *sinthome* into the dialectical version of Lacan's theory from the middle period. A complete breach exists between the two periods when it comes to the *sinthome*.

Unlike ordinary symptoms, the *sinthome* is not the indication of an underlying neurosis. It is rather a structure that allows the subject to stave off a psychotic break. The psychoanalyst can liberate the subject from its more debilitating symptoms, but it leaves the *sinthome* intact. The absence of a master signifier leaves the subject vulnerable to falling into full-blown psychosis. According to Lacan's theory, psychosis is the usual destiny for those that lack psychic access to a master signifier. The lack of the master signifier leaves psychotics unable to orient themselves within the symbolic order, so that they relate to this order through the imaginary. But the *sinthome* compensates for this absence and gives the subject an ordering principle for its existence, which is why psychoanalysis doesn't try to interpret the *sinthome* away.[153]

In *Seminar XXIII*, Lacan focuses on James Joyce for his way of compensating for the absence of a paternal metaphor or master signifier in his psyche. As Lacan sees it, Joyce writes *Finnegans Wake* in the way that he does – inventing his own language in the act of writing – to give himself a structure that would rescue him from the absence of a master signifier. Even though Joyce writes an unreadable novel, the writing itself creates an individualized *sinthome* that saves him from falling into psychosis. The unreadable nature of *Finnegans Wake*, a fact that Lacan appreciates rather than derides, is essential to its status as a *sinthome*. The *sinthome* organizes the subject's jouissance but itself has no signification. The nonsense of the *sinthome* provides a point of anchorage for the world of sense. Joyce's form of writing is a symptom of his own psyche, and yet it gives an order to his subjectivity.[154]

Lacan emphasizes the failure of the paternal metaphor for Joyce. This is what necessitates the form of writing that he adopts. According to Lacan, "Joyce came up with a compensation for the paternal failing."[155] In the abeyance of the Name-of-the-Father, the *sinthome* gives the subject the ability to orient itself in the world, which is why Lacan finds the *sinthome* so important.

The subject has recourse to the *sinthome* in order to hold together the symbolic, imaginary, and real registers. It plays a part in knotting subjectivity together – specifically through a Borromean knot, the figure that fascinates Lacan throughout his late period. The Borromean knot shows how the imaginary, symbolic, and real interlock as three separate pieces of string. But in *Seminar XXIII*, Lacan introduces the idea that the figure of the Borromean knot would fall apart without the addition of the *sinthome*. It is a fourth agency that keeps the subject from disintegrating.[156] It saves the contemporary subject that exists in a world lacking a clear master signifier. The *sinthome* makes up for the failure of the paternal function in the social order.

We can see an instance of the *sinthome* in the way that dialogue functions in Quentin Tarantino's films. His films include long sequences of dialogue that exist for their own sake, as a site for enjoyment that doesn't advance the narrative. The exchange that hitmen Jules (Samuel L. Jackson) and Vincent (John Travolta) have before they go to shoot their next victims shows how dialogue works as a *sinthome* in *Pulp Fiction* (Quentin Tarantino, 1994). Vincent regales Jules with a description of different customs in Europe, including what the French call a McDonald's Quarter Pounder with Cheese – a *Royale with Cheese*.

The discussion between Jules and Vincent doesn't have anything to do with the upcoming hit or their ultimate destinies in the film. It is a narrative detour, but it is nonetheless one of the most quoted scenes in Hollywood history. As a *sinthome*, it holds the film together in a way that the narrative structure does not. The filmic narrative is atemporal and fragmented, but the scene of dialogue enables spectators to structure their enjoyment of the film. The dialogue as *sinthome*, not the narrative or of the ideas driving the films, is what makes Tarantino an appealing filmmaker to some. The predominance of the *sinthome* over the narrative and the form in his films is also what turns others off.

Lacan theorizes the *sinthome* at the time when he claims that nonrelation has the last word on relation. In the late period of his philosophy, the signifying chain ceases to be a chain at all. The sexual nonrelation interrupts it, so that the master signifier can have no way at all of relating to the other signifiers. The triumph of nonrelation causes the master signifier to stop playing its structuring role for the psyche. Set adrift by nonrelation, the subject cannot orient itself through this signifier. This is where the *sinthome* comes to the subject's aid.

The turn to the *sinthome* is itself symptomatic of Lacan's late sexuation period. In contrast to the Name-of-the-Father or master signifier, the *sinthome* is particular to the individual subject. While many subjects can have a master signifier in common, no one can share a *sinthome* with another subject. Each subject must form its own *sinthome* as a way of compensating for the absence of a structuring master signifier.

When analysis allows the subject to recognize its *sinthome* as the way that it structures its jouissance, this recognition does not lead the subject out of its sense of isolation. It ensconces the subject in its particular form of jouissance and doesn't enable the subject to recognize the inherent connection between this jouissance and the Other. What provides coherence for one subject cannot provide it for any other. Conceptualizing the *sinthome* as an individualized version of the master signifier bespeaks the absence of any dialectical relation.[157] Isolation replaces contradiction.

When discussing the *sinthome*, Lacan insists that one cannot interpret it away. To do so would risk depriving the subject of what holds it together. This turn away from interpretation marks a dramatic departure from Lacan's earlier thinking, which foregrounded both the subject's interpretation of the Other's desire and the analyst's interpretation of the subject. The *sinthome* doesn't require interpretation because it is a site of jouissance, not a gap or contradiction where desire might emerge.

The abandonment of interpretation is simultaneously a turn away from theorizing the social totality. Granting the subject its *sinthome* allows it to find its singularity apart from a struggle with the master signifier. Theorizing the *sinthome* as a replacement for the master signifier eliminates the emphasis on the failure of the master signifier. Rather than seeing subjectivity emerge where the master signifier fails, Lacan gives up on the relation between them.

The late Lacan's insistence on nonrelation represents a step backward both philosophically and politically. According to this late theory, the subject acquires coherence through its own particular *sinthome* and avoids the confrontation with the desire of the Other. The interpretation of desire that the middle Lacan insists on gives way to a prohibition on interpretation when it comes to the *sinthome.* While it is possible to discover a radical edge to the formulas of sexuation in the way that Joan Copjec does, the *sinthome* has no such bright side. It is a theoretical dead end because it treats the subject as an isolated entity.[158] Its emergence indicates Lacan's abandonment of dialectics, which involves the confrontation of the subject with the failure of the social totality, for the isolated subjectivity of liberalism. When the *sinthome* appears in Lacan's philosophy, the radicality of his project disappears.

Notes

1 The symbolic order humanizes the world, even though it introduces a signifier between the subject and everything it encounters. Lacan claims, "Everything which is human has to be ordained within a universe constituted by the symbolic function." Jacques Lacan, *The Seminar of Jacques Lacan, Book II: The Ego in Freud's Theory and in the Technique of Psychoanalysis, 1954–1955*, ed. Jacques-Alain Miller, trans. Sylvana Tomaselli (New York: Norton, 1991 [1978]), 29. We have no experience of our humanity outside symbolic mediation.

2 Lacan contends that the subject's choice to enter the symbolic order is a forced choice, a choice that never appears as a choice in the present. One cannot refuse the symbolic order because the capacity to refuse becomes evident only after the fact. It is only a choice retroactively.

3 To explain the power of the structure over individual lives, Lévi-Strauss examines marital decisions. He contends that such decisions are never just a matter of individual proclivities. Instead, the choice of a spouse adheres to structural rules, even if these rules have become relatively invisible in modern societies. The structural determinations proclaim who must marry whom.

4 One of the primary philosophical quarrels in France during the middle of the twentieth century took place between Jean-Paul Sartre and Claude Lévi-Strauss, and it centered on the problem of the subject. Sartre made the subject the linchpin of his philosophy, whereas Lévi-Strauss dismissed subjectivity as an illusion that disappeared with a recognition of the underlying structure. Despite his personal and theoretical allegiance to Lévi-Strauss, Lacan's system necessarily ends up on the side of Sartre, not that of Lévi-Strauss. For Lacan, the power of the symbolic order produces subjectivity rather than eliminating the subject.

5 Richard Boothby, *Freud as Philosopher: Metapsychology after Lacan* (New York: Routledge, 2001), 87.

6 The relationship between the symbolic order and unconscious desire is paradoxical. The symbolic order conveys unconscious desire, but it must do so indirectly because the unconscious cannot appear in a direct form and remain unconscious. It is always elsewhere relative to what is directly graspable. Signifiers reveal the unconscious but don't say it. I can never proclaim, "My unconscious is x." I must instead interpret the unconscious through the distortion of the symbolic order that occurs when I speak.

7 Joan Copjec notes that signifiers deceive us by suggesting that a plenitude of reality exists just beyond them. Although we treat signifiers as if they are transparent, they aren't. As Copjec puts it,

"*Since signifiers are not transparent, they cannot demonstrate that they are not hiding something behind what they say – they cannot prove that they do not lie.* Language can only present itself to the subject as a veil that cuts off from view a reality that is other than what we are allowed to see." Joan Copjec, *Read My Desire: Lacan Against the Historicists* (Cambridge, MA: MIT Press, 1994), 54. Or, signifiers hide that they aren't hiding anything.

8 In his first seminar, Lacan points out that what we do with the signifier *elephant* is much more important than what people do to actual elephants in the world. The fate of the signifier plays a decisive role in the fate of the animal.

9 The signifier *homeless* has come into such disrepute that people have begun to replace it with the nicer-sounding *houseless*. They do so with the belief – tied to the early Lacan – that changing the signifier will transform the social reality.

10 The symbolic order has an inherent political status because it creates a public in which people can interact. When we lose touch with the importance of the symbolic order, our sense of a life in common disappears. In *Wrestling with the Angel*, Tracy McNulty dedicates herself to pointing out the crucial position that the symbolic has in all political aspirations, precisely because it provides a common ground for our interaction. She writes, "the symbolic sustains life in common by supporting the conditions of credibility for social coexistence and constraining our subjective desires to find a public expression." Tracy McNulty, *Wrestling with the Angel: Experiments in Symbolic Life* (New York: Columbia University Press, 2014), 9. McNulty feels the need to write this book due to the absence of emphasis on the symbolic, even among those indebted to Lacan. Her view is that most theorists put too must stress on the real at the expense of the symbolic, a verdict that she would undoubtedly extend to the present work.

11 Although it took years of struggle to change the most widely used terms in English, it happened more rapidly in English than in languages where gender plays a more prominent role, such as French, German, or Spanish.

12 Jacques Lacan, *Le Séminaire, livre XIV: La logique du fantasme, 1966–1967*, ed. Jacques-Alain Miller (Paris: Seuil, 2023), 29.

13 Although Lacan is more famous for the mirror stage than any other idea, he borrows most of the insights in "The Mirror Stage" from Henri Wallon. For a chronicle of Wallon's influence on Lacan, see Juan Pablo Lucchelli, *Lacan: De Wallon à Kojève* (Paris: Éditions Michèle, 2017).

14 Richard Boothby sees Lacan's critique of the imaginary status of the ego as perhaps his central insight. As he puts it in *Death and Desire*, "Lacan's first and arguably most original and far-reaching innovation in psychoanalytic theory was to characterize the Freudian 'ego' as a formation of the imaginary." Richard Boothby, *Death and Desire: Psychoanalytic Theory in Lacan's Return to Freud* (London: Routledge, 1991), 18. What Boothby is getting at here is the recognition that it is possible to read Freud and view the path of psychoanalysis as that of shoring up the ego. Not so with Lacan.

15 Although we typically weigh what we see more heavily than where we see from, this is an error. And not an innocuous one. It is one that Jennifer Friedlander aims to correct in *The Feminine Look*. There, she insists, "The subject is . . . constituted less by what it sees than it is by what it cannot see." Jennifer Friedlander, *Feminine Look: Sexuation, Spectatorship, Subversion* (Albany: SUNY Press, 2008), 9. For Friedlander, shifting the emphasis from what is seen to where it is seen from is a feminist political task. This task aligns Lacan's project, especially as it appears in Friedlander's work, with feminism.

16 Lacan makes this point in his first seminar. He states, "The primary imaginary relation provides the fundamental framework for all possible erotism. It is a condition to which the object of Eros as such must be submitted. The object relation must always submit to the narcissistic framework and be inscribed in it." Jacques Lacan, *The Seminar of Jacques Lacan, Book I: Freud's Papers on Technique, 1953–1954*, ed. Jacques-Alain Miller, trans. John Forrester (New York: Norton, 1988 [1975]), 174. When Lacan grants the imaginary the primary role in forming the subject's desire, he conceptualizes narcissism as the model for desire. Desire emerges through the imaginary formation of the ego. In later seminars when the imaginary becomes more marginal, desire runs counter to ego identification.

17 For ego psychology, adaptation is the primary aim. This is a point that central thinker of ego psychology Heinz Hartman makes clear in *Ego Psychology and the Problem of Adaptation*. He writes, "Knowledge of reality must be subordinated to adaptation to reality." Heinz Hartmann, *Ego Psychology and the Problem of Adaptation*, trans. David Rapaport (Madison:

International Universities Press, 1958 [1939]), 66. In the formula of ego psychology, nothing outweighs adaptation because failing to adapt leads to the subject's suffering. For Lacan, however, adaptation is a fool's errand: It is neither achievable nor desirable because there is no substantial figure to which we might conform ourselves.

18 Jacques Lacan, *The Seminar of Jacques Lacan, Book II: The Ego in Freud's Theory and in the Technique of Psychoanalysis, 1954–1955*, ed. Jacques-Alain Miller, trans. Sylvana Tomaselli (New York: Norton, 1991 [1978]), 306.

19 Joan Copjec, Mari Ruti, Slavoj Žižek, and Alenka Zupančič almost never make reference to the imaginary, although they seldom go long without discussing the real. This evinces their theoretical commitment to the Lacan of the middle or, in some cases, late period. In contrast, Richard Boothby, for whom *Seminar VII* represents the crucial text, does give considerable attention to the imaginary register.

20 Jacques Lacan, *The Seminar of Jacques Lacan, Book II: The Ego in Freud's Theory and in the Technique of Psychoanalysis, 1954–1955*, ed. Jacques-Alain Miller, trans. Sylvana Tomaselli (New York: Norton, 1991 [1978]), 297.

21 Lacan's early conception of the real jibes with the old expression "Get real!" One says this to someone too caught up in self-image or symbolic status. The real that we tell this person to return to is a real that stays the same regardless of imaginary flights of fancy or symbolic pretensions.

22 In *Real Deceptions*, Jennifer Friedlander shows the distance between the real of the middle period and that of the early and late. Her definition of the real holds only for the middle Lacan because it emphasizes the dialectical relation between the real and the symbolic. She writes, "the Real is the *effect* of the constitutive failure of the symbolic to flawlessly render reality." Jennifer Friedlander, *Real Deceptions: The Contemporary Reinvention of Realism* (Oxford: Oxford University Press, 2017), 14. For Friedlander, one must think of the real through the symbolic failure, not as existing on a separate plane from the symbolic.

23 Jacques Lacan, *The Seminar of Jacques Lacan, Book I: Freud's Papers on Technique, 1953–1954*, ed. Jacques-Alain Miller, trans. John Forrester (New York: Norton, 1988 [1975]), 262.

24 Lacan's early theorization of the real as self-identical partakes in the philosophical common sense in France in the mid-twentieth century. Both Alexandre Kojève and Jean-Paul Sartre insist on a rigid distinction between the subject and being. For them, being is what it is – what Sartre calls the in-itself – and has no capacity for any negativity. The subject, in contrast, negates everything all the time. Lacan links subjectivity to the symbolic order in a way that Sartre doesn't, but his early conception of the real is Sartrean.

25 It is Lacan's early version of the real that Judith Butler argues with in *Bodies That Matter*, which sees that Lacan's theorization of the real as a realm external to the symbolic order can only occur within this symbolic order. The supposed outside emerges from the inside. Butler states, "To claim that the real resists symbolization is still to symbolize the real as a kind of resistance." Judith Butler, *Bodies That Matter: On the Discursive Limits of "Sex"* (New York: Routledge, 1993), 207. This line of argument represents an effective response to Lacan's early conception of the real. To theorize the real on a separate plane from that of the symbolic is to miss their dialectical interrelation. We must see how the real emerges out of the contradictions that the symbolic itself produces, which is the position that Lacan comes to in the middle period.

26 Despite earlier identifying the unconscious with the structure of language, in *Seminar XXII: R. S. I., 1973–1974*, Lacan links it to the real. He says, "The unconscious is the real." Jacques Lacan, *Le Séminaire, livre XXII: R. S. I., 1973–1974*, unpublished manuscript, session of April 15, 1975. Colette Soler considers this shift the most dramatic in Lacan's trajectory. See Colette Soler, *Lacan – The Unconscious Reinvented*, trans. Esther Faye and Susan Schwartz (London: Routledge, 2014 [2009]).

27 Jacques Lacan, *Le Séminaire, livre XXI: Les non-dupes errent, 1972–1973*, unpublished manuscript, session of February 12, 1974.

28 One can see this dynamic in the penultimate seminar. See Jacques Lacan, *Le Séminaire, livre XXVI: La topologie et le temps, 1978–1979*, unpublished manuscript.

29 As Lacan turns his focus to the Borromean knot, he simultaneously begins to privilege the matheme as the form through which psychoanalytic theory can be transmitted. Mathemes are mathematical formulas using variables and numerals to express theoretical insights. In *Seminar XX: Encore, 1972–1973*, he states, "Mathematical formalization is our goal, our ideal. Why? Because it alone is matheme, in other words, it alone is capable of being integrally transmitted."

Jacques Lacan, *The Seminar of Jacques Lacan, Book XX: Encore, 1972–1973*, ed. Jacques-Alain Miller, trans. Bruce Fink (New York: Norton, 1998 [1975]), 119. Lacan's investment in mathemes stems from his late belief that one can transmit ideas in a way that doesn't require a common symbolic order. The matheme, he wagers, bypasses the problem of desire, which is what it has in common with the Borromean knot.

30 The real makes its absence felt throughout Žižek's writings. But for his most detailed examination of it, see Slavoj Žižek, *The Puppet and the Dwarf: The Perverse Core of Christianity* (Cambridge, MA: MIT Press, 2003).

31 While he speaks constantly about the unconscious, Freud seldom uses the German term for desire (*Verlangen* or *Begierde*) but instead tends to refer to a wish (*Wunsch*). *Wunsch* can also signify *desire*, but it doesn't align wholly with the unconscious in Freud's writings. It has an ambiguous status in, say, the *Interpretation of Dreams*, where Freud discusses many conscious wishes that dreams fulfill, not just unconscious ones.

32 There is no reality for Lacan outside of our unconscious desire. He goes so far as to claim that "desire is the essence of reality." Jacques Lacan, *Le Séminaire, livre XIV: La logique du fantasme, 1966–1967*, ed. Jacques-Alain Miller (Paris: Seuil, 2023), 21. If we want to explore the nature of our reality, we cannot ignore the desire that animates it but must take its transformative effects into account.

33 Joan Copjec claims that theorizing the world through the lacking subject constitutes the major discovery of psychoanalysis. She writes, "One of psychoanalysis's deepest insights is that we are born not into an already constituted world that impinges on our senses to form perceptions, but in the wake of a primordial loss; it is not, then our relation to the *order of things*, but our relation to *das Ding* that decides the objectivity of our reality or its collapse." Joan Copjec, *Imagine There's No Woman: Ethics and Sublimation* (Cambridge, MA: MIT Press, 2002), 192. Objects are not just there to be perceived but appear through the negativity that the subject introduces. The subject doesn't belong to the world but always relates to it through what it doesn't have.

34 Jacques Lacan, *The Seminar of Jacques Lacan, Book I: Freud's Papers on Technique, 1953–1954*, ed. Jacques-Alain Miller, trans. John Forrester (New York: Norton, 1988 [1975]), 146.

35 Jacques Lacan, "Kant with Sade," *Écrits: The Complete Edition*, trans. Bruce Fink (New York: Norton, 2006 [1966]), 652–653.

36 Jacques Lacan, *The Seminar of Jacques Lacan, Book XI: The Four Fundamental Concepts of Psychoanalysis, 1963–1964*, ed. Jacques-Alain Miller, trans. Alan Sheridan (New York: Norton, 1978 [1973]), 176.

37 Perhaps more than any other theorist taking up Lacan's theory of desire, Mari Ruti locates singularity in the subject's desire. She contends, "we individuate ourselves through the specificity of our desire." Mari Ruti, *Distillations: Theory, Ethics, Affect* (New York: Bloomsbury, 2018), 188.

38 Thinking along these lines, Walter Davis once said to me, "We invent fascism out of our desire to capitulate." Walter Davis, private conversation.

39 As he theorizes desire, Lacan distinguishes unconscious desire from conscious wishes. No matter how much we reflect on our desire, we cannot bring unconscious desire to consciousness. It is never reducible to what we wish or will. Instead, unconscious desire disrupts the conscious plans of our will. The more we will a conscious aim, the more our unconscious desire subverts it. Unconscious desire satisfies itself through this subversion of the conscious will that allows it to repeat its trajectory, not from the attainment of any specific object.

40 For Kant, not only must we follow our duty without regard to the good, but we must heed it no matter how deleterious the consequences. Even if we end up hanged for doing our duty (as his example has it), we must do it.

41 Although this isn't the explicit aim of the book, Alenka Zupančič's *Ethics of the Real* brings Kantian morality and Lacanian ethics together by focusing on their shared formal structure. At times, this marriage forces Zupančič to criticize certain aspects of Kant's thought where they deviate too far from Lacan's claims. Where Kant rejects the possibility of diabolical evil – doing evil for evil's sake – Zupančič insists on it. See Alenka Zupančič, *Ethics of the Real: Kant, Lacan* (London: Verso, 2000).

42 Jacques Lacan, *The Seminar of Jacques Lacan, Book VII: The Ethics of Psychoanalysis, 1959–1960*, ed. Jacques-Alain Miller, trans. Dennis Porter (New York: Norton, 1992 [1986]), 319.

43 By not giving ground relative to one's desire and acceding to a symbolic death, one enters what Lacan in *Seminar VII* calls the zone between two deaths. This is a zone of freedom because it exists beyond the reach of any symbolic authority.

44 Darian Leader laments the slipperiness of the concept of jouissance, which leads him to advocate replacing it with multiple, more precise, concepts. In his book devoted to jouissance, strangely titled *Jouissance*, Leader writes, "out of all the Lacanian concepts, it is the one that is the least coherent and the least rigorous, despite the fact that it is taken to mark a level of sophistication that only advanced Lacanians can attain." Darian Leader, *Jouissance: Sexuality, Suffering and Satisfaction* (Cambridge: Polity, 2021), 132–133. Those who invoke the term *jouissance* think that they're being clever, but, according to Leader, they are really being obscurantists. There is much to be said for Leader's position.

45 Néstor Braunstein, "Desire and Jouissance in the Teachings of Lacan," *The Cambridge Companion to Lacan*, ed. Jean-Michel Rabaté (Cambridge: Cambridge University Press, 2003), 103.

46 To give an idea of how stark the contrast is between different periods of Lacan's thought, at one point he claims that there is only a jouissance of the body. At another time, he insists that jouissance occurs through the signifier, as what he calls *jouis-sens*. What's most troubling is that at no time in any of his writings or while giving his seminars did Lacan say that he had changed his understanding of the term.

47 We suffer our jouissance, but it gives a purpose to our existence. As Lacan puts it, "it is Jouissance whose absence would render the universe vain." Jacques Lacan, "The Subversion of the Subject and the Dialectic of Desire in the Freudian Unconscious," *Écrits: The First Complete Edition in English*, trans. Bruce Fink (New York: Norton, 2006 [1966]), 694.

48 Jacques-Alain Miller, "Paradigms of *Jouissance*," trans. Jorge Jauregui, *Lacanian Ink* 17 (2000): 18. Miller finds a total of six different paradigms of jouissance operative at one point or another. It is in the second paradigm of jouissance, according to Miller, that Lacan makes the link between the phallus and jouissance.

49 Miller, "Paradigms of *Jouissance*," 23.

50 There are some followers of Lacan who contend that the conception of jouissance from *Seminar VII* is one that Lacan never abandons. For them, the association of jouissance with transgression becomes the last word on how Lacan theorizes it. This is not my position.

51 Slavoj Žižek, *The Fragile Absolute, or, Why Is the Christian Legacy Worth Fighting For?* (London: Verso, 2000), 150, 152.

52 Although the middle Lacan's conception of jouissance was likely not at the fore of her thinking when she titled her book, bell hooks' *Feminist Theory: From Margin to Center* nicely captures the path that jouissance takes after Lacan stops associating it with the phallus and turns to what doesn't fit.

53 Alenka Zupančič, *What IS Sex?* (Cambridge, MA: MIT Press, 2017), 117.

54 Lacan's term in French for this surplus is *plus-de-jouir*. In some translations of the later seminars, *plus-de-jouir* becomes *surplus jouissance* in English. When one commits to translating *jouissance* as *jouissance*, this is what one gets: the absurdity of using a French word in English to convey a different (albeit related) word from the French.

55 While commenting on Strachey's English translation, Lacan states that "*Trieb* and *instinct* have nothing in common." Jacques Lacan, *The Seminar of Jacques Lacan, Book XI: The Four Fundamental Concepts of Psychoanalysis, 1963–1964*, ed. Jacques-Alain Miller, trans. Alan Sheridan (New York: Norton, 1978 [1973]), 49. This mistranslation into English has historically played an important part in the reduction of Freud to a biological thinker, which makes it easier to claim that his ideas are out of date or even just wrongheaded about the body.

56 In *Seminar XI*, Lacan stresses the distance between the satisfaction of the drive and the satisfaction of a biological instinct for reproduction. He states, "If the drive may be satisfied without attaining what, from the point of view of a biological totalization of function, would be the satisfaction of reproduction, it is because it is a partial drive, and its aim is simply this return into circuit." Lacan, *Seminar XI*, 179. The drive repeats its circuit with a constant force.

57 Although Freud always claims to espouse a dualistic theory of the drive, he actually takes a dialectical approach. When he opposes the death drive to Eros after 1920, the dialectic of the drive becomes evident through the priority that the death drive has over Eros. Eros emerges as an interruption of the death drive, as a countervailing tendency that ultimately serves the more fundamental death drive. They are not simply two opposing forces in Freud's theory, despite what Freud himself claims.

58 This image of a struggle between Eros and the death drive is how Freud concludes *Civilization and Its Discontents*. He writes, "Men have gained control over the forces of nature to such an extent

that with their help they would have no difficulty in exterminating one another to the last man. They know this, and hence comes a large part of their current unrest, their unhappiness and their mood of anxiety. And now it is to be expected that the other of the two 'Heavenly Powers,' eternal Eros, will make an effort to assert himself in the struggle with his equally immortal adversary. But who can foresee with what success and with what result?" Sigmund Freud, *Civilization and Its Discontents*, trans. James Strachey, in *The Standard Edition of the Complete Psychological Works of Sigmund Freud*, ed. James Strachey, vol. 21 (London: Hogarth, 1961 [1930]), 145.

59 One can refer to an orgasm in French as *la petite mort*, which would be the "little death" in English. Despite the obvious link here between libidinal discharge and death, this term misleads us about the role that the death drive plays in our sexuality. The death drive doesn't manifest itself in the big finish but in the various sexual tensions that we create leading up to *la petite mort*.

60 The recognition that there is only a singular drive is one of Lacan's most important recognitions. When he discovers this, he doesn't move beyond Freud but sees the logic at work in psychoanalytic thinking that Freud himself doesn't recognize. The reduction of the libido to the death drive marks the triumph of dialectic over dualism. In Lacan's essay "The Position of the Unconscious," he writes, "every drive is virtually a death drive." Jacques Lacan, "The Position of the Unconscious," *Écrits: The First Complete Edition in English*, trans. Bruce Fink (New York: Norton, 2006 [1966]), 719. Lacan doesn't talk so much about the libido because he recognizes the death drive at the base of it.

61 Between *Seminar II* and *Seminar XI*, Lacan takes a brief detour in his thinking about the drive. After identifying the death drive with the signifier in the early seminars, Lacan reconceptualizes it in *Seminar VII: The Ethics of Psychoanalysis*, a reconceptualization that he would never return to, making the understanding of the death drive in this seminar, like so much in it, a one-off. The idea of the death drive in *Seminar VII* functions as a point of transition from his early position to his mature one. In this seminar, the death drive becomes an impulse toward total destruction, but this total destruction also is complete rebirth. As Lacan puts it, "If everything that is immanent or implicit in the chain of natural events may be considered as subject to the so-called death drive, it is only because there is a signifying chain. Freud's thought in this matter requires that what is involved be articulated as a destruction drive, given that it challenges everything that exists. But it is also a will to create from zero, a will to begin again." Jacques Lacan, *The Seminar of Jacques Lacan, Book VII: The Ethics of Psychoanalysis, 1959–1960*, ed. Jacques-Alain Miller, trans. Dennis Porter (New York: Norton, 1992 [1986]), 212. Destructiveness is at once creativity. It goes beyond the signifier, and yet it depends on signification. By laying things out in this way, Lacan opens up the path to a recognition that the death drive takes the subject beyond the symbolic realm, which he develops in *Seminar XI*.

62 Alenka Zupančič has a unique way of thinking about the relationship between desire and drive that avoids conceiving of them as opposed. As she writes in *Ethics of the Real*, "In order to arrive at the drive, one must pass through desire and insist on it until the very end." Alenka Zupančič, *Ethics of the Real: Kant, Lacan* (London: Verso, 2000), 239. Zupančič develops an ethics of desire that has a place for the drive as the result of insisting on one's desire. In this way, Zupančič bridges the divide between the Lacan who champions desire and the Lacan who sides with the drive.

63 Martin Heidegger did not have a decisive influence on Lacan's thought. But Heidegger's conception of the they (or *das Man*) anticipates Lacan's theorization of the big Other. For Heidegger, the they is a social force that demands conformity from everyone. It strips people of the existential burden by offering a route to identify with the collective. One of the terrible ironies of the history of Western philosophy is that the theorist of the they devoted himself enthusiastically to one of the most conformist ideologies in human history. Heidegger's allegiance to Nazism marks a betrayal of his critique of the they.

64 Jacques Lacan, *The Seminar of Jacques Lacan, Book VI: Desire and Its Interpretation, 1958–1959*, ed. Jacques-Alain Miller, trans. Bruce Fink (Cambridge: Polity, 2019 [2013]), 33.

65 Although the big Other has a symbolic status, it is not simply reducible to the symbolic order, which is why we should be wary of using them interchangeably as synonyms. It's important to maintain the distinction between the two concepts, even though some people writing on Lacan do not. The symbolic order gives the subject a field of signification, while the big Other slants this field in a particular direction. The big Other tilts the symbolic order in the direction of its authority, but there is no possibility for a neutral form of the symbolic order, one without the tilt that the big Other introduces. The deviation of this tilt creates the space for subjectivity.

66 Jacques Lacan, *Le Séminaire, livre XIV: La logique du fantasme, 1966–1967*, ed. Jacques-Alain Miller (Paris: Seuil, 2023), 151.

67 Molly Rothenberg describes psychoanalysis as a process through which the subject breaks the psychic hold that the big Other has on it. This hold exists through the role that it plays in the subject's fantasy. According to Rothenberg's description of psychoanalysis, "Its purpose is to help the subject recognize and work through its own idiosyncratic fantasy that someone, some Other, knows the truth about the world and the subject, and for that reason deserves to be in a position of mastery." Molly Anne Rothenberg, *The Excessive Subject: A New Theory of Social Change* (Cambridge: Polity, 2010), 149. Once one works through this process, mastery loses its appeal. It's not that one sees that the emperor has no clothes. The emperor wears clothes, but the subject recognizes itself as the weaver of those clothes.

68 The greatness of *Heathers* consists in both its unrelenting depiction of the oppressiveness of the big Other and the vision of an alternative that it offers. The film ends with Veronica (Winona Ryder) instituting a new regime at Westerburg High School, a regime that reaches out to those the big Other ostracizes. It is not a vision in which the big Other disappears, but one in which its insubstantiality becomes foregrounded.

69 According to Lacan, the infant doesn't start out experiencing its own omnipotence and subsequently modifying its expectations when it confronts the external world. Instead, it initially invests itself in the omnipotence of the parental big Other and later transfers this belief in omnipotence to a big Other operating as a social authority. In *Seminar IV: The Object Relation, 1957–1958*, he says, "the structure of almightiness, contrary to what people believe, lies not in the subject but in the mother, that is, in the primal Other. The Other is the one who is almighty." Jacques Lacan, *The Seminar of Jacques Lacan, Book IV: The Object Relation, 1957–1958*, ed. Jacques-Alain Miller, trans. A. R. Price (Cambridge: Polity, 2020 [1994]), 161. As it becomes socialized, the child swaps one big Other for another. The conflicts that occur during this process involve the competition between these two authorities much more than the child's reluctance to conform. It's a question of which authority will win the subject's adherence.

70 It is the lasting merit of the television series *The Sopranos* that it displays so clearly the obedience to the big Other at work in the criminality of the participants in organized crime. Tony Soprano (James Gandolfini) wants everything that the contemporary capitalist big Other tells him to want. His violations of the law hide his obedience to the big Other.

71 The absence of widespread picture dictionaries tells us something about the symbolic order, especially about the relationship between the signifier and the signified. We tend to think of the signified as the mental image or picture that corresponds to the signifier, but we actually determine signification through the relationship that signifiers have with each other. The unpopularity of the picture dictionary relative to the traditional one provides evidence for the correctness of the latter theory.

72 Tautology is often immediately evident when one looks up a definition. For instance, one discovers that *human* is what has to do with humanity, or something similarly helpful.

73 The Name-of-the-Father is most evident in countries where a single party dominates, but this doesn't mean that it is any less determinative in multiparty democracies. Capitalism appears to do away with the Name-of-the-Father as it violates all prohibitions and allows people to give in to their most rapacious impulses. But there is no society possible without some founding metaphorical signifier. The most predatory society still depends on some fundamental prohibition.

74 Lacan comes to believe that there are multiple master signifiers, of which the Name-of-the-Father is one. This is evident in one of the only statements that he makes concerning the two concepts, which occurs in *Seminar XVIII: On a Discourse That Would Not Be a Semblance, 1970–1971*. He states, "the master signifier of analytic discourse up to the present is the Name-of-the-Father." Jacques Lacan, *Le Séminaire, livre XVIII: D'un discours qui ne serait pas du semblant, 1970–1971*, ed. Jacques-Alain Miller (Paris: Seuil, 2006), 173. This might be the only case where the term that Lacan comes to in the late period, *master signifier*, captures the structure better than the earlier term because it explains structures not centered around masculine authority. For this reason, we should privilege *master signifier* and S_1 over *Name-of-the-Father* and *paternal metaphor*.

75 Shifting the figure of prohibition from an actual person to a signifier frees Lacan from the heterosexual model that operates in Freud's theory. Although Freud doesn't endorse this model

of the family and even recognizes it as a problem – he is not a heteronormative thinker – it is the point of departure for Freud's theorizing. Once Lacan turns from the father to the Name-of-the-Father, from the person to the signifier, the link to the traditional family structure dissipates. This delinking becomes more apparent when he adopts the terms *master signifier* and S_1 in lieu of *Name-of-the-Father* and *paternal metaphor*.

76 One can see a clear connection between Lacan's grasp of the nonsensical status of the Name-of-the-Father and Hegel's belief in the purely formal status of the monarch. In the *Philosophy of Right*, Hegel contends that the monarch doesn't provide any guidance for the state but just plays the structurally necessary role of "someone to say 'yes' and to dot the 'I.'" G. W. F. Hegel, *Elements of the Philosophy of Right*, ed. Allen W. Wood, trans. H. B. Nisbet (Cambridge: Cambridge University Press, 1991 [1820]), 323. Because the monarch is purely formal, Hegel believes that stupidity in the monarch is a virtue rather than a vice. Lacan never alludes to Hegel when discussing the Name-of-the-Father, but Hegel's monarch lies in the theoretical background of this concept.

77 Jacques Lacan, *The Seminar of Jacques Lacan, Book V: Formations of the Unconscious, 1957–1958*, ed. Jacques-Alain Miller, trans. Russell Grigg (Cambridge: Polity, 2017 [1998]), 132.

78 One of the great feminist insights of psychoanalysis consists in its separation of the impossibility of desire from the prohibition enacted by the Name-of-the-Father. The prohibition always occurs subsequent to the impossibility, which means that patriarchy cannot have an ontological – or even a historical – priority.

79 Jacques Lacan, *Le Séminaire, livre XXI: Les non-dupes errent, 1972–1973*, unpublished manuscript, session of December 11, 1973.

80 "The Signification of the Phallus" stands out as the only one of the *Écrits* that Lacan wrote in German.

81 The phallic signifier signifies the possibility of meaning. As Lacan puts it in "The Signification of the Phallus," "For the phallus is a signifier, a signifier whose function, in the intrasubjective economy of analysis, may lift the veil from the function it served in the mysteries. For it is the signifier that is destined to designate meaning effects as a whole, insofar as the signifier conditions them by its presence as signifier." Jacques Lacan, "The Signification of the Phallus," *Écrits: The First Complete Edition in English*, trans. Bruce Fink (New York: Norton, 2006 [1966]), 579. Lacan formulates this same idea more concisely in *Seminar V*, where he states that the phallus is "the signifier of the signified in general." Jacques Lacan, *The Seminar of Jacques Lacan, Book V: Formations of the Unconscious*, ed. Jacques-Alain Miller, trans. Russell Grigg (Cambridge: Polity, 2017 [1998]), 240. The contrast between these two statements nicely illustrates the obfuscation at work in Lacan's written essays and the relative clarity of the seminars.

82 Jennifer Friedlander, *Feminine Look: Sexuation, Spectatorship, Subversion* (Albany: SUNY Press, 2008), 64.

83 I have modified this joke from a classic one among psychoanalysts about Freud.

84 There are many feminists who take this psychoanalytic insight as a central tenet of their feminism. The list includes Joan Copjec, Jennifer Friedlander, Hilary Neroni, Jacqueline Rose, Mari Ruti, and Alenka Zupančič, among others.

85 Sigmund Freud, *An Outline of Psychoanalysis*, trans. James Strachey, in *The Standard Edition of the Complete Psychological Works of Sigmund Freud*, vol. 23, ed. James Strachey (London: Hogarth Press, 1964 [1938]), 192–193.

86 During his early seminars and writings, Lacan distinguishes between the symbolic and imaginary phallus. While the symbolic phallus is a signifier, the imaginary phallus is what the subject loses in the process of symbolic castration. Lacan points out the child learns sexual distinctiveness not through the real presence or absence of the penis but through its relation to the imaginary phallus. He states, "this is certain not to be gathered, in any case whatsoever, from anything that originates in any physiological leaning of either of the two sexes. One has to start with the existence of an imaginary phallus." Jacques Lacan, *The Seminar of Jacques Lacan, Book IV: The Object Relation, 1956–1957*, ed. Jacques-Alain Miller, trans. A. R. Price (Cambridge: Polity, 2020 [1994]), 182. The imaginary phallus is what the child believes that it has lost and what the parents appear to have.

87 The distinction between the Name-of-the-Father and the phallic signifier has its basis in the exceptional status of the former and the role of the latter as the signifier of all signification. The Name-of-the-Father is a signifier without a signified, a signifier that signifies only itself, whereas the phallic signifier signifies the entire field of signifieds. The former lacks signification, and the

latter has an excess of signification. In Lorenzo Chiesa's terms, this is a difference "between the Name-of-the-Father as the signifier of signifiers and the phallus as the signifier of signifieds as such." Lorenzo Chiesa, *Subjectivity and Otherness: A Philosophical Reading of Lacan* (Cambridge, MA: MIT Press, 2007), 100. As Chiesa sees it, this is the view that Lacan arrives at in the late 1950s, but soon thereafter, he recognizes that this position is no longer theoretically tenable and begins to merge the Name-of-the-Father with the phallic signifier, so that there ceases to be a distinction between them from the 1960s onward. For the middle and the late Lacan, the phallic signifier is the Name-of-the-Father. The signifier that signifies itself also signifies all signifieds.

88 Jacqueline Rose translates "The Signification of the Phallus" as "The Meaning of the Phallus." The title in German is "Die Bedeutung des Phallus."

89 Alenka Zupančič, *The Odd One In: On Comedy* (Cambridge, MA: MIT Press, 2008), 205.

90 The fact that Fink would introduce a new English term for the *point de capiton* indicates how inessential this concept seemed to people engaging with Lacan's philosophy. If it were considered a central concept, a translator would not hazard an alternative, especially when the original was already accurate.

91 The quilting point reveals a difference between Lacan's thought and Derrida's. For Lacan, the quilting point is necessary for signification to function in a nonpsychotic way. Derrida, in contrast, views the quilting point as a theoretical abridgment of the openness of signification.

92 In Saussure's most famous statement about the structure of language, he indirectly evinces his belief that signifiers and signifieds are intrinsically coupled with each other. He states, "in language there are only differences. Even more important: a difference generally implies positive terms between which the difference is set up; but in language there are only differences *without positive terms*. Whether we take the signified or the signifier, language has neither ideas nor sounds that existed before the linguistic system, but only conceptual and phonic differences that have issued from the system." Ferdinand de Saussure, *Course in General Linguistics*, ed. Charles Bally and Albert Sechehaye, trans. Wade Baskin (New York: Philosophical Library, 1959 [1915]), 120. Saussure's insistence that language is a system of pure differences is what almost everyone retains from this passage. Lacan accepts this claim but rejects the subsequent implication that the signifier and signified are bonded together. For him, their relationship must constantly be forged and always threatens to break apart, as we see happening in the case of the psychotic.

93 Jacques Lacan, *The Seminar of Jacques Lacan, Book III: The Psychoses, 1955–1956*, trans. Russell Grigg, ed. Jacques-Alain Miller (New York: Norton, 1993 [1981]), 261.

94 As Lacan explains it in *Seminar III*, introducing a quilting point has the effect of replacing a series of fears with one central fear. Rather than fearing disparate threats, one fears only the father. In the example that he gives from Jean Racine's play *Athalie* (1691), the quilting point transforms all random fears to the fear of God. Lacan states, "This famous fear of God completes the sleight of hand that transforms, from one minute to the next, all fears into perfect courage. All fears – *I have no other fear* – are exchanged for what is called the fear of God, which, however constraining it may be, is the opposite of a fear." Lacan, *Seminar III*, 267. The turn to the quilting point doesn't just change what we fear. It can, as in this case, deliver us from fear.

95 To be sure, Lacan invented the short session for solid theoretical reasons. But he subsequently abused the practice with his analysands. Often, Lacan would stop sessions after only a couple of minutes while still charging the analysands full price. This enabled him to see tens of analysands per hour, when other psychoanalysts restricted themselves to one. It's safe to say that this aided his financial situation much more than the psyche of any of his analysands.

96 Jacques Lacan, "The Field and Function of Speech and Language in Psychoanalysis," *Écrits: The First Complete Edition in English*, trans. Bruce Fink (New York: Norton, 2006 [1966]), 259.

97 Slavoj Žižek, *For They Know Not What They Do: Enjoyment as a Political Factor* (London: Verso, 1991), 18.

98 See Sigmund Freud, *Project for a Scientific Psychology*, trans. James Strachey, in *The Complete Psychological Works of Sigmund Freud*, vol. 1, ed. James Strachey (London: Hogarth Press, 1966), 281–397; and Martin Heidegger, "The Thing," in *Poetry, Language, Thought*, trans. Albert Hofstader (New York: Harper & Row, 1975 [1971]), 163–180.

99 Lacan points out that the overvaluation of the figure of the Lady in courtly love has nothing at all to do with a feminist sense of equality for women. Courtly love coexisted with a system of oppression that devalued women in the social order.

100 In *Imagine There's No Woman*, Joan Copjec provides a succinct formulation of the contrast between Freud and Lacan on sublimation. She writes, "sublimation is not something that happens to the drive under special circumstances; it is the proper destiny of the drive." Joan Copjec, *Imagine There's No Woman: Ethics and Sublimation* (Cambridge, MA: MIT Press, 2002), 30. Lacan recognizes that the deviation that sublimation introduces is what makes objects desirable in the first place.

101 Jacques Lacan, *The Seminar of Jacques Lacan, Book VII: The Ethics of Psychoanalysis, 1959–1960*, ed. Jacques-Alain Miller, trans. Dennis Porter (New York: Norton, 1992 [1986]), 112.

102 Although much has been written on Lacan and the term *extimacy*, he uses it only a few times. This occurs primarily in *Seminar VII* during Lacan's discussion of courtly love.

103 Some thinkers who follow Lacan deemphasize the contrast between *das Ding* and the *objet a*. Lorenzo Chiesa claims that Lacan sustains the distinction between *das Ding* and the *objet a* for only a brief period. After the introduction of *das Ding* in *Seminar VII*, the two concepts blend together. Chiesa notes, "the distinction between the Thing and the object *a* holds only in Seminar VII." Lorenzo Chiesa, *Subjectivity and Otherness: A Philosophical Reading of Lacan* (Cambridge, MA: MIT Press, 2007), 132. While many interpreters insist on the importance of this distinction, Chiesa's inclination to merge Lacan's objects is not without theoretical justification. Both objects play a similar role relative to the subject's desire, which is undoubtedly why Chiesa links them. For his part, Daniel Cho argues that there is an error in seeing the two "as separate concepts." He states, "*objet a* [is] the schematization or formalization of *das Ding*." Daniel Cho, private communication, 30 January 2020. The problem with the claims of Chiesa and Cho is that Lacan himself discusses the two concepts in relation to each other in *Seminar XVI: From an Other to the other, 1968–1969*.

104 Jacques Lacan, *The Seminar of Jacques Lacan, Book XVI: From an Other to the other, 1968–1969*, ed. Jacques-Alain Miller, trans. Bruce Fink (Cambridge: Polity, 2024 [2006]), 201.

105 As Boothby sees it, religious difference comes down to our distinct relationships to what we don't know. He says, "religion can be defined as the culturally-mediated relation to the unknown beyond that Lacan has called *das Ding*." Richard Boothby, *Embracing the Void: Rethinking the Origin of the Sacred* (Evanston, IL: Northwestern University Press, 2022), 103. There is a commonality among all religions that lies in what exceeds their grasp.

106 For Ruti, our ethical being depends on our relationship to the Thing. When we listen to what she describes as the call of character, "we can learn to distinguish between things that transmit the echo of the Thing and those that do not." Mari Ruti, *The Call of Character: Living a Life Worth Living* (New York: Columbia University Press, 2014), 162. Our desire oriented around *das Ding* is, as Ruti sees it, opposed to the desire of the Other that immerses us in banal things.

107 Jacques Lacan, *Le Séminaire, livre XXI: Les non-dupes errent, 1973–1974*, unpublished manuscript, session of April 9, 1974.

108 In his book on the *objet a*, Juan-Pablo Lucchelli insists on the priority of the absent *objet a* to the present object of desire (and to all the objects in the visual field). He says, "The cause of vision is not the object seen but instead what pushes the subject to see." Juan Pablo Lucchelli, *Introduction à l'objet a de Lacan* (Paris: Éditions Michèle, 2020), 228. What pushes me to see is the *objet a*, the object nowhere visible as an object. What we can't see drives us to look.

109 If someone doesn't take the time to wrap a present, we rightly see this as an indication this person doesn't care about the recipient of the gift. It is tempting to argue that wrapping without a gift inside evinces more care than an unwrapped gift, although it's possible that a child would dispute this conclusion on Christmas morning.

110 One could also say that the *objet a*, in the terms of Sheila Kunkle, "reveals in a traumatic way how our subjectivity is split." Sheila Kunkle, "Introduction: On the Subject of Endings," in *Cinematic Cuts: Theorizing Film Endings*, ed. Sheila Kunkle (Albany: SUNY Press, 2016), 8. As the distortion of the *objet a* makes itself manifest, the division of the subject appears externally.

111 Kojève believes that the desire for recognition is Hegel's solution to the riddle of history, but it is actually Kojève's solution that he imputes to Hegel. For Hegel, the desire for recognition always fails and points beyond itself. In Kojève's view, we can achieve recognition and satisfy our only desire. In his lectures on the *Phenomenology of Spirit*, he claims, "it is the first and the only human Desire, the desire for recognition." Alexandre Kojève, *Introduction à la lecture de Hegel*, ed. Raymond Queneau (Paris: Gallimard, 1947), 126. The invention of the *objet a* allows Lacan to

conceptualize desire in terms beyond recognition – closer to Hegel than to Kojève, although Lacan himself could not see any difference between the two.

112 Guy Le Gaufey notes the difficulty of pinning down the exact moment when Lacan invents the *objet a*, even though we can be sure that it is an invention of the middle period. In the early period, Lacan uses the small *a* to refer to the imaginary other, and then in *Seminar VIII*, the first seminar of the middle period, he uses the term *ágalma* to indicate an object that resembles what will become the *objet a*. As Le Gaufey points out, "the term *objet a* is never encountered, with the value and signification that we give it today, before the beginning of the 1960s. And contrary to Lacan's other inventions or discoveries, it is not easy to date this appearance in a clear and simple fashion." Guy Le Gaufey, *L'objet a: Approches de l'invention de Lacan* (Paris: Epel, 2012), 13.

113 Whenever Lacan describes the *objet a*, he emphasizes its irreducibility to what the subject can perceive. We can't represent it because it creates the possibility of representation. As Lacan puts it in *Seminar XIII: The Object of Psychoanalysis, 1965–1966*, "the *objet a is* there, in that space of the hole that is properly, let us say representable, properly in the sense that it is never represented." Jacques Lacan, *Le Séminaire, livre XIII: L'objet de la psychanalyse, 1965–1966*, unpublished manuscript, session of June 1, 1966.

114 Mladen Dolar points out the excessive status of the voice relative to what the Other demands. It is the form of enjoyment in the demand that outstrips its content. He writes, "The voice is the excess of the signifier, initially displayed as the excess of the demand of the Other, the demand beyond any particular demands, demand as such." Mladen Dolar, *A Voice and Nothing More* (Cambridge, MA: MIT Press, 2006), 81. This excess in every demand is what compels our obedience.

115 In *Read My Desire*, Joan Copjec addresses the deformation of the gaze that occurs with psychoanalytic film theory. She claims that "film theory operated a kind of 'Foucauldinization' of Lacanian theory." Joan Copjec, *Read My Desire: Lacan Against the Historicists* (Cambridge, MA: MIT Press, 1994), 19. The interpretation of the gaze in the terms of mastery has the effect of eliminating its fundamental disruptiveness.

116 The distinction between look and gaze was not available to Lacan, so he didn't employ it. French has only a single term, *le regard*, for the two terms in English. This is a case where the translation into a second language offers the opportunity for greater conceptual precision. Unfortunately, what we got instead was conceptual confusion.

117 For Foucault, power in the modern world works through making those it controls visible. Beginning with this idea, Foucault theorizes the concentration camp as the structural paradigm for this world. In the camp, everything that one does is seen. In *Discipline and Punish*, Foucault writes, "The camp is the diagram of a power that acts by means of general visibility." Michel Foucault, *Discipline and Punish: The Birth of the Prison*, trans. Alan Sheridan (New York: Vintage, 1979 [1975]), 171. Lacan's conception of the gaze, in contrast, concerns the invisible, not what looks on the visual field but what is subtracted from it.

118 Jacques Lacan, *The Seminar of Jacques Lacan, Book XI: The Four Fundamental Concepts of Psychoanalysis, 1963–1964*, ed. Jacques-Alain Miller, trans. Alan Sheridan (New York: Norton, 1978 [1973]), 96 (translation corrected).

119 It is tempting to postulate that the entire misapprehension of the gaze perpetuated in film theory resulted from this mistranslation. But alas, the gaze became a concept in film theory before Alan Sheridan published the mistranslation of this sentence from *Seminar XI*. We have to find someone else to blame.

120 Lacan links the development of perspective painting to the emergence of anamorphic tricks within the painting. As Guy Le Gaufey points out in his discussion of the *objet a*, "Anamorphoses are monsters *engendered* by the technique of perspective." Guy Le Gaufey, *L'objet a: Approches de l'invention de Lacan* (Paris: Epel, 2012), 160. The attempt to paint from the perspective of the looking subject leads directly to the introduction of the gaze as a disruption of the visual field.

121 When Lacan talks about *Las Meninas* in his thirteenth seminar, Foucault attends. But at the session where Lacan plans to give his interpretation of the painting, Foucault doesn't show up, which disappoints Lacan, who expresses the wish to present his ideas to Foucault. Despite directly undermining Foucault's interpretation, Lacan presents his analysis as complementing that of Foucault, which is probably why he thinks it will go over well with the latter.

122 Richard Boothby, *Freud as Philosopher: Metapsychology after Lacan* (New York: Routledge, 2001), 275.

123 Slavoj Žižek, *The Parallax View* (Cambridge, MA: MIT Press, 2006), 40. Because of the role that fantasy plays in providing a map for how to relate desire to the world of objects, it must be operative from the beginning. It is not as if we first desire and then subsequently create a fantasy to solve the problem of desire. The fantasy solution brings the problem of desire into existence. Or, as Žižek puts it in an earlier work, "It is only through fantasy that the subject is constituted as desiring: *through fantasy, we learn how to desire.*" Slavoj Žižek, *Looking Awry: An Introduction to Jacques Lacan through Popular Culture* (Cambridge, MA: MIT Press, 1991), 6. The way that fantasy retreats from desire teaches the subject how to desire in the first place.

124 Jacques Lacan, *The Seminar of Jacques Lacan, Book VI: Desire and Its Interpretation, 1958–1959*, ed. Jacques-Alain Miller, trans. Bruce Fink (Cambridge: Polity, 2019 [2013]), 19.

125 The absence of any reference to the real in the early theory of fantasy becomes clearest in *Seminar V: Formations of the Unconscious, 1957–1958*, where Lacan defines fantasy in terms of the relationship between the imaginary and the symbolic. In *Seminar V*, he states, "Fantasy is essentially an imaginary embedded in a particular signifying function." Jacques Lacan, *The Seminar of Jacques Lacan, Book V: Formations of the Unconscious, 1957–1958*, ed. Jacques-Alain Miller, trans. Russell Grigg (Cambridge: Polity, 2017 [1998]), 388. Here, fantasy is simply the way that an image acquires the symbolic form of a narrative.

126 In *Seminar VI*, Lacan leaves no doubt that he uses the letter *a*, which will later become the *objet a* of the real, to indicate an imaginary entity. He states that in "the formula of fantasy . . . the subject appears elided in it. It is not him, inasmuch as there is another there, an imaginary other, little *a*." Lacan, *Seminar VI*, 167. The fact that the *a* here appears in apposition to the imaginary other should not be surprising because it indicates Lacan's thinking at the time. In a couple of years, it would change completely. He would come to designate the imaginary other as i(a) to contrast it with the *objet a*.

127 As Juan-David Nasio points out, "the motor of fantasy is a core of enjoyment around which is organized the fantasmatic staging." Juan-David Nasio, *Le Fantasme: Le plaisir de lire Lacan* (Paris: Petite Bibliothèque Payot, 2005), 44.

128 Jacques Lacan, *The Seminar of Jacques Lacan, Book XI: The Four Fundamental Concepts of Psychoanalysis, 1963–1964*, ed. Jacques-Alain Miller, trans. Alan Sheridan (New York: Norton, 1978 [1973]), 273.

129 Boothby, *Freud as Philosopher*, 275–276.

130 Because she recognizes the role that fantasy plays in opening up the avenues to new possibilities, Molly Rothenberg claims, "the *politics* of social change is irremediably fantasmatic." Molly Anne Rothenberg, *The Excessive Subject: A New Theory of Social Change* (Cambridge: Polity, 2010), 206. As Rothenberg further notes, social change depends on adopting a position on fantasy that ceases to identify the other with the enjoyment that should rightfully be ours.

131 Lacan's conception of the hysteric's discourse leads him to dismiss the possibility of radical political action leading to an egalitarian social arrangement. The view is evident in his critique of the student revolt in the late 1960s in Paris as the expression of the desire for a new master. Lacan gave a talk to the students at the Université de Paris VIII (Vincennes) on December 3, 1969, during the middle of the seminar where he theorizes the four discourses. He concludes this talk with a prediction of the failure of their revolt, as he says to them, "the revolutionary aspiration has only a single possible outcome – of ending up as the master's discourse . . . What you aspire to as revolutionaries is a master. You will get one." Jacques Lacan, "Analyticon," in *The Seminar of Jacques Lacan, Book XVII: The Other Side of Psychoanalysis, 1969–1970*, ed. Jacques-Alain Miller, trans. Russell Grigg (New York: Norton, 2007 [1991]), 207. Despite his association with many egalitarian theorists and activists, Lacan believes that only psychoanalytic practice, performed with individual subjects, can break the hold of mastery. This position becomes more ensconced in his theorizing after the turn to the four discourses. The timing of the speech at Vincennes is not coincidental.

132 In his early seminars prior to the invention of the *objet a*, Lacan views the task of the psychoanalyst as that of taking up the position of the big Other. In this earlier theory, the primary danger in analysis is imaginary identification with the analyst, an identification that adopting the symbolic position of the big Other helps to thwart. When he changes his mind and associates the analyst with the *objet a*, Lacan comes to see the big Other as a trap for the subject and focuses on the real point at which the big Other fails. This is the theoretical position that Lacan has when he develops the four discourses in *Seminar XVII*.

133 Jacques Lacan, *The Seminar of Jacques Lacan, Book XVII, 1969–1970: The Other Side of Psychoanalysis*, ed. Jacques-Alain Miller, trans. Russell Grigg (New York: Norton, 2007 [1991]), 176.

134 Molly Rothenberg points out that the knowledge that one acquires in psychoanalysis is distinct from ordinary knowledge. She writes, "Only in the fourth discourse, the discourse of the Analyst, does the subject acquire a knowledge (by the signifiers produced in the analysis) that tells the truth about the impossible of *objet a* and the uniqueness of the master-signifier that governs the subject's life." Molly Anne Rothenberg, *The Excessive Subject: A New Theory of Social Change* (Cambridge: Polity, 2010), 149. By paying attention to the *objet a*, analysis opens up a path out of mastery.

135 For Lacan's theorization of the capitalist discourse, see Jacques Lacan, "Du discours psychanalytique," in *Lacan en Italie 1953–1978*, ed. Giacomo B. Contri (Milan: La Salamandra, 1972), 27–39.

136 Levi Bryant takes Lacan's theory of the four discourses to its end point, multiplying the discourses in ways that Lacan could not have foreseen but nonetheless makes possible. Bryant envisions a discourse of biopower and a discourse of immaterial production, to name just two of the multitude he identifies. Although Bryant's new discursive formulations never caught on, they represent the danger of multiplicity gone amok that results from the abandonment of the focus on a single contradictory structure. See Levi Bryant, "Žižek's New Universe of Discourse: Politics and the Discourse of the Capitalist," *International Journal of Žižek Studies* 2.4 (2008): https://zizekstudies.org/index.php/IJZS/article/view/141/216.

137 Samo Tomšič makes the ultimately compelling claim that the capitalist discourse "is not a fifth discourse – it is a fake discourse." Samo Tomšič, *The Capitalist Unconscious: Marx and Lacan* (London: Verso, 2016), 221. This explains why Lacan articulates it only on an ad hoc basis and not at the same time that he develops the four primary discourses.

138 Jacques Lacan, *The Seminar of Jacques Lacan, Book XIX: . . . or Worse, 1971–1972*, ed. Jacques-Alain Miller, trans. A. R. Price (Cambridge: Polity, 2018 [2011]), 4.

139 Lacan's first statement about the sexual nonrelation occurs in his *Seminar XVIII: Of a Discourse That Would Not Be a Semblance, 1970–1971*. Here, he insists on "the non-existence of the sexual relation." Jacques Lacan, *Le Séminaire, livre XVIII: D'un discours qui ne serait pas du semblant, 1970–1971*, ed. Jacques-Alain Miller (Paris: Seuil, 2006), 74.

140 Lacan's formulas of sexuation are the most controversial part of his doctrine. Even a devoted Lacanian thinker such as Darian Leader finds the formulas a complex way for Lacan to articulate commonplaces concerning sexual difference. In *Jouissance*, he says, "there is surely a hypnotic logico-mathematical gloss here on some old cliches about the sexes." Darian Leader, *Jouissance: Sexuality, Suffering and Satisfaction* (Cambridge: Polity, 2021), 119. Leader's scorn for the purported logical structure of the formulas is a minority report among thinkers in Lacan's orbit, but his is not a completely isolated voice.

141 Lacan would see the turn to an emphasis on gender as a neutering of the antagonism of sex. As Joan Copjec puts it in "The Sexual Compact," "The psychoanalytic category of sexual difference was . . . deemed suspect and largely forsaken in favor of the neutered category of gender. Yes, neutered, I insist on this; for it was specifically the sex of sexual difference that dropped out when this term was replaced by *gender*." Joan Copjec, "The Sexual Compact," *Angelaki* 17.2 (2012): 31–32. The trouble that occurs in gender is always trouble between genders, which is why gender is, for Copjec, neuter. In contrast, the trouble with sex is not just between sexes but internal to each sex, which is exactly what Lacan's formulas of sexuation illustrate.

142 Jacques Lacan, *The Seminar of Jacques Lacan, Book XX: Encore, 1972–1973*, ed. Jacques-Alain Miller, trans. Bruce Fink (New York: Norton, 1998 [1975]), 74.

143 According to Nathalie Jaudel, there are exceptions on both sides of sexuation. The male side has one exception. On the female side, there are only exceptions. She states that Lacan draws attention to "two fashions of being an exception: the fashion of the man, side of the father of the horde, side of the *at-least-one-that-is-not*, the at-least-one supposing thus that there are others of them – and the fashion of the woman, the side of not-all, in which *each one* is an exception." Nathalie Jaudel, *La Légende noire de Jacques Lacan: Élisabeth Roudinesco et sa méthode historique* (Paris: Navarin, 2014), 218. Understanding female sexuation as a universe of exceptionality is one way of interpreting the feminine not-all.

144 Copjec describes the contrast between the two logical structures. She writes, "Rather than defining a universe of men that is complemented by a universe of women, Lacan defines man as the

prohibition against constructing a universe and woman as the impossibility of doing so." Joan Copjec, *Read My Desire: Lacan Against the Historicists* (Cambridge, MA: MIT Press, 1994), 235. Impossibility has a structural and political priority over prohibition because prohibition exists only to obscure the fact of impossibility.

145 The formulas first appear in *Seminar XVIII*, but Lacan spends more time explaining how to read them in *Seminar XX*.

146 Guy Le Gaufey, *Lacan and the Formulae of Sexuation: Exploring Logical Consistency and Clinical Consequences*, trans. Cormac Gallagher (London: Routledge, 2020 [2006]), 67. For a discussion of the importance of the failure of complementarity for feminism, see Hilary Neroni, *The Violent Woman: Femininity, Narrative, and Violence in Contemporary American Cinema* (Albany: SUNY Press, 2005).

147 Copjec, *Read My Desire*, 204.

148 Judith Butler, "Competing Universalities," in Judith Butler, Ernesto Laclau, and Slavoj Žižek, *Contingency, Hegemony, Universality: Contemporary Dialogues on the Left* (London: Verso, 2000), 148.

149 Patricia Gherovici, *Transgender Psychoanalysis: A Lacanian Perspective on Sexual Difference* (London: Routledge, 2017), 33. For more on Lacan and trans, see Patricia Gherovici, *Please Select Your Gender: From the Invention of Hysteria to the Democratizing of Transgenderism* (London: Routledge, 2010).

150 After connecting feminine jouissance to mysticism, Lacan cryptically states, "Mysticism isn't everything that isn't politics." Lacan, *Seminar XX*, 76. He then leaves any account of what this politics might look like completely up in the air.

151 There is a clear difference between insisting on feminine jouissance as a political position and proclaiming the sexual nonrelation itself as political. Lacan himself tends to idealize feminine jouissance, but this tendency runs contrary to the proclamation of the sexual nonrelation, which is where the real political discovery in his late work lies.

152 Alenka Zupančič, *What IS Sex?* (Cambridge, MA: MIT Press, 2017), 25.

153 Lacan continues to discuss the refusal to treat the symptom in the years after he introduces the concept. In *Seminar XXV: The Moment to Conclude, 1977–1978*, he states, "Analysis doesn't consist in one being liberated of one's *sinthomes*." Jacques Lacan, *Le Séminaire, livre XXV: Le moment de conclure, 1977–1978*, unpublished manuscript, session of January 10, 1978.

154 Symptoms are signifiers, but the *sinthome* is real. As Colette Soler notes, "the *sinthome* . . . is itself outside of meaning, is existential." Colette Soler, *Lacanian Affects: The Function of Affect in Lacan's Work*, trans. Bruce Fink (London: Routledge, 2016 [2011]). Coler is the Lacanian theorist who focuses most intensely on the *sinthome*. See also Colette Soler, *Lacan – The Unconscious Reinvented*, trans. Esther Faye and Susan Schwartz (London: Routledge, 2014 [2009]).

155 Jacques Lacan, *The Seminar of Jacques Lacan, Book XXIII: The Sinthome, 1975–1976*, ed. Jacques-Alain Miller, trans. A. R. Price (Cambridge: Polity, 2016 [2005]), 77.

156 Slavoj Žižek emphasizes how the *sinthome* gives the subject whatever consistency it has. He states, "symptom, conceived as *sinthome*, is literally our only substance, the only positive support of our being, the only point that gives consistency to the subject." Slavoj Žižek, *The Sublime Object of Ideology* (London: Verso, 1989), 75.

157 Lorenzo Chiesa sees the turn from the master signifier to the *sinthome* as a part of Lacan's turn to individualism. According to Chiesa, the *sinthome* offers the subject a "process of symbolic reinscription through a new, individualized Master-Signifier." Lorenzo Chiesa, *Subjectivity and Otherness: A Philosophical Reading of Lacan* (Cambridge, MA: MIT Press, 2007), 189. While Chiesa is certainly correct in his assessment, this move is something we should rue rather than celebrate.

158 Slavoj Žižek attempts to integrate the concept of the *sinthome* into his philosophy alongside the rest of Lacan's thought. He views the *sinthome* as just another part of the Lacanian edifice, the logical end point of Lacan's theoretical trajectory. He even employs the *sinthome* as a way to theorize how enjoyment works in totalitarianism. His creative efforts to make the *sinthome* fit alongside the earlier Lacanian conceptual system are laudable, but they don't take into account the incompatibility between Lacan's different periods, even though, at times, Žižek works out a periodization of Lacan's philosophy. To make sense of Lacan as a thinker, one must divide him from himself. Otherwise, the philosophy becomes a group of parts that don't form a whole.

Conclusion

Lacan reveals what is possible when one brings the insights of psychoanalysis into philosophy and the insights of philosophy into psychoanalysis. He is both a philosophical psychoanalyst and a psychoanalytic philosopher. Although he wouldn't call himself a philosopher, he is one nevertheless. In his theoretical work, a new conception of subjectivity emerges that pushes previous ideas of the subject in an unforeseen direction. With Lacan, the subject acquires an unconscious that displaces the subject's essence outside of itself. One finds oneself as a subject when the unconscious derails one's most intimate intentions. The discovery of the unconscious doesn't eliminate the subject but allows us to understand it anew.

Lacan's background in philosophy allows him to do what Freud could not – create a genuinely psychoanalytic philosophy. At his most radical, Lacan shows how the subject's unconscious desire leaves it unable to fit in the social order that demands its conformity. The subject desires what the social order cannot give it and tries to give the social order what it doesn't want. This desire protrudes from the social order and in this way acts as the basis for the subject's political being. Lacan creates a vision of subjectivity at odds with its social determinants. Subjectivity is the expression of society's contradictory failure, not the measure of its success.

Lacan's transformation of psychoanalysis into a full-blown philosophy occurs through his socialization of Freud's insights. By turning Freud's notion of castration into symbolic castration, Lacan opens up thinking about the subject's unconscious desire in terms of its failed relation to the social order. The unconscious isn't just a product of the Oedipal triangle but emerges out of a signifying structure that runs through the social order. Grasping the importance of signification leads Lacan outward in his thinking. Even when the family has a crucial role in his theory, its position is a metaphorical one, as is evident with the Name-of-the-Father. The parent is a social function.

The emphasis on the social order didn't lead Lacan himself to political radicality. He was wary about any translation of psychoanalytic insights into political speculation. But in the years since his death, political theorizing has become the most fecund arena for the development of Lacan's ideas. Led by Slavoj Žižek, Lacanian political theory has come to the fore among psychoanalytic engagements in politics. Lacan's ability to link subjectivity to the point of contradiction within the symbolic order gives him a theoretical radicality that others would take up.

Lacan's philosophy of contradiction reaches its apogee with the discovery of the *objet a*. Through the encounter with this object, we confront how our unconscious distorts what we perceive, how what appears to be a neutral world bears the mark of our unconscious desire. We grasp our connection to others through the object that indicates our failure to belong. The contradictions of the perceptual field manifest our unconscious involvement in what we perceive. Lacan makes clear how we are connected to our world through our very alienation from it. We are what doesn't fit within the world, and that's how we relate to the world. This is Lacan's reformulation of dialectics. In Lacan's philosophy, the unconscious has a part to play in dialectical analysis. No one else before him had made this leap – and few after him have sustained it.

Unfortunately, the radical version of Lacan had a limited lifespan. It corresponded to the middle period after his turn away from structuralism and before his insistence that the sexual division leaves masculine sexuation completely separated from feminine sexuation. At this point, he ceased to be a dialectical thinker as he gave up on a universal theory of subjectivity. He stopped theorizing the failure of relations and privileged the sexual nonrelation. Nonrelation trumps all relation, with the consequence that Lacan's importance as a political thinker dissipates. In the late Lacan, there is no desiring subject. Instead, there is a phallic form of subjectivity and a feminine form. One doesn't emerge out of the other, but their nonrelation bespeaks the absence of the universality that enlivens Lacan's middle period. These two forms of subjectivity do not exist in the same signifying universe. This is why Lacan began to theorize different discursive structures and to turn away from the master signifier as a shared necessity of the symbolic order. It turns out, Lacan comes to believe, that nothing is shared. Hegel's insistence on universality disappears in the late Lacan. When he loses this, Lacan loses what allows him to come up with his most important insights.

When we take stock of Lacan's contributions, we are not obliged to follow him down the ultimate path that he took. We can stop and find some value in what Lacan moved beyond. Not every movement forward represents progress. There is no rule that says the final position a thinker comes to represents the greatest insight. This is one of the major lessons of psychoanalysis, a lesson that we must apply to Lacan's own thinking. Perhaps he reached his theoretical high point when he believed he was just at a way station. The moment when Lacan theorized the importance of the distortion turned out to be a moment of distortion in his own philosophical trajectory, a moment that he ultimately abandoned. Lacan moved on from an emphasis on the subject's unconscious desire as a distortion of the perceptual field because he didn't recognize that he had reached a point worthy of a lifetime of philosophical speculation. It makes sense that a theorist who prioritized the effect of the unconscious on subjectivity would not recognize where his own greatest insights lie. It is only from the outside that one sees when a thinker gets it right.

Bibliography

Althusser, Louis. 1971 [1964]. "Freud and Lacan." *Lenin and Philosophy and Other Essays*. Trans. Ben Brewster. New York: Monthly Review Press. 133–150.

Althusser, Louis. 1971 [1969]. "Ideology and Ideological State Apparatuses." *Lenin and Philosophy and Other Essays*. Trans. Ben Brewster. New York: Monthly Review Press. 85–126.

Baudry, Jean-Louis, 1974–1975. "Ideological Effects of the Basic Cinematic Apparatus." Trans. Alan Williams. *Film Quarterly* 28.2: 39–47.

Bellour, Raymond. 1989. "Cher amis de *Hors Cadre* . . .," *Hors Cadre* 7: 51–68.

Berkeley, George. 1998 [1710]. *A Treatise on the Principles of Human Knowledge*. Oxford: Oxford University Press.

Boothby, Richard. 1991. *Death and Desire: Psychoanalytic Theory in Lacan's Return to Freud*. London: Routledge.

Boothby, Richard. 2001. *Freud as Philosopher: Metapsychology after Lacan*. New York: Routledge.

Boothby, Richard. 2022. *Embracing the Void: Rethinking the Origin of the Sacred*. Evanston, IL: Northwestern University Press.

Borch-Jacobsen, Mikkel. 1991 [1990]. *Lacan: The Absolute Master*, trans. Douglas Brick. Stanford: Stanford University Press.

Braunstein, Néstor. 2003. "Desire and Jouissance in the Teachings of Lacan." *The Cambridge Companion to Lacan*. Ed. Jean-Michel Rabaté. Cambridge: Cambridge University Press. 102–115.

Bryant, Levi. 2008. "Žižek's New Universe of Discourse: Politics and the Discourse of the Capitalist." *International Journal of Žižek Studies* 2.4: https://zizekstudies.org/index.php/IJZS/article/view/141/216.

Butler, Judith. 1993. *Bodies That Matter: On the Discursive Limits of "Sex."* New York: Routledge.

Butler, Judith. 2000. "Competing Universalities." *Contingency, Hegemony, Universality: Contemporary Dialogues on the Left*. Ed. Judith Butler, Ernesto Laclau, and Slavoj Žižek. London: Verso. 136–181.

Chiesa, Lorenzo. 2007. *Subjectivity and Otherness: A Philosophical Reading of Lacan*. Cambridge, MA: MIT Press.

Chomsky, Noam. 1989. "An Interview." *Radical Philosophy* 53: 31–40.

Copjec, Joan. 1994. *Read My Desire: Lacan Against the Historicists*. Cambridge, MA: MIT Press.

Copjec, Joan. 2002. *Imagine There's No Woman: Ethics and Sublimation.* Cambridge, MA: MIT Press.
Copjec, Joan. 2012. "The Sexual Compact." *Angelaki* 17.2: 31–48.
Davis, Walter A. 2006. *Death's Dream Kingdom: The American Psyche Since 9–11.* London: Pluto Press.
Dayan, Daniel. 1974. "The Tutor-Code of Classical Cinema." *Film Quarterly* 28.1: 22–31.
Deleuze, Gilles, and Félix Guattari. 1983 [1972]. *Anti-Oedipus: Capitalism and Schizophrenia.* Trans. Robert Hurley, Mark Seem, and Helen R. Lane. Minneapolis: University of Minnesota Press.
Derrida, Jacques. 1998 [1966]. *Resistances of Psychoanalysis.* Trans. Peggy Kamuf, Pascale-Ann Brault, and Michael Naas. Stanford, CA: Stanford University Press.
Descartes, René. 1985 [1637]. *Discourse on the Method of Rightly Conducting One's Reason and Seeking the Truth in the Sciences.* Trans. Robert Stoothoff. *The Philosophical Writings of Descartes.* Vol. 1. Cambridge: Cambridge University Press.
Dolar, Mladen. 2006. *A Voice and Nothing More.* Cambridge, MA: MIT Press.
Fink, Bruce. 1997. *A Clinical Introduction to Lacanian Psychoanalysis: Theory and Technique.* Cambridge: Harvard University Press.
Foucault, Michel. 1979 [1975]. *Discipline and Punish: The Birth of the Prison.* Trans. Alan Sheridan. New York: Vintage.
Freud, Sigmund. 1953 [1900]. *The Interpretation of Dreams.* Trans. James Strachey. *The Complete Psychological Works of Sigmund Freud.* Vols. 4–5. Ed. James Strachey. London: Hogarth Press.
Freud, Sigmund. 1953 [1913]. *Totem and Taboo.* Trans. James Strachey. *The Standard Edition of the Complete Psychological Works of Sigmund Freud.* Vol. 13. Ed. James Strachey. London: Hogarth Press. 1–162.
Freud, Sigmund. 1955 [1917]. "A Difficulty in the Path of Psycho-Analysis." Trans. Joan Riviere. *The Complete Psychological Works of Sigmund Freud.* Vol. 17. Ed. James Strachey. London: Hogarth Press. 135–144.
Freud, Sigmund. 1955 [1920]. *Beyond the Pleasure Principle.* Trans. James Strachey. *The Standard Edition of the Complete Psychological Works of Sigmund Freud.* Vol. 18. Ed. James Strachey. London: Hogarth Press. 1–64.
Freud, Sigmund. 1961 [1930]. *Civilization and Its Discontents.* Trans. James Strachey. *The Standard Edition of the Complete Psychological Works of Sigmund Freud.* Vol. 21. Ed. James Strachey. London: Hogarth Press. 57–145.
Freud, Sigmund. 1964 [1938]. *An Outline of Psychoanalysis.* Trans. James Strachey. *The Standard Edition of the Complete Psychological Works of Sigmund Freud.* Vol. 23. Ed. James Strachey. London: Hogarth Press. 139–207.
Friedlander, Jennifer. 2008. *Feminine Look: Sexuation, Spectatorship, Subversion.* Albany: SUNY Press.
Friedlander, Jennifer. 2017. *Real Deceptions: The Contemporary Reinvention of Realism.* Oxford: Oxford University Press.

Gherovici, Patricia. 2010. *Please Select Your Gender: From the Invention of Hysteria to the Democratizing of Transgenderism*. London: Routledge.
Gherovici, Patricia. 2017. *Transgender Psychoanalysis: A Lacanian Perspective on Sexual Difference*. London: Routledge.
Harman, Graham. 2018. *Object-Oriented Ontology: A New Theory of Everything*. New York: Penguin.
Hartmann, Heinz. 1958 [1939]. *Ego Psychology and the Problem of Adaptation*. Trans. David Rapaport. Madison, WI: International Universities Press.
Hegel, G. W. F. 2010 [1817]. *Encyclopedia of the Philosophical Sciences in Basic Outline, Part I: Science of Logic*. Trans. Klaus Brinkman and Daniel O. Dahlstrom. Cambridge: Cambridge University Press.
Hegel, G. W. F. 1991 [1820]. *Elements of the Philosophy of Right*. Ed. Allen W. Wood. Trans. H. B. Nisbet. Cambridge: Cambridge University Press.
Jaudel, Nathalie. 2014. *La Légende noire de Jacques Lacan: Élisabeth Roudinesco et sa méthode historique*. Paris: Navarin.
Johnston, Adrian. 2017. *Irrepressible Truth: On Lacan's "The Freudian Thing."* London: Palgrave.
Kojève, Alexandre. 1947. *Introduction à la lecture de Hegel*. Ed. Raymond Queneau. Paris: Gallimard.
Kunkle, Sheila. 2016. "Introduction: On the Subject of Endings." *Cinematic Cuts: Theorizing Film Endings*. Ed. Sheila Kunkle. Albany: SUNY Press. 1–18.
Lacan, Jacques. 1988 [1975]. *The Seminar, Book I: Freud's Papers on Technique, 1953–1954*. Ed. Jacques-Alain Miller. Trans. John Forrester. New York: Norton.
Lacan, Jacques. 1991 [1978]. *The Seminar of Jacques Lacan, Book II: The Ego in Freud's Theory and in the Technique of Psychoanalysis, 1954–1955*. Ed. Jacques-Alain Miller. Trans. Sylvana Tomaselli. New York: Norton.
Lacan, Jacques. 1993 [1981]. *The Seminar of Jacques Lacan, Book III: The Psychoses, 1955–1956*. Ed. Jacques-Alain Miller. Trans. Russell Grigg. New York: Norton.
Lacan, Jacques. 2020 [1994]. *The Seminar of Jacques Lacan, Book IV: The Object Relation, 1957–1958*. Ed. Jacques-Alain Miller. Trans. A. R. Price. Cambridge: Polity.
Lacan, Jacques. 2017 [1998]. *The Seminar of Jacques Lacan, Book V: Formations of the Unconscious, 1957–1958*. Ed. Jacques-Alain Miller. Trans. Russell Grigg. Cambridge: Polity.
Lacan, Jacques. 2019 [2013]. *The Seminar of Jacques Lacan, Book VI: Desire and Its Interpretation, 1958–1959*. Ed. Jacques-Alain Miller. Trans. Bruce Fink. Cambridge: Polity.
Lacan, Jacques. 1992 [1986]. *The Seminar of Jacques Lacan, Book VII: The Ethics of Psychoanalysis, 1959–1960*. Ed. Jacques-Alain Miller. Trans. Dennis Porter. New York: Norton.
Lacan, Jacques. 2017 [1991]. *The Seminar of Jacques Lacan, Book VIII: Transference, 1960–1961*. Ed. Jacques-Alain Miller. Trans. Bruce Fink. Cambridge: Polity.

Lacan, Jacques. 1961–1962. *Le Séminaire, livre IX: L'Identification, 1961–1962.* Unpublished manuscript.

Lacan, Jacques. 2014 [2004]. *The Seminar of Jacques Lacan, Book X: Anxiety, 1962–1963.* Ed. Jacques-Alain Miller. Trans. A. R. Price. Cambridge: Polity.

Lacan, Jacques. 1978 [1973]. *The Seminar of Jacques Lacan, Book XI: The Four Fundamental Concepts of Psychoanalysis, 1963–1964.* Ed. Jacques-Alain Miller. Trans. Alan Sheridan. New York: Norton.

Lacan, Jacques. 1964–1965. *Le Séminaire, livre XII: Problèmes cruciaux pour la psychanalyse, 1964–1965.* Unpublished manuscript.

Lacan, Jacques. 1965–1966. *Le Séminaire livre XIII: L'objet de la psychanalyse, 1965–1966.* Unpublished manuscript.

Lacan, Jacques. 2023. *Le Séminaire, livre XIV: La logique du fantasme, 1966–1967.* Ed. Jacques-Alain Miller. Paris: Seuil.

Lacan, Jacques. 2024. *Le Séminaire, livre XV: L'Acte psychanalytique, 1967–1968.* Paris: Seuil.

Lacan, Jacques. 2024 [2006]. *The Seminar of Jacques Lacan, Book XVI: From an Other to the other, 1968–1969.* Ed. Jacques-Alain Miller. Trans. Bruce Fink. Cambridge: Polity.

Lacan, Jacques. 2007 [1991]. *The Seminar of Jacques Lacan, Book XVII: The Other Side of Psychoanalysis, 1969–1970.* Ed. Jacques-Alain Miller. Trans. Russell Grigg. New York: Norton.

Lacan, Jacques. 2006. *Le Séminaire, livre XVIII: D'un discours qui ne serait pas du semblant, 1970–1971.* Ed. Jacques-Alain Miller. Paris: Seuil.

Lacan, Jacques. 2018 [2011]. *The Seminar of Jacques Lacan, Book XIX: . . . or Worse, 1971–1972.* Ed. Jacques-Alain Miller. Trans. A. R. Price. Cambridge: Polity.

Lacan, Jacques. 1998 [1975]. *The Seminar of Jacques Lacan, Book XX: Encore, 1972–1973.* Ed. Jacques-Alain Miller. Trans. Bruce Fink. New York: Norton.

Lacan, Jacques. 1972–1973. *Le Séminaire livre XXI: Les non-dupes errent, 1972–1973.* Unpublished manuscript.

Lacan, Jacques. 1973–1974. *Le Séminaire, livre XXII: R. S. I., 1973–1974.* Unpublished manuscript.

Lacan, Jacques. 2016 [2005]. *The Seminar of Jacques Lacan, Book XXIII: The Sinthome, 1975–1976.* Ed. Jacques-Alain Miller. Trans. A. R. Price. Cambridge: Polity.

Lacan, Jacques. 1976–1977. *Le Séminaire, livre XXIV: L'insu que sait d'une bévue s'aile à mourre, 1976–1977.* Unpublished manuscript.

Lacan, Jacques. 1977–1978. *Le Séminaire, livre XXV: Le moment de conclure, 1977–1978.* Unpublished manuscript.

Lacan, Jacques. 1978–1979. *Le Séminaire livre XXVI: La topologie et le temps, 1979–1980.* Unpublished manuscript.

Lacan, Jacques. 2006 [1966]. *Écrits: The First Complete Edition in English.* Trans. Bruce Fink. New York: Norton.

Lacan, Jacques. 2006 [1966]. "The Field and Function of Speech and Language in Psychoanalysis." *Écrits: The First Complete Edition in English.* Trans. Bruce Fink. New York: Norton. 197–268.

Lacan, Jacques. 2006 [1966]. “Kant with Sade.” *Écrits: The First Complete Edition in English*. Trans. Bruce Fink. New York: Norton. 645–668.

Lacan, Jacques. 2006 [1966]. “The Mirror Stage as Formative of the *I* Function as Revealed in Psychoanalytic Experience.” *Écrits: The First Complete Edition in English*. Trans. Bruce Fink. New York: Norton. 75–81.

Lacan, Jacques. 2006 [1966]. “On My Antecedents.” *Écrits: The First Complete Edition in English*. Trans. Bruce Fink. New York: Norton. 51–57.

Lacan, Jacques. 2006 [1966]. “The Position of the Unconscious.” *Écrits: The First Complete Edition in English*. Trans. Bruce Fink. New York: Norton. 703–721.

Lacan, Jacques. 2006 [1966]. “The Signification of the Phallus.” *Écrits: The First Complete Edition in English*. Trans. Bruce Fink. New York: Norton. 575–584.

Lacan, Jacques. 2006 [1966]. “The Subversion of the Subject and the Dialectic of Desire in the Freudian Unconscious.” *Écrits: The First Complete Edition in English*. Trans. Bruce Fink. New York: Norton. 671–702.

Lacan, Jacques. 1972. “Du discours psychanalytique.” *Lacan en Italie 1953–1978*. Ed. Giacomo B. Contri. Milan: La Salamandra.

Lacan, Jacques. 2001. *Autres écrits*. Paris: Seuil.

Leader, Darian. 2021. *Jouissance: Sexuality, Suffering and Satisfaction*. Cambridge: Polity.

Le Gaufey, Guy. 2020 [2006]. *Lacan and the Formulae of Sexuation: Exploring Logical Consistency and Clinical Consequences*. Trans. Cormac Gallagher. London: Routledge.

Le Gaufey, Guy. 2012. *L’objet a: Approches de l’invention de Lacan*. Paris: Epel.

Lévi-Strauss, Claude. 1969 [1949]. *The Elementary Structures of Kinship*. Trans. James Harle Bell, John Richard von Sturmer, and Rodney Needham. Boston: Beacon Press.

Lucchelli, Juan-Pablo. 2014. *Lacan avec et sans Lévi-Strauss*. Paris: Éditions Nouvelles Cécille Defaut.

Lucchelli, Juan-Pablo. 2017. *Lacan: De Wallon à Kojève*. Paris: Éditions Michèle.

Lucchelli, Juan-Pablo. 2020. *Introduction à l’objet a de Lacan*. Paris: Éditions Michèle.

Mathews, Peter D. 2020. *Lacan the Charlatan*. London: Palgrave, 2020.

McNulty, Tracy. 2014. *Wrestling with the Angel: Experiments in Symbolic Life*. New York: Columbia University Press.

Miller, Jacques-Alain Miller. 2000. “Paradigms of *Jouissance*.” Trans. Jorge Jauregui. *Lacanian Ink* 17: 8–47.

Milner, Jean-Claude. 2021 [1995]. *A Search for Clarity: Science and Philosophy in Lacan’s Oeuvre*. Trans. Ed Pluth. Evanston, IL: Northwestern University Press.

Moi, Toril. 1985. *Sexual/Textual Politics: Feminist Literary Theory*. London: Routledge.

Nancy, Jean-Luc, and Philippe Lacoue-Labarthe. 1992 [1973]. *The Title of the Letter: A Reading of Lacan*. Trans. Francois Raffoul and David Pettigrew. Albany: SUNY Press.

Nasio, Juan-David. 2005. *Le Fantasme: Le plaisir de lire Lacan*. Paris: Petite Bibliothèque Payot.
Neroni, Hilary. 2005. *The Violent Woman: Femininity, Narrative, and Violence in Contemporary American Cinema*. Albany: SUNY Press.
Nobus, Dany. 2000. *Jacques Lacan and the Freudian Practice of Psychoanalysis*. London: Routledge.
Nobus, Dany. 2017. *The Law of Desire: On Lacan's "Kant with Sade."* London: Palgrave.
Ronen, Ruth. 2018. *Lacan with the Philosophers*. Trans. Michal Sapir. Toronto: University of Toronto Press.
Rose, Jacqueline. 1986. *Sexuality in the Field of Vision*. London: Verso.
Rothenberg, Molly Anne. 2010. *The Excessive Subject: A New Theory of Social Change*. Cambridge: Polity.
Roudinesco, Élisabeth. 1990 [1986]. *Jacques Lacan & Co.: A History of Psychoanalysis in France, 1925–1985*. Trans. Jeffrey Mehlman. Chicago: University of Chicago Press.
Roudinesco, Élisabeth. 1997 [1993]. *Jacques Lacan*. Trans. Barbara Bray. New York: Columbia University Press.
Roudinesco, Élisabeth. 2003. "The Mirror Stage: An Obliterated Archive." *The Cambridge Companion to Lacan*. Ed. Jean-Michel Rabaté. Trans. Barbara Bray. Cambridge: Cambridge University Press, 25–34.
Ruti, Mari. 2014. *The Call of Character: Living a Life Worth Living*. New York: Columbia University Press.
Ruti, Mari. 2015. *The Age of Scientific Sexism*. New York: Bloomsbury.
Ruti, Mari. 2017. *The Ethics of Opting Out: Queer Theory's Defiant Subjects*. New York: Columbia University Press.
Ruti, Mari. 2018. *Distillations: Theory, Ethics, Affect*. New York: Bloomsbury.
Saussure, Ferdinand de. 1959 [1915]. *Course in General Linguistics*. Ed. Charles Bally and Albert Sechehaye. Trans. Wade Baskin. New York: Philosophical Library.
Silverman, Kaja. 1983. *The Subject of Semiotics*. Oxford: Oxford University Press.
Soler, Colette. 2014 [2009]. *Lacan – The Unconscious Reinvented*. Trans. Esther Faye and Susan Schwartz. London: Routledge.
Soler, Colette. 2016 [2011]. *Lacanian Affects: The Function of Affect in Lacan's Work*. Trans. Bruce Fink. London: Routledge.
Stavrakakis, Yannis, ed. 2019. *Routledge Handbook of Psychoanalytic Political Theory*. London: Routledge.
Tomšič, Samo. 2016. *The Capitalist Unconscious: Marx and Lacan*. London: Verso.
Turkle, Sherry. 1992. *Psychoanalytic Politics: Jacques Lacan and Freud's French Revolution*. 2nd ed. New York: Guilford Press.
Vanheule, Stijn, Derek Hook, and Calum Neill. 2018. *Reading Lacan's Écrits from "The Signification of the Phallus" to "Metaphor of the Subject."* London: Routledge.
Vanheule, Stijn, Derek Hook, and Calum Neill. 2019. *Reading Lacan's Écrits from "The Freudian Thing" to "Remarks on Daniel Lagache."* London: Routledge.

Vanheule, Stijn, Derek Hook, and Calum Neill. 2022. *Reading Lacan's Écrits from "Logical Time" to "Response to Jean Hyppolite."* London: Routledge.
Zafiropoulos, Markos. 2003. *Lacan et Lévi-Strauss, ou le retour à Freud, 1951–1957*. Paris: Presses Universitaires de France.
Žižek, Slavoj. 1989. *The Sublime Object of Ideology*. London: Verso.
Žižek, Slavoj. 1991. *Looking Awry: An Introduction to Jacques Lacan through Popular Culture*. Cambridge, MA: MIT Press.
Žižek, Slavoj. 1991. *For They Know Not What They Do: Enjoyment as a Political Factor*. London: Verso.
Žižek, Slavoj. 2000. *The Fragile Absolute, or, Why Is the Christian Legacy Worth Fighting For?* London: Verso.
Žižek, Slavoj. 2003. *The Puppet and the Dwarf: The Perverse Core of Christianity*. Cambridge, MA: MIT Press.
Žižek, Slavoj. 2006. *The Parallax View*. Cambridge, MA: MIT Press.
Zupančič, Alenka. 2000. *Ethics of the Real: Kant, Lacan*. London: Verso.
Zupančič, Alenka. 2008. *The Odd One In: On Comedy*. Cambridge, MA: MIT Press.
Zupančič, Alenka. 2017. *What IS Sex?* Cambridge, MA: MIT Press.

Index

For EU product safety concerns, contact us at Calle de José Abascal, 56–1°, 28003 Madrid, Spain or eugpsr@cambridge.org.

www.ingramcontent.com/pod-product-compliance
Lightning Source LLC
Chambersburg PA
CBHW032024050726
47590CB00006B/2299

* 9 7 8 1 0 0 9 3 0 0 7 5 9 *